BUFFALO BILL IN BOLOGNA

Postcard depicting Buffalo Bill in Bologna, 1906. Courtesy Jack and Susan Davis,
Olde America Antiques, Bozeman, MT.

Buffalo Bill in Bologna

THE AMERICANIZATION OF
THE WORLD, 1869–1922

ROBERT W. RYDELL
AND ROB KROES

THE UNIVERSITY OF CHICAGO PRESS
CHICAGO AND LONDON

Robert W. Rydell is professor of history at Montana State University–Bozeman. He is the author of six books, including *All the World's a Fair* and *World of Fairs*, both published by the University of Chicago Press. Rob Kroes is professor of American studies and director of the Amerika Instituut at the University of Amsterdam. He is the author of eleven books, including, most recently, *If You've Seen One, You've Seen the Mall* and *Us and Them: Questions of Citizenship in a Globalized World.*

The University of Chicago Press, Chicago 60637
The University of Chicago Press, Ltd., London
© 2005 by The University of Chicago
All rights reserved. Published 2005
Printed in the United States of America
14 13 12 11 10 09 08 07 06 05   1 2 3 4 5
ISBN: 0-226-73242-8 (cloth)

An earlier version of a portion of chapter 2 was previously published as "The Pledge of Allegience and the Construction of the American Nation" *Rendezvous* 30, no. 2 (spring 1996), 13–26.
Portions of chapter 3 appeared in *Paris 1900: The "American School" at the Universal Exposition,* ed. Diane Fischer (New Brunswick, NJ: Rutgers University Press, 1999). Courtesy of Rutgers University Press.
Portions of chapters 1, 3, and 6 appeared in *If You've Seen One, You've Seen the Mall: Europeans and American Mass Culture,* Rob Kroes (Urbana, Ill.: University of Illinois Press, 1996). Courtesy of University of Illinois Press.

Library of Congress Cataloging-in-Publication Data

Rydell, Robert W.
    Buffalo Bill in Bologna : the Americanization of the world, 1869–1922 / Robert W. Rydell and Rob Kroes.
        p.   cm.
    Includes bibliographical references and index.
    ISBN 0-226-73242-8 (alk. paper)
    1. Popular culture—United States.   2. United States—Civilization.
  3. United States—Relations—Foreign countries.   4. Amercanization.
  5. Civilization, Modern—American influences.   I. Kroes, Rob.   II. Title.

E 169.1 .R95 2005
303.48'273'009034—dc22   2004024389

♾ The paper used in this publication meets the minimum requirements of the American National Standard for Information Sciences—Permanence of Paper for Printed Library Materials, ANSI Z39.48-1992.

TO OUR FAMILIES AND FRIENDS

CONTENTS

6

DEBATING AMERICAN MASS CULTURE IN THE
UNITED STATES AND EUROPE
142

ILLUSTRATIONS

ACKNOWLEDGMENTS

The idea for this book originated in a cross-disciplinary, trans-Atlantic research project on the reception of American mass culture in Europe that was sponsored by the Netherlands Institute for the Advanced Studies in the Humanities and Social Sciences. The project never would have been possible without the support of the Institute's rector, Prof. Dr. D. J. van de Kaa, and his fine staff. We are also grateful for the participation of many scholars from a wide range of disciplines who participated in seminars we organized and contributed essays to multiple publications published by the VU University Press in Amsterdam. In addition to the authors, the core research team consisted of Hans Bertens, Doeko F. J. Bosscher, David Ellwood, Mel van Elteren, Mick Gidley, and David Nye. Their insights, as well as those of the scholars who participated in our seminars, helped us frame the basic questions of this book and contributed in no small way to its content.

A book like this draws on the work of many scholars who have produced pioneering research about American cultural forms. The endnotes and bibliographical essay underscore our profound indebtedness to historians, sociologists, anthropologists, and cultural studies specialists. We have also drawn on some of our previously published work and are grateful to the Rutgers University Press and the University of Illinois Press for permission to republish it here in revised form.

Over the years, several friends have read this book either in whole or in part. We are especially grateful to George Cotkin, Jonathan McLeod, and Alexander Saxton for their insights and suggestions for improvement. The readers for the University of Chicago Press also offered excellent criticism along the way. With their keen sense for the visual, Eric Breitbart and Mary Lance provided important leads to photographic and film archives. We are also indebted to the many archivists and librarians in both Europe and the United States who helped us find materials in their collections.

We would be remiss not to acknowledge another group of people who never previewed this book, except as they heard us talk about it at professional meetings. These are the "usual suspects," as we have come to call them, and they include, in addition to some of the aforementioned individuals, John Blair, Marc Chenetier, Kate Delaney, Heinz Ickstadt, Berndt Ostendorf, and Richard Pells. Indeed, we are especially grateful to the European Association of American Studies, the Organization of American Historians, the American Historical Association, and the American Studies Association for their support of international professional meetings and collaborations. It is also important to thank our students and colleagues at the University of Amsterdam and Montana State University–Bozeman, who helped us clarify our ideas in many seminar discussions.

The editorial staff at the University of Chicago Press worked wonders. We are especially grateful to Douglas Mitchell for his support and Russell D. Harper for his eye for detail in copyediting our work. Timothy McGovern and Monica Holliday kept us on schedule—no small task given the distances involved.

Finally, we also wish to acknowledge the support of our families. They have contributed to this book in countless ways, and it is to them and our friends on both sides of the Atlantic that we dedicate this work.

INTRODUCTION

"There is no there there," wrote novelist Gertrude Stein about the city of Oakland, California.[1] The same has often been said of the subject of this book. Mass culture, in the eyes of some critics, exists in name but lacks a core identity. Lacking the clear focus of traditional fields such as political, diplomatic, and economic history, mass culture often has not been considered a fit subject for serious historical scholarship. High versus low, legitimate versus illegitimate, substance versus ephemera, racially charged ideas about "civilization" versus "otherness"—these are some of the dichotomies that have been used to set the study of mass culture apart from the rest and to dismiss it as a subject unworthy of serious scholarly attention.

Such suspicions, while not entirely absent at the beginning of the twenty-first century, have receded over the past twenty years as historians, together with specialists in a constellation of disciplines that are called cultural studies, have produced an impressive body of scholarship that has moved mass culture from the periphery toward the center of contemporary scholarship.

Scholarship, of course, does not occur in a vacuum. A number of events have underscored the need to understand the ways that mass culture has become central to the political life of Americans. For instance, President Richard Nixon's appearance on *Rowan and Martin's Laugh-In* and his meeting with Elvis Presley at the White House; President Jimmy Carter's interview in *Playboy* magazine; former president Gerald Ford and former secretary of state Henry Kissinger's appearance on *Dynasty*; President Ronald Reagan's deep immersion in the world of Hollywood's dream factories; the U.S. military's use of rock 'n' roll music blaring over loudspeakers to force Panamanian ruler Manuel Noriega out of hiding in the Vatican Embassy in 1989 during the U.S. invasion of Panama; President Bill Clinton's appearance on MTV and the juxtaposition of Clinton with Elvis Presley on a postage stamp issued by the Republic of Chad; appearances by presidential candidates Al Gore and George W. Bush on popular late-night comedy shows; California's election of film star Arnold Schwarzenegger as governor; not to mention the U.S. Postal Service's decision to issue a set of stamps commemorating the centennial of the comic strip. Since Americans have often looked to Europe for validation of their culture, it is also worth recalling that, in 1994, Oxford University's renowned debating society, the Oxford Union, invited Kermit the Frog to address its members, giving the *Sesame Street* puppet the same forum as world leaders.[2]

Science, no less than politics, has been affected by American mass cultural influences. When casting about for a name for a newly discovered species of spider that uses a sticky ball to catch its prey, an entomologist reached into baseball's Hall of Fame and came up with *Mastophora dizzydeani.*[3]

Events abroad have also underscored the significance of American mass culture. Revolutions in central Europe and the Soviet Union in the 1980s and early 1990s drew heavily on American and European mass cultural exports, especially rock 'n' roll, blue jeans, and Willis Conover's popular Voice of America radio show that broadcast jazz to Communist Bloc countries. The pervasiveness of American mass culture overseas was clear when U.S. soldiers captured former Iraqi president Saddam Hussein in a cellar outfitted with a supply of Bounty candy bars, 7 UP, and hot dogs and, upon entering the home of Iraq's deputy prime minister, Tariq Aziz, found videotapes of *The Sound of Music* and copies of *Vanity Fair* magazine. Or one might think of Japanese prime minister Junichiro Koizumi's recent CD release of his karaoke versions of Elvis Presley songs or French prime minister Lionel Jospin's rendition of *Autumn Leaves* during his last and failed campaign for reelection.[4]

In the late 1980s, on the occasion of a lecture tour in what was then East Germany, one of the authors met with a high official in the East German cultural ministry. When he asked him why, given the level of censorship in Eastern Bloc countries, the East German government allowed American soap operas to be transmitted, his response was revealing: "Because shows like *Dallas* reveal the depravity of the West better than anything we could do." Were the intentions of the cultural ministry fully realized? Subsequent events culminating in the destruction of the Berlin Wall and the creation of the Stalin World Theme Park in Lithuania might suggest otherwise.[5]

All of these episodes drawn from recent experience call attention to the pervasiveness—a better term might be globalization—of American mass culture at the close of the twentieth century. In the eyes of many people abroad, mass culture has become America's chief defining characteristic. Whether or not that observation is in fact true, there is no denying the significance of mass culture for contemporary Americans or for the way people around the world perceive the United States.[6] But how has mass culture gained such dominance within the United States and how has American mass culture attained such a presence overseas? How has mass culture functioned? Has it been the agent of liberation or manipulation? Is mass culture even the right term? Would it be more accurate to speak of popular culture?[7]

These questions, of course, are not new. As literary historian Patrick Brantlinger reminds us, debates about the meaning and function of mass culture date to the ancient world, where the writer Juvenal coined the phrase "bread and circuses" to condemn the retreat of citizens from politics that made the rise of the Roman Empire possible. In more recent times, the debate, often referred to as the mass society debate, has taken shape between positions staked out by the Frankfurt School and a group of cultural populists. According to Frankfurt School theorists Theodor Adorno and Max Horkheimer, writing in the context of the Second World War, mass cultural forms had replaced religion as the opiate of the masses. But are audiences always passive receivers, mere Play-Doh in the hands of media moguls? Cultural studies specialist and cultural populist John Fiske, for one, rejects that viewpoint, arguing that people make their own meanings out of popular—he rejects as pejorative the adjective "mass"—culture.[8]

But for a historical study like this one, which looks at the period between 1869 and 1922, there are good reasons to use the phrase "mass culture" to describe the transformation of American culture, although it is important to add that the term itself seems not to have come into common usage until the 1930s. To those who might object that ours imposes present categories on the past, we would remind them that the logic of their argument would also make it impossible to use the word "racism"—a term also coined between the world wars—to characterize white attitudes toward nonwhites in the nineteenth century.[9] Words like "racism" and phrases like "mass culture" came into being to describe social practices and attitudes already in existence. While difficult and unpleasant, these terms are important because they call attention to the fundamental importance of ideology for cultural formations. Indeed, it seems hardly accidental that "racism" and "mass culture" were coined at approximately the same time to describe practices that, in the United States at least, had been historically conjoined since the Civil War in manufacturing a new national identity for a country that had suffered four years of bloody conflict. Precisely because mass culture played a historically specific role in reconstructing the United States, it is important to distinguish it from popular culture—a term that has been used to describe more locally produced cultural formations in both pre- and postindustrial societies.

So what exactly is mass culture? Historian Susan Davis offers this clue in her definition of what popular culture is not: "popular culture does not mean the industrially produced, standardized cultural forms produced for cheap sale to 'mass' audiences." Mass culture, on the other hand, means exactly that—and more. Mass culture means the mobilization of cultural and ideological resources on a scale unimaginable in a preindustrial society lacking mass transportation and communication facilities. It also means the mobilization of those resources for purposes of maintaining in society what cultural critic Dick Hebdidge calls a "moving equilibrium" between the political interests of contending classes. Mass culture, in other words, often serves a hegemonic function within advanced, industrialized societies.[10]

Like "mass culture," "ideology," and "racism," the term "hegemony" often sends readers running for cover, in part because its origins in cultural theory are traced to an Italian Communist, Antonio Gramsci. Gramsci asked some hard questions of his Marxist, mostly Leninist, peers. Why, he wondered, had the collapse of capitalism predicted by Karl Marx and his followers failed to occur, as predicted, in the most advanced capitalist countries? The answer, Gramsci posited, was rooted in the ability of the ruling classes to maintain their control, or hegemony, through the exercise of authority through cultural means and thereby win the hearts and minds—Gramsci called it the "spontaneous consent"—of the masses to the general direction they set for society. Hegemony, as many scholars have cautioned, can often be read as a variant of social control theory, which argues that social and cultural institutions, including everything from public schools to holiday festivals, function primarily to control people's behavior, usually in the interest of powerful elites. Like these critics, we would insist that cultural hegemony has never been absolute and has always involved struggle between those with access to power and those without. That is one of the chief lessons to be learned from the history of American mass culture.[11]

To put this matter in slightly different terms, it is clear that by the end of the First World War, the United States boasted a network of culture industries that produced increasingly standardized entertainment forms for consumption within accelerating mass markets at home and abroad. It is equally apparent that these mass cultural forms were hardly value-free or neutral. They often expressed and conveyed ideologies of race, gender, empire, and consumption and played a pivotal role in the process of reconstructing the American national identity after the Civil War. Millions—indeed, tens of millions of people—"took in" movies, fairs, circuses, amusement parks, and dime novels. But in the course of "taking in" these mass cultural forms, were they "taken in" by their ideological messages? Were the so-called culture industries all-powerful and their audiences passive sponges? Or were audiences more resilient and creative than we often think? Many recent scholars, by shifting the focus of attention away from the culture industries to consumers and by calling attention to the crucial variables of the class, gender, and race of audiences, have cast doubts on "trickle down" models of mass culture, preferring instead to liken mass culture to a tool kit or menu from which one makes selections according to one's preferences and goals. Far from being a monolithic monoculture, mass culture is pluralistic and, in the hands of the oppressed, can be selectively appropriated and refashioned into "weapons of the weak."[12]

There is yet another perspective on mass culture, one which holds that mass culture industries do not so much mold as respond to popular tastes and interests. In a free market, so the argument goes, people choose what they want to see or what they want to consume from a variety of commodities provided to them by industries that would cease to exist if demand for their products ceased. This is a plausible argument if one thinks in terms of short-term market actions. But what happens over the long term, especially as people are culturally conditioned about the choices available to them? If the market, say, through advertising, shapes people's desires, is it right to speak of free choice without some measure of qualification?[13]

The same questions can be asked of a related argument that, in validating the importance of taking audience experiences into account, emphasizes how consumers make their own meanings out of cultural commodities like music, clothing, television, and film. Mass cultural forms, so the reasoning goes, afford people pleasure—a realm of experience and fantasy where the intentions of the producers of cultural forms are routinely negotiated and even subverted. While there is little doubt that mass culture affords contradictory experiences depending on one's social position, there is good reason to remember that the pleasures afforded by mass culture are rarely unmediated. Indeed, the power of mass cultural forms—from advertisements for Buffalo Bill's Wild West productions (frontispiece) to modern-day commercials for beer—may well lie in their cumulative capacity to define particular activities as pleasurable.

Questions about definition and function—and these run through any discussion of mass culture—are further complicated when we expand our lens to examine the export and reception of American mass cultural forms in a transatlantic context. From a bare trickle in the middle of the nineteenth century, some American mass cultural exports, like motion pictures, reached a flood stage by the First World War, when American films captured a large share of global markets. How should we understand these developments? Should they be seen in the context of American neo-imperialism, whereby American mass cultural exports are located in a matrix of growing efforts by the United States government to expand its economic and political power overseas? Or should these developments be seen in a context that emphasizes the ability of people on the receiving end to make their own meanings out of

U.S. cultural imports through a process of cultural recycling or creolization? In other words, should the emphasis be on imperialism, with its focus on domination, or on creolization, which stresses human creativity in cultural matters? Or, as we suggest in this book, might there be a third alternative, one that emphasizes the processes of creating cultural hybrids within a global context increasingly shaped by the rise of the United States to the stature of a global political, economic, and military power? To put this in slightly different terms, perhaps it is best to think of mass culture along fluid, symbiotic, and dialectical lines, rather than in terms of mutually exclusive categories that decontextualize complex historical processes.[14]

Putting the rise of American mass culture in a transatlantic setting is illuminating in another respect. American innovations in mass culture certainly had their counterparts in Europe (think, for instance, of the film industry). So why did American mass culture make such inroads in Europe? The Americanness of American cultural products is at the core of an answer to this question. By the end of the nineteenth century, at least some Americans were embracing vernacular cultural forms as self-conscious alternatives to elitist cultural formations. Ragtime music and jazz, not classical music, railway stations and movie theaters, not private castles, articulated an expressive individualism that challenged existing cultural hierarchies and created cultural tensions that receptive Europeans could deploy in their struggles against hierarchical social structures and communitarian structures of feeling.[15]

Clearly, this is not the first book to address these issues, but it does try to frame them historically, specifically with reference to the ascent and proliferation of mass cultural forms between the Civil War and the end of the First World War. Why this periodization? Just as there is no consensus among scholars about the definition of mass culture, so there is no consensus about its chronology. Most historians, however, to the extent they are comfortable using the term "mass culture" at all, believe that it is a mid-twentieth-century phenomenon. What existed earlier, as Michael Kammen argues, was, at best, "proto mass culture." Indeed, he suggests that many of the cultural formations we examine in this book, such as wild west shows and silent films, were "so radically different in nature from what we consider mass culture in the last four decades of the twentieth century" that they do not deserve the name.[16] By implication, these cultural formations were closer to the world of popular entertainments that characterized eighteenth-century London and Paris than to the electronically mediated world of the late twentieth century. To be sure, there is some merit in this argument, but it sidesteps an epoch-making (and culture-transforming) event that occurred in Utah Territory on May 10, 1869. On this date, time and space were utterly reconfigured when the "golden spike" joined two sections of railroad tracks, creating the world's first trans-

Fig. intro.-1. "The Last Rail is Laid! The Last Spike is Driven! The Pacific Railroad is Completed!" From the May 10, 1869, telegram sent to President U.S. Grant from Promontory Point, Utah. Photograph by A. J. Russell. Courtesy of the Andrew J. Russell Collection, the Oakland Museum of California.

continental railway. As one twentieth-century cultural critic put it: "With the barrier of mountain and desert breached, the United States were now physically, as well as legally, united. The world's most expansive single-language, single landmass culture had taken the most crucial step toward becoming a communicative unity, in which all parts were in effective contact."[17] Historian David Haward Bain puts the matter more succinctly: "For all intents and purposes, the entire nation was now connected in one great electrical circuit."[18] Of course existing forms of popular culture did not disappear overnight. Most, in fact, like circuses, adapted to new mass market opportunities, new production technologies, and new expectations by consumers or risked extinction. At the same time, wholly new forms of cultural production (motion pictures, for instance) came into being in response to the new mass market opportunities made possible by the transcontinental railroad, its corporate forms of organization, its communication support system, and the ensuing mass immigration to the United States that made late nineteenth-century America resemble late twentieth-century America in more ways than not.[19] In this respect, it is worth thinking about what historian David Kunzle has to say about the relationship between the advent of railroad transportation and the rise of motion pictures. "It has been said," Kunzle observes, "that the cinema is the product of the railway experience and the demand for accelerated vision, a moving picture seen through a frame as it were through a train window; even the celluloid itself, running on little wheels and tracks, has been compared to the train on its great iron rail."[20] Is this to say that the transcontinental railroad caused the rise of mass culture? No, but, along with the telegraph (the first line was strung in 1844) and the transatlantic cable (completed between 1858 and 1866), the transcontinental railroad became the central node in a complex communication network that facilitated the expansion and export of American business and American mass culture industries.[21]

There were, to be sure, other variables that paved the way in the United States for the creation of mass cultural forms that would unite people across time, space, and cultures. With the massive increase in immigration in the last half of the nineteenth century, the American population as a whole trebled, while the industrial labor force doubled. Between 1870 and 1910, over twenty million immigrants arrived in the United States. Put in different terms, that meant that about fifteen hundred persons arrived in the United States each day. By the turn of the century, Americans could boast of some fifty cities with populations greater than 100,000, while fifty years earlier there were not even ten. Another part of the answer is that between 1850 and 1920, the work week for Americans became shorter. In the middle of the nineteenth century, the average work week was about sixty to seventy hours and encompassed six full days of labor. By the end of the First World War, the direction of American society was clearly set toward the forty-hour week and growing parity between work and leisure. In this social context, new technologies of production (especially Henry Ford's perfection of mass production techniques) and new institutions of distribution and consumption (especially department stores, world's fairs, advertising agencies, and installment buying) reconfigured American culture around values associated with leisure and amusement.

We could conclude this book with any number of cultural or technological moments that would indicate the embeddedness of American mass culture in American life by the 1920s (think, for instance, of the production of Henry Ford's ten millionth Model T automobile in 1924). But one such moment stands out: George Owen Squier's application of radio technology to the transmission of music, which, in 1922, resulted in the creation of a music service called "Wired Radio," which he renamed Muzak. Utilized initially to transmit music to the home and to increase the productivity of workers on the job, Muzak may be regarded as background, but it provides us the opportunity to foreground the pervasiveness of mass culture in the United States much earlier than is often thought to have been the case.[22]

Fig. intro.-2. Chromolithograph representing the completion of the trans-Atlantic cable. Courtesy of the Library of Congress.

It is no secret that, by the early 1920s, American culture had dimensions that were so arresting that they were becoming the subject of an intense debate among European and American intellectuals concerned about the implications of these novel cultural forms for modern political systems. In the 1920s, American and European critics were joined by Japanese writers concerned about the Americanization of Japan through advertising and film images. But as early as 1901, an English journalist, W. T. Stead, had written a book entitled *The Americanization of the World*, in which he shrewdly argued that American economic organization had already reached such an advanced stage of development that England and, eventually, the rest of the world would be inevitably swamped by American products and American cultural values. Whether or not he was right about its effects, it is clear that, at the beginning of the twentieth century, American mass culture, blooming in the United States, was already pollinating shores on the other side of the Atlantic Ocean, creating some interesting cultural hybrids in the process.

Why was the United States the first nation to develop mass culture? Or, to put this question differently, why did the "massification of leisure" occur first in the United States?[23] The transcontinental railroad and communica-

Kladderadatsch.]   [Berlin.

The Americanisation of England.

Ships, railways, meat, cigars, matches, etc., all these John Bull receives from the many-handed Uncle Sam Buddha, but naturally in return for suitable gifts to the Priests.

Fig. intro.-3. This cartoon from the London magazine *Review of Reviews* (July 15, 1902, p. 101) captures the gist of W. T. Stead's articles, and later book, about the Americanization of the world. Courtesy of the General Research Division, New York Public Library, Astor, Lenox, and Tilden Foundations.

tion innovations associated with it are part of the answer; mass immigration is also part of the explanation; so is the rise of the American corporation. But we also need to step back to antebellum America and briefly survey the economic, technological, political, and religious forces that fostered the search for and development of a national culture that would override local and regional cultural loyalties. The first chapter does just that. It then proceeds to examine the development of circuses, wild west shows, dime novels, and vaudeville—all of which facilitated the commercialization of American culture and its packaging for a mass, ethnically diverse, transcontinental audience. As the second chapter makes clear, this process received an enormous boost from a series of world's fairs organized between 1876 and 1916, especially from the 1893 Chicago World's Columbian Exposition, a world's fair that, in addition to functioning as a hothouse for germinating future mass cultural forms, opens a revealing window on the complex interactions between the producers and consumers of mass culture. The third chapter maps the range of mass cultural forms that proliferated in the wake of the World's Columbian Exposition and examines how amusement parks, advertising, and popular music reconfigured American culture at the dawn of the twentieth century. The fourth chapter takes up the export of American mass culture to Europe, focusing especially on Buffalo Bill's Wild West performances in Europe, on the American exhibits at the 1900 Paris Universal Exposition,

Fig. intro.-4. A sign of modernity, the New York Building, Dutch headquarters of the New York Metropolitan Insurance Company, in Amsterdam's city center. Photograph ca. 1880s. Courtesy of the Gemeentearchief Amsterdam.

and on the popularity of American chromolithographs in Europe. The fifth chapter, "The Triumph of American Mass Culture," examines two momentous developments in American mass culture: D. W. Griffith's film *The Birth of a Nation* and President Woodrow Wilson's creation of the Committee on Public Information as the propaganda arm of the U.S. government during the First World War. Because of the perceived power of film, the Committee on Public Information devoted significant resources to film censorship and to fashioning the various modular components of American mass culture into vehicles for projecting positive images of the United States around the globe. Precisely because American mass culture was becoming a force with which to be reckoned in Europe as well as America, it began attracting serious attention from intellectuals on both sides of the Atlantic. It is to this subject that the final chapter of this book turns.

By examining a variety of mass cultural forms—from world's fairs to wild west shows to motion pictures—these chapters, along with the accompanying photographs and captions, insist that mass culture can never be understood as a static construct and that its constantly shifting boundaries have involved struggles between dominant and subordinate groups for the prerogative of giving meaning to the culture in which all Americans lived their lives. Our book concludes with a short epilogue, carrying the story of American mass culture and its reception in Europe into the middle third of the twentieth century, and a bibliographical essay that, in addition to providing a guide to further reading and reflection, suggests that the next step in the debate over the form, function, and meaning of mass culture must consider the globalizing dimensions of American mass culture and its implications for the future of the modern construct known as the nation-state.

Clearly a short book on a subject so complex cannot be comprehensive. Indeed, our aim is not to survey the expansion of American mass culture around the globe. But if we provide a basic introduction to the origins of American mass culture and its rise to prominence in America and Europe before the 1920s, and encourage further collaborative work across oceans into the multiple meanings of mass culture around the world, we will have accomplished our primary objectives.

Indeed, *Buffalo Bill in Bologna* is the product of one such collaboration, begun almost twenty years ago when Robert Rydell was selected by the U.S. Fulbright Commission to serve as John Adams Chair in American Studies at the University of Amsterdam and when Rob Kroes was promoted to the position of chaired professor of American Studies at the same university. Since then, we have worked together on many projects, including one sponsored by the Netherlands Institute for Advanced Studies in the Social Sciences and Humanities that enabled us to assemble a group of international scholars to study the reception of American mass culture in Europe. We would be remiss not to acknowledge again their contributions that helped make this book possible. Collaborations, of course, are built on respect and friendship; they can also involve differences. Rydell, if the truth be told, is rather more inclined, following the work of historian Alexander Saxton, to think of mass culture in terms of cultural imperialism and ideology, while Kroes, following the lead of social anthropologist Ulf Hannerz, is more inclined to think of mass culture in terms of hybridity and creolization. Rydell is more inclined to emphasize structures, institutions, and audiences; Kroes is more inclined to give primacy to processes and individual experiences. We maintain our inclinations but have always been willing to question them.

AMERICAN MASS CULTURE TAKES FORM

It is notoriously difficult, often impossible, to pin dates to cultural developments. As anthropologists and cultural historians remind us, cultures are
systems and processes, not events that can be dated.[1] But events can sometimes transform and redirect cultures. That is exactly what happened on
May 10, 1869, at Promontory, Utah, when a nationwide media event was
staged to join Americans on both coasts in celebrating the completion of the
transcontinental railroad. As telegraph wires carried the news of the golden
spike being hammered into the last tie, mass parades erupted in cities around
the United States. Marchers, forgetting the horrific costs in human life ex-
acted by the breakneck pace of the railroad's construction, hailed the railroad
as an engineering feat that rivaled that of the British construction of the Suez
Canal. A telegraph operator and poet, Walt Whitman, who had followed
news of the railroad's construction as it came in over the wires, wrote "Passage to India" to convey his understanding of what the transcontinental railway meant for the future:

> I see over my own continent the Pacific railroad surmounting every barrier,
> I see continual trains of cars winding along the Platte carrying freight and
>   passengers,
> . . . .
> . . . I behold enchanting mirages of waters and meadows,
> Marking through these and after all, in duplicate slender lines,
> Bridging the three or four thousand miles of land travel,
> Tying the Eastern to the Western sea,
> The road between Europe and Asia.[2]

Afire with the same kind of technological utopianism that would spark the
imagination of late twentieth-century Internet enthusiasts, Whitman believed

the transcontinental railroad would hasten the realization of the dream of human brotherhood.

Whitman's faith in technology may have been misplaced, but he certainly understood the epoch-making significance of the transcontinental railroad. In economic terms, the completion of the railroad, together with the passage of the Homestead Act, which opened America's vast interior to agricultural development, gave potential farmers access to both urban and foreign markets, while additional federal railroad acts connected the Midwest to Chicago and St. Louis, making these urban population centers in their own right. Population growth in the nation's interior, resulting, in part, from mass migrations from Europe and Asia, meant new, expanded markets for America's merchants and manufacturers, at least for those able and willing to take risks and acquire sufficient capital to gain access to these markets. By the 1880s, thanks to the large-scale investments necessary to foster industrial development, the era of entrepreneurial capitalism would give way to the rise of corporate capitalism, which limited the liability of investors for economic failure while holding the prospect of fabulous wealth for those with the means to invest in the nation's industrial growth. By the early 1900s, a growing number of American corporations were becoming multinational, establishing offices in major English, French, and German cities. Whether they understood all of its dynamics or not, Americans—and Europeans—were witnessing what historian Alan Trachtenberg has aptly termed "the incorporation of America."[3]

The rise of the corporation at home had important consequences abroad. As Emily Rosenberg has made clear, American corporations like General Electric, Westinghouse, and Singer Sewing Machines set up production facilities around the world. Food companies did the same, setting up processing plants in foreign countries in order to have better access to foreign markets. No less important was the level of U.S. foreign investments. Between 1897 and 1914, as Rosenberg notes, "American direct investments abroad more than quadrupled, rising from an estimated $634 million to $2.6 billion." American dollars promoted economic growth overseas, and at home, but America's overseas investments also had the effect of causing "varying degrees of economic, cultural, and political dependence on America, the ultimate source of capital and management decisions." As one English journalist lamented in his 1901 book, *The American Invaders:* Americans "have acquired control of almost every new industry created during the past fifteen years . . ."[4]

The rise of corporations, the creation of a nationwide and globalizing mass market for American products, linked to an increasingly intricate web of railroad and telegraph networks, had profound consequences for American culture. Within fourteen years of the completion of the transcontinental railroad, one of the most fundamental components of human culture, the conception of time, was utterly transformed as the railroads, to avoid unfortunate delays and collisions, standardized time and imposed uniform time zones across the United States. Standardized time, developed to facilitate access to mass markets, had its broader cultural corollaries as the basic rule of the new industrial economy, low unit cost and increased volume of production, came to be applied to the production of cultural as well as industrial products. To state the matter plainly, the same forces that were generating the incorporation of the American economy were also generating the incorporation of American culture.[5] By the 1890s, distinctive forms of industrially produced and increasingly standardized forms of entertainment were coming into being to capture national and even international markets. There were, to be sure, economic reasons for this "takeoff" of American mass culture, but there were equally compelling political reasons for its rapid development and triumph in American life.

Chief among these was the not so simple fact that, from the moment of its founding, the term "united" in United States had been an ideal to be hoped for, not a reality that could be assumed. The American colonies, after all, had replicated virtually every religious and political schism known to European societies since the beginnings of the Reformation. In addition, Americans were divided by race as descendants of Europeans imposed their rule on Native Americans and Africans. Given these divisions, compounded by emerging class divisions among European Americans within urban centers and regional and economic differences between the North, South, and West, an immediate question presented itself to the architects of the American republic: what would unite Americans? If, as Seymour Martin Lipset asserted, America was the "first new nation" that had broken the chains of colonial rule, how would it cope with its internal divisions and plan for its future?[6] Constructing and, over time, reconstructing a national identity would become a central characteristic of American life. Religion, politics, economics—all of these played a part in building the American nation prior to the Civil War. So did popular culture. In fact, over the course of the antebellum period, American popular culture increasingly served as an important vehicle for giving meaning to American politics.

By the 1830s, when French aristocrat and prison reformer Alexis de Tocqueville toured the United Stated and published his *Democracy in America*, the modern American political system—predicated on the ability of political parties to build coalitions among Americans across class and geographical lines—was in place. Driven by their coalition-building imperatives, the Democratic and, belatedly, Whig parties sought to win mass support for their particular ideological formulations. To do so, Jacksonian

Democrats, as Alexander Saxton has documented in *The Rise and Fall of the White Republic*, turned to an assortment of popular cultural media like newspapers, the theater, and minstrel shows to transmit their political ideas to a broad national audience.[7]

The linkage of politics and culture was apparent in the first mass circulation newspapers in the 1830s. Before the Age of Jackson, newspapers circulated on a subscription basis to a limited and generally elite audience. By 1830, according to Saxton, "there were sixty-five dailies in the United States with an average circulation of 1,200 ... In 1840, there were 138 dailies; in 1850, 254," with average circulation rising to around 3,000 in 1850. Made possible in part by the steam-powered press, the "penny press," with stories featuring urban crime reports and sex scandals, transformed journalism and helped cement urban working-class support within the Jacksonian coalition.[8]

No less important to the conflation of Democratic Party politics and culture in the Jacksonian period was blackface minstrelsy—an entertainment form that disseminated racist stereotypes of African Americans as a way of winning mass support among white urban audiences for the Democratic Party's emphasis on racial equality among whites regardless of class. Performed before largely white male audiences in urban centers by troupes organized by E. P. Christy, Thomas Rice, Dan Emmett, and Stephen Foster, these shows featuring white actors with blackened faces perfectly complemented Jacksonian political attacks on upper-class privilege and the broader defense of the institution of slavery that formed the ideological cornerstones of the Democratic Party in antebellum America.[9]

Coextensive with the rise of the penny press and blackface minstrelsy were transformations in American theater, especially the growing popularity of melodrama as a genre with a distinctive stock of lower-class vernacular characters who, as Saxton explains, were associated with the Jacksonian "upsurge" in national politics. Rough in action and speech, Jacksonian vernacular heroes, whether "Mose," the urban firefighter, or Nimrod Wildfire, the frontier hero modeled on David Crockett, rehearsed the racial calculus of the Jacksonian coalition and emphasized a racial democracy among whites to the exclusion of nonwhites.

The democratizing and nationalizing propensities within antebellum American culture generally and in the theater found graphic expression in New York City in 1849 when rivalry between two Shakespearian actors and their followers culminated in the bloody Astor Place Riot. Why would rivalry between Shakespearian actors lead to a riot that would leave at least twenty-two people dead and scores wounded? The short and not so simple answer is that in antebellum America, Shakespeare's plays were fundamentally intertwined with what it meant to be an American. As popular enter-

Fig. 1-1. 1849 Riot at the Astor Place Opera House. Courtesy of the Library of Congress.

tainment, they helped give meaning to America. As Lawrence Levine puts it, Shakespeare's plays, widely read and performed throughout the nation, "had meaning to a nation that placed the individual at the center of the universe and personalized the large questions of the day."[10] Leading actors like Edwin Forrest and Edwin Booth helped pioneer the development of the "star" system and cultivated extraordinary loyalties among their followers. Boisterous theater crowds that would, for example, interrupt performances by demanding that actors repeat favorite passages reflected the leveling tendencies of the Jacksonian period. When English or Anglophile actors refused to perform or were reported to have made degrading comments about American audiences, the consequences ranged from rotten fruit and vegetables being rained upon actors to mob action.

The latter fate befell English actor William Charles Macready, Edwin Forrest's chief Shakespearian rival. Macready, a talented actor with a strong bent for aristocratic sympathies, and Forrest, a hero of the Jacksonian urban working classes because of his animated style and militant championship of American nationalism, scheduled performances of *Macbeth* on the same day in rival New York theaters. Forrest played to an enthusiastic audience. Macready, on the other hand, never had a chance. When he opened in the Astor Place Opera House, boos, hisses, taunts, and ultimately projectiles forced him offstage. He immediately announced that he would leave for England, but a group of prominent civic leaders and notable American writers, including

Washington Irving and Herman Melville, convinced him that his departure would give the "mob" just what they wanted. Three days later, Macready announced he would give another performance in the same theater. When nearly two thousand affluent people jammed into the theater and another ten thousand gathered outside, the performance quickly became a staging ground for festering class antagonisms. As the crowd outside became convinced that the performance was being held to spite them, they threatened to burst through the doors and torch the theater and its aristocratically inclined patrons. When the militia prevented that from happening by firing point blank at the protesters and killing several, the opening volley in America's cultural wars had been fired. When the smoke cleared, Shakespeare still remained a presence in American popular culture, but his position of preeminence would be challenged by the novel cultural innovations pioneered by an American original—Phineas T. Barnum.[11]

Fig. 1-2. P. T. Barnum and James E. Bailey circus poster. 1897. Courtesy of the Library of Congress.

Born in 1810 in rural Connecticut to a family that lived in meager economic circumstances, Barnum became a Jacksonian partisan and man on the make. Convinced that he could make money in the world of popular amusements, with its mixture of animal shows and disabled people who were displayed as "freaks," he sold his grocery store and, with borrowed money, purchased an elderly African American woman, Joice Heth, from a showman who had been putting her on display with the claim that she was 161 years old and had been George Washington's nurse. Barnum added his own touch—publicity, and a lot of it. And it worked. Thousands flocked to see her, earning Barnum nearly fifteen hundred dollars a week. Then, when Heth died and an autopsy revealed her age to be about half what Barnum had advertised, Barnum, in response to one newspaper's scathing denunciation of his deceits, continued his publicity operation. Barnum told another newspaper publisher, James Gordon Bennett, that Heth was still alive and that the rival newspaper had been duped. Bennett unwittingly published one correction after another before finally coming to the realization that Barnum had been using him to keep the showman's name before the public and to whet its appetite for more of Barnum's productions.

They did not have long to wait. In 1841, he took over Scudder's American Museum—an old-fashioned cabinet of curiosities that had fallen on hard times—and converted the institution into an entertainment factory for New Yorkers eager for amusement. Barnum enumerated the exhibits at his dime museum, which he charged twenty-five cents instead of the usual dime to enter, as follows: "Educated dogs, industrious fleas, automatons, jugglers, ventriloquists, living statuary, tableaux, gipsies, Albinoes, fat boys, giants, dwarfs, rope-dancers, live Yankees, pantomime, instrumental music, singing and dancing in great variety, dioramas, panoramas, models of Niagara, Dublin, Paris, and Jerusalem; Hannington's dioramas of the Creation, the Deluge, Fairy Grotto, Storm at Sea; the first English Punch-and-Judy in this country, Italian Fantoccini, mechanical figures, fancy glass-blowing, knitting machines, and other triumphs in the mechanical arts; dissolving views, American Indians who enacted their warlike and religious ceremonies on the stage—these, among others, were all exceedingly successful." But what made the museum such a triumph was a combination of Barnum's genius for promotion and a lucky discovery, a midget, Charles S. Stratton, whom Barnum would call General Tom Thumb.

On Thanksgiving Day, 1842, Barnum put Tom Thumb on display in his museum and drew an enormous crowd. In many respects, there was nothing novel about Tom Thumb. People, especially those considered to be "other" by virtue of race or physical handicaps, were commonplace exhibits in the world of Victorian-era shows. What made Tom Thumb stand out was Barnum's ad-

Fig. 1-3. P. T. Barnum's American Museum, New York City. 1855. Courtesy of the Library of Congress.

vertising prowess. Through newspaper publicity, billboards, and biographies, Barnum promoted "the General" to the hilt and kept the American Museum in the forefront of the popular imagination.[12]

Barnum's scams are legendary. On one occasion, he joined a monkey's head to a fish tail and, calling his creation a mermaid, delighted thousands who paid to see this piece of humbug. On another, while managing Jenny Lind, "the Swedish Nightingale," he convinced the public that the singer gave all of her salary to charities. His chief discovery, as Daniel Boorstin explains, "was not how easy it was to deceive the public, but rather, how much the public enjoyed being deceived."[13] Neil Harris carries Boorstin's insight one step farther, insisting that Barnum, while the master of the humbug, achieved success because he appealed to the high value Jacksonian democrats placed on the ability of ordinary men and women to understand the world through their common sense. Barnum's hoaxes, in other words, were appealing because they flattered his audience, especially the widespread conviction among the middle classes in Jacksonian America that a commonsensical understanding of the world would guarantee the republic's survival into the future.[14]

To sum up, America, on the eve of the Civil War, nurtured a lively range of rapidly evolving popular cultural forms that, in their nationalizing and democratizing propensities, accompanied and complemented the rapid development of mass politics. Yet, like America's political, economic, and religious institutions, America's emerging popular cultural formations proved incapable of resolving the long simmering problem of slavery. The result was a civil war that registered enormous destruction of life and property.

As the single greatest failure of the American political system, the Civil War had profound consequences for the future of American culture. In particular, the war led to a redoubling of efforts to nationalize American culture and to rationalize the emergence of social hierarchy in the United States. Why? Because despite the euphoria that came with the completion of the transcontinental railroad, between 1873 and the First World War the American economy rocked between boom and bust. Industrial violence increased. Railroad workers launched a nationwide strike in 1877; alleged anarchists threw a bomb into a political rally at Chicago's Haymarket Square in 1886; steelworkers returned the violence directed at them by their employers at Homestead, Pennsylvania, in 1892; and federal troops were used to crush the 1894 strike by workers in George Pullman's company town. With millions of immigrants streaming into the United States, about one immigrant a minute between 1870 and 1910, a new and menacing question presented itself to many Americans. Had one civil war been fought between regions only to make way for another between classes?

In the context of the fault lines spreading across the American landscape, the organization of cultural meaning on a nationwide scale assumed newfound importance, and mass—industrially produced—cultural forms emerged as crucial institutions for manufacturing new values—and a new national identity—rooted in leisure, consumerism, and the doctrines of scientific racism. The point here is not that popular culture disappeared. Rather, the crucial point is that after the Civil War, American culture as a whole was transformed. By the 1890s, what was popular in American culture was increasingly the product of culture industries that, like American corporations, required a great deal of capitalization and increasingly sophisticated strategies for controlling resources and markets. The theater was one of the first arenas where these transformations became evident.

THE THEATER

Between the Civil War and the 1880s, according to historian Robert Toll, a veritable industrial revolution occurred in the theater business. Prior to the Civil War, most theater companies were locally based and independently owned and managed. After the Civil War, the same processes of consolidation that were occurring in industry were transforming the theater. The proliferation of railroads made it possible to organize so-called combination companies that required centralized managerial and booking operations as well as easy access to investment capital. By the 1870s, several large New

York City–based theater corporations were buying independent theaters across the country and linking them into theater "chains" that had to book their productions. By the early 1890s, the Theatrical Syndicate, a trust that operated in the mold of steel or oil trusts brought into being by Andrew Carnegie and John D. Rockefeller, owned over five hundred theaters nationwide and held a virtual monopoly over bookings in major cities and small towns alike. These transformations in the American theater from an entrepreneurial to a corporate-capitalist endeavor mirrored changes in the economic structure of the United States itself and resulted in the creation of a new theatrical product—vaudeville.[15]

Vaudeville—the exact origin of the term remains obscure—came into existence through the efforts of three individuals. The "father of vaudeville" was Tony Pastor, a former circus clown who, during the Civil War, developed a variety of acts and performed them in New York City's tenderloin saloons. After the war, Pastor, following Barnum's example, determined that he could make much more money if he cleaned up his acts and made them palatable to a Victorian middle-class audience. With his repertoire of songs and dances and trapeze performances, not to mention door prizes like sewing machines, Pastor opened several new theaters offering "high-class" family entertainment. In so doing, he opened the eyes of Benjamin Franklin Keith and Edward Franklin Albee, circus and dime-museum impresarios, who superimposed corporate-capitalist modes of organization on Pastor's more limited entrepreneurial visions.

Like Pastor, they targeted their variety shows for family audiences. But where Pastor was content with controlling one theater at a time, Keith and Albee set out to develop a vaudeville empire. Beginning with their palatial Colonial Theater in Boston, which cost over half a million dollars and boasted a dazzlingly opulent interior, they created a network of nearly two dozen theaters, including the fabled Palace Theater at 47th and Broadway in New York City, and helped organize other vaudeville producers into the United Booking Office. Through this latter arrangement, they tried to monopolize the national vaudeville circuit by agreeing to allow only actors who belonged to their organization to perform in their theaters.

Typically, a vaudeville show included eight or nine acts featuring comedians, acrobats, magicians, animal acts, and song-and-dance routines in various combinations. As vaudeville became ever more formulaic, it became standard practice to save the big-name performers, usually a comedy team like Joe Weber and Lew Fields, for the finale. And, more often than not, comedy routines turned on ethnic or racial humor. At the beginning of their careers, Weber and Fields, for instance, both products of New York's Lower East Side Jewish ghetto, performed in blackface before shifting their emphasis to ethnic

Fig. 1-4. Poster depicting the popularity of vaudeville. The origin of the term is obscure but may well have originated in the Vau de Vire (Valley of the Vire River) in Normandy, renowned for its popular music and fairs. Courtesy of the Library of Congress.

humor in the 1890s, probably to capitalize on growing public concern over the increasing number of immigrants to the United States. In one of their acts, the Pool Room Sketch, they used their own dialect to poke fun at immigrants. "Vatever I don't know, I teach you," Fields, playing a pool-hall hustler, assured the unsuspecting Weber before trying to cheat him out of his money.

Through the stereotypes perpetrated by immigrant actors, middle-class Victorians could certainly laugh at foreigners, who were increasingly perceived as a threat to the United States. But laughter could cut in a variety of ways. By getting middle-class audiences to laugh, immigrant comedians also subtly effected a shock of recognition of the immigrants' shared human qualities and gained cognizance of their ability to succeed in American society. And for working-class families who heard these jokes, immigrant vaudeville comedians may well have underscored something they already knew, namely the power of language to manipulate social reality.

With its legion of famous performers like magician Harry Houdini, blackface comedian Al Jolson, comic operatic star Lillian Russell, and a host of burlesque entertainers to be discussed in the next chapter, vaudeville, by the turn of the century, had become a staple in the lives of millions of Americans. According to one study, roughly 15 percent of America's urban population attended at least one vaudeville show a week, enabling theaters to gross around $20,000 per week.[16]

From the vantage point of many performers, the profitability of the shows seemed to go hand-in-hand with crass exploitation by theater owners. As Toll relates in *On with the Show*, film actor Groucho Marx, who, like so many other movie stars, got his start in vaudeville, derisively called Albee "Ol Massa" because of the latter's absolute control over the lives of actors. As was the case in other industries, vaudeville actors tried to organize for better wages and control over their working conditions. In 1900, following the precedent of British actors who had organized themselves into the Water Rats, a group of American actors banded together. Calling themselves the White Rats, they threatened to strike if the theater owners failed to change their practices. In the short term, they were outmaneuvered by the owners, who, following the example of other industrialists, made clear that they would "blacklist," that is, share the names of unionized actors and ban them from their theaters. But in the long run, the efforts of the White Rats did bear fruit, in the theater actors' strike of 1919 and the formation of the Actors' Equity Association.[17]

What accounts for vaudeville's success? Part of the answer has to do with the ability of producers to supply a seemingly inexhaustible array of fresh actors and acts who could provide socially acceptable entertainment for an emerging middle class increasingly interested in the political and social reforms associated with the Progressive era. Another part of the answer is more complex. In the first place, while vaudeville, with its lavish theaters, encouraged people to spend their time and money on entertainment, and thereby encouraged the commercialization of American culture, its lighthearted performances provided audiences with an opportunity to transcend the anxieties associated with America's growing consumer-oriented civilization. Vaudeville left audiences feeling good both about themselves and the culture of abundance that characterized middle-class existence. In the second place, vaudeville, through its standard fare of racial and ethnic comedy routines, helped sustain dominant beliefs about the presumed elite status of whites, while holding out the possibility that room could be made in American society for at least some white ethnic groups. These shows, in short, assured middle-class Progressive-era audiences of their prerogative to uplift and otherwise reform American society.

As important as it was, vaudeville was just one of the many bright constellations in an ever-widening galaxy of ideologically supercharged entertainments for the masses that made representations of racial hierarchy crucial to the process of national reconstruction after the Civil War. Others were the circus and the wild west show.

THE CIRCUS

Like its counterpart in outdoor theatrical entertainment, the wild west show, the circus became a crucial agent in what Terence Ranger and Eric Hobsbawm have aptly characterized as "the invention of tradition."[18] A characteristic of all societies, the invention and reinvention of tradition became especially important in America after the Civil War, when social conflict threatened to spill over every wall designed to restrain it. In addition to threats of class warfare manifested in waves of industrial violence that swept the country after the 1877 railroad strikes, mass immigration from southern and southeastern Europe and Asia seemed to be threatening the dominant position of Americans who claimed Anglo-Saxon supremacy as their birthright. As it gained popularity after the Civil War, the circus did not so much alleviate this anxiety as redirect it into an affirmation of America's imperial prowess.

The circus, of course, had its distant origins in antiquity, but historians more properly date the rise of the modern circus to London in 1770 when Philip Astley opened his hippodrome—a one-ring circus—featuring trained horses and other amusements including clowns and acrobats. With Astley's success, entrepreneurs in other cities followed suit and the circus medium spread across Europe and to the United States as a form of entertainment fixed to a particular site. With the opening of the Erie Canal in 1825, mobility, not fixity, began to characterize the American circus, and the tent rapidly became the American circus's defining architectural feature. Between 1825 and 1871, numerous circuses traveled around the United States and became a characteristic form of American popular culture.

After the Civil War, the same economy of scale and pressures of consolidation that affected the American economy as a whole reconfigured tent shows and circuses. With railroads giving greater access to wider markets in rural America, some entertainment entrepreneurs, notably P. T. Barnum, saw possibilities for increasing circus profits by adjusting the circus to new methods of transportation and corporate organization. After joining the circus world in 1871, Barnum formed several partnerships, culminating in 1887, when, with James E. Bailey, he created the Barnum & Bailey Greatest Show on Earth, which in turn would be purchased in 1908 by the five Ringling brothers and consolidated in 1918 as Ringling Brothers and Barnum & Bailey Combined Shows. Exactly what Barnum had in mind for a consolidated circus was clear from the title of his 1873 show: "P. T. Barnum's Great Traveling World's Fair Consisting of Museum, Menagerie, Caravan, Hippodrome, Gallery of Statuary and Fine Arts, Polytechnic Institute, Zoological Garden, and 100,000 Curiosities, Combined with Dan Castello's, Sig. Sebastian's and Mr. D'Atelie's Grand Triple Equestrian and Hippodromatic Exposition." The circus, in other words, would incorporate aspects of a vast array of American popular entertainments, including museums, fairs, animal exhibitions, and sideshow amusements, that could not be contained by one ring. In 1873, circuses added a second ring. Eight years later, when Bailey added a third ring to his massive circus operation, the form of the circus would be utterly reshaped, following a strategy that was a far cry from the one Barnum had pursued in the old days of the American Museum. At that institution, Barnum had tried to engage audiences with exhibits that cried out for exercising commonsense faculties. With "The Greatest Show on Earth," Barnum and his cohorts now emphasized the overwhelming of audiences with spectacle.

Reportedly, Barnum said of Americans: "There is a sucker born every minute." But, as several historians have noted, he is more accurately remembered for his dying words in 1891: "What were the gate receipts at Madison Square Garden last night?"[19] Clearly, the post–Civil War circus was becoming a big business, but it was about much more than widening profit margins or giving audiences what they wanted. With Gilded Age Americans engaged in what one historian has called a marked "search for order," the circus, with its enthralling pageantry and spectacle, functioned as a key institution in the effort to reconstruct an American national identity out of the rubble left by four years of civil war and in the face of mounting class conflict. To accomplish this end, circus organizers raised the tent poles for their cultural canopies on footings set in America's most durable ideological cement, white racism, which by the close of the century was also undergirding the national drive to develop an overseas empire.[20]

The racism of the circus was clear in the circular generated by the Ringling Brothers Circus entitled *The Plantation Darkey at the Circus*. "Everybody on this earth enjoys the circus to a greater or less extent," the showmen claimed, "but there is one individual who reels in the delights that come with the sawdust-sprinkled ring just a little more than anybody else. He is the nimble autocrat of the whisk-broom, the dining room, the whitewash brush and the Southern cotton field—in short, the great and only, Afro-American." What fascinated African Americans, according to the publicity release, were the clowns and the monkeys. "The monkeys," the circular insisted, "which to everyone else are queer little specimens of the animal kingdom, full of motion and pranks, are to the negro miniature old men and women from some far away lands where they have everything their own way and by some strange superstition usually connected with Ireland, and, stranger still, the darkey in looking at one will invariably exclaim, 'Looks just like a' Irishman.'"[21] In the context of growing concern about the assimilability of some Europeans that would lead to growing agitation for immigration restriction, the circus demonstrated the fluidity of racist stereotyping and its centrality for re-constructing a racially-based American national identity after the Civil War.

Circuses, importantly, not only reflected but shaped dominant thinking about race. They wove racism into the promotion of consumerism and imperialism. Continuing a tradition that reached into the antebellum period, American circuses featured displays of people from the Middle East, fostering images of "otherness" that coalesced in a set of beliefs that Edward Said aptly terms "orientalism." An 1880 advertisement from the Barnum & Bailey Circus was typical: "REAL WILD MOORISH CARAVAN! Scenes of Barbaric Splendor, Skilled Warriors, Daring Sheiks and Fearless Horsemen . . ." With their exotic harem dancers, circuses outfitted audiences with an imperialist vocabulary a full decade before the 1898 Spanish American War propelled America onto the world's stage as a colonial power. In the 1890s, the imperialist references of circuses became even more explicit as they increasingly made the Egyptian and Roman Empires the themes of their programs. The official program for the 1893 Ringling Brothers' circus, for instance, gushed with imperial rhetoric:

> The most imposing, glorious and majestic display ever beheld . . . At the blare of trumpets and blast of bugles, a tremendous outpouring and outspreading of a vast bannered army and motley throng of mailed marching warriors, gladiators, charioteers, steel-clad knights, royal grandees, mounted cavaliers and ladies, helmeted spearmen, civilians, squires, pontifical high-priests and wandering Jews, actors courting the dramatic muse, Moors and Mamelukes, Bedouins of the desert . . . Magnificent ostentation. The flash of sword and helmet, spear and shield. Garments rich with the dyes of the Indies; cloth of gold and glitter of silver . . . ; Displaying all the pageantry and pride of Rome's victorious legions . . . Imperial ballets and stupendous statues in one bewildering blaze of unisonous spectacular action and moving in majestic march, manoeuvre, dance and tableau obedient to the trumpet's call.[22]

With their three rings looping together a national vision of imperial abundance, and with America's "splendid little war" with Spain just around the corner, circuses gave proof to the proposition that life sometimes imitates art. The same could be said for the wild west show.

THE WILD WEST

Like an earlier hero of the American frontier, David Crockett, William Cody was born twice—the second time at the hands of a popular writer. The life that followed from Cody's natural birth in 1846 led him from Iowa to Kansas, where his father died fighting in the antislavery cause. After a brief stint in the U.S. army during the Civil War, Cody pegged his future to the industrialization of the American West and its concomitant—the extermination of Native Americans. He obtained a grading contract from one railroad corporation seeking to build a spur line that would join the transcontinental route. Once, in response to demands from his workers for fresh meat, Cody exhibited astonishing skills in slaughtering bison, killing eleven animals in quick succession. His hunting prowess on horseback earned him the moniker "Buffalo Bill" from admiring troops stationed nearby to protect railroad workers from attacks by Indians enraged by white encroachments on their territory. In 1868, with warfare erupting across the Great Plains between Indians and whites, Cody agreed to serve as a scout with the U.S. army and was quickly designated chief scout for the Fifth Cavalry, a position that earned him the admiration of General Philip Sheridan, a Civil War hero who had turned his talents to the pacification of the plains.[23]

Between 1869 and 1871, Cody's life took a dramatic turn. In 1869, popular writer of dime novels Edward Zane Carroll Judson, better known as Ned Buntline, met Cody and wrote a popular adventure story, *Buffalo Bill, King of the Border Men*, that, together with a melodramatic production based on the book, made Cody into an overnight sensation. Cody, however, did not show any immediate interest in capitalizing on his newfound fame. Not until newspaper publisher James Bennett invited him to New York City did Cody have a change of heart. At that point, he decided to team up with Buntline and agreed to star in *Scouts of the Prairie*, a play that Buntline scripted in several hours. Between 1873 and 1876 Cody pursued a career in show business, but the sudden death of his son, Kit Carson Cody, made him receptive to invitations to resume his position as scout for U.S. army forces prosecuting all-out warfare against Sioux Indians trying to repel the influx of gold seekers into the Black Hills of South Dakota. Three weeks after the Sioux defeated General George Armstrong Custer at the Battle of the Little Big Horn, Cody shot Cheyenne chief Hay-o-Wei through the head, scalped him, and yelled: "The first scalp for Custer!" The theatrical possibilities of the Sioux campaign registered immediately. Within weeks, Cody was seeking a script writer and soon thereafter determined to write several dime novels himself as well as his autobiography.

Cody was not alone in seeking to capitalize on public fascination with the events surrounding the Battle of the Little Big Horn and more general interest in the American West. Countless aspiring playwrights, authors, and show business entrepreneurs sought new ways to reach the massive audience galvanized by Custer's defeat at the hands of the Plains Indians. Part of the problem was scale—representing battles in the confined spaces of indoor theater just seemed inappropriate. But there were alternatives. As early as 1843, P. T. Barnum had organized an outdoor Buffalo hunt complete with Indian dancers in New Jersey that attracted over twenty thousand spectators. Circuses were well established as outdoor theatrical media, and rodeo, a relatively new form of outdoor entertainment featuring the roping and riding skills of cowboys, was taking hold. In 1882, Cody helped organize "The Old Glory Blowout" in Omaha, Nebraska—an event that combined equestrian showmanship with a buffalo hunt. On the basis of its success, Cody announced his intention to organize a show that would shortly be incorporated as "Buffalo Bill's Wild West, America's National Entertainment."

Cody did not organize his show on his own. He teamed up with two men with established show business credentials: Nate Salsbury and John Burke. Salsbury was an occasional actor, playwright, and aspiring theater manager who had long wanted to manage Buffalo Bill. Burke had been an actor in blackface minstrel shows before turning his talents to theatrical management and promotion. With Cody as star, these men organized a spectacle that bore one of the central characteristics of modern mass culture: what media critic David E. James terms "the consolidated integration of one medium with another and of art with social reality."[24]

The integration accomplished by Buffalo Bill's Wild West was multifaceted. Through his contacts with the army, Cody secured a steady supply of Native Americans willing to perform in exchange for higher wages than they could earn on reservations. Through their show business contacts, Cody's partners had access to skilled rodeo performers and to the latest technologies of transport and display. In addition to this vertical integration that paralleled the integration of raw materials and finished products in a growing number of large industries, the Wild West, through its press division under Burke's control, moved horizontally in the effort to build a market not only for Wild West performances but for souvenirs as well. Several decades before the phrase "public relations" came into common parlance and saturation advertising became routine, the Wild West boasted a prototypical public relations division that generated increasingly sophisticated advertising designed to equate a product—the show—with a way of life defined as heroic. By attending the show and buying souvenirs imprinted with Buffalo Bill's name, audiences were told they could live out fantasies of heroic action in the American West at the very moment government census-takers and prominent historians were proclaiming the end of the frontier. Billed as an authentic representation of the West, what the Wild West represented most accurately were the forces of industrialization that by the late twentieth century would render the American West the most industrialized section of the nation.

The industrial basis for Buffalo Bill's Wild West was clear from the start. Transporting the show required a minimum of eighteen railroad cars to carry the performers, work crews, animals, and equipment. Unless performances took place in already existing arenas like Madison Square Garden, work crews had to set up prefabricated grandstands, load and unload props that ranged from Gatling guns to stagecoaches, and set up tents for performers and concessionaires. As Sarah J. Blackstone points out, the show "carried with it the largest private electrical plant in existence at the time" and required an enormous food service capable of feeding seven hundred people three times a day. In one week, Blackstone relates, the show's storeroom disbursed:

> Beef 5,694 pounds; veal 1,259 pounds; mutton 750 pounds; pork 966 pounds; bacon 350 pounds; hams 410 pounds; chicken 820 pounds; bread 2,100 loaves; milk 3,260 quarts; ice 10 tons; potatoes 31 barrels; cabbage 7 barrels ... Worcestershire sauce 15 gallons; mustard 6 gallons; powdered mustard 15 pounds ... pig's feet 1 barrel; flour 4 barrels; cornmeal 200 pounds; syrup 10 gallons; and pies 500.[25]

Operating on a military-industrial scale, the Wild West became a mobile dream factory capable of producing narratives of heroic conquest for mass audiences numbering in the millions.

Those narratives took form in the pageantry of the Wild West—pageantry that reproduced the essential ideological messages of western dime novels, making those messages visible and therefore more powerful. As Blackstone makes clear, the basic structure of the Wild West was set as early as 1886, when Buffalo Bill opened a show in Madison Square Garden that ran for several months. Entitled *The Drama of Civilization*, the show turned on five acts—called "epochs." The first epoch, "The Primeval Forest," featured Indians and animals borrowed from a circus living together before the arrival of whites. The second epoch, "The Prairie," centered on an emigrant train coping with an array of natural disasters, including a prairie fire. "Cattle Ranch," the third epoch of civilization, showed Buffalo Bill coming to the rescue of a beleaguered pioneer family under attack from Indians. "Mining Camp," the final epoch, announced the arrival of "civilization" with the Pony Express and a variety of cowboy entertainments. As if to underscore the importance of "civilization," *The Drama of Civilization*, before completing its run, included a final "epoch," Custer's Last Stand, that concluded with Buffalo Bill arriving at the scene of the "massacre" with the words "Too Late!" projected on a screen behind the cyclorama painting of the battle.[26]

This drama of the triumph of civilization over savagery would be replayed many times during the life of the Wild West, but the theater of battle soon extended from the Little Big Horn to encompass much of world history. While on tour in Europe, Buffalo Bill included a grand review of mounted troops from a variety of countries and featured a troupe of African Zulu men and women. The success of these features resulted in the rechristening of the show for its debut alongside the 1893 Chicago world's fair. Called "Buffalo Bill's Wild West and Congress of Rough Riders of the World," the Wild West took on the character of an imperial pageant. By the close of the century, the show included "exotic" components—Arab acrobats and an "Indian from Africa" segment featuring an African or African American riding an elk— that nurtured the same underlying worldview that world's fairs were projecting. To underscore its function as an imperial showcase, the Wild West included Filipinos from America's first overseas colony and an act featuring some of the Rough Riders who had charged up San Juan Hill. Little wonder that Theodore Roosevelt admired the Wild West, especially the way its opening anthem, "The Star Spangled Banner," brought crowds to their feet cheering the entrance of Buffalo Bill's performers. As president, Roosevelt would help inaugurate the drive to make "The Star Spangled Banner"—an old English drinking melody that came to Francis Scott Key's head during the War of 1812—America's national anthem. By the close of the nineteenth century, wild west shows joined the panoply of mass entertainments that were creating, sometimes consciously, sometimes not, a national culture rooted in the shared conviction that "to be a people of plenty" Americans would have to accept "empire as a way of life."[27]

This, at least, was the central message of the wild west show script. But was it the only message audiences could come away with? Certainly not, especially if the performer happened to be female. Proper women in the Victorian era were supposed to be the guardians of American morality. They were supposed to be angelic and submissive, content to nurture their children and fashion their homes into places where their husbands could take refuge from the ravages of the get-ahead world of business. But several Wild West performers did not exactly fit this stereotype, despite the efforts of publicity men to make them conform.

Annie Oakley, Lillian Smith, May Lillie, and Annie Schafer were cases in point. Billed as "The Peerless Wing and Rifle Shot," Oakley consistently de-

Fig. 1-5. Poster depicting Buffalo Bill's Wild West Congress of Rough Riders. 1899. Courtesy of the Library of Congress.

feated males who challenged her shooting prowess. As evidence of her skill, her act included shooting a cigarette from her husband's lips and a dime held by his fingertips. Smith and Lillie also specialized in dazzling audiences with their sharpshooting skills, while Schafer performed in equestrian events that included roping and bronco busting.[28]

Because women performing in wild west shows challenged prevailing stereotypes, showmen did their best to contain the threatening potential of women sharpshooters and rodeo riders by emphasizing their femininity. One program went out of its way to insist that the women performers were "not of the new woman class—not of the sort that discards her feminine attributes and tries to ape the man . . ."[29] But through their performances, in which they abandoned the side saddle and dressed in cowboy attire, and matched their equestrian and shooting skills with men, the women performers in the wild west shows revealed the ability of performers to edit—if not rewrite—cultural scripts and to test the limits of Victorian values.

A similar argument has been made about the Indians who performed in wild west shows. While there is no doubt that wild west showmen used Indian performers to lend legitimacy to America's imperialism on both domestic and foreign fronts, it would be an exaggeration to regard Indian performers as helpless victims of the showmen's wiles. According to historian Lester G. Moses, wild west shows, especially Buffalo Bill's, afforded Indians the opportunity to negotiate for higher wages than they received for work on reservations, empowered Indians to educate white American audiences about native cultures, and essentially afforded Indian performers an opportunity to "make do" in a society that seemed hell-bent on their extermination.[30] American Indian and women performers revealed one of the fundamental truths about mass culture, namely that the producers of mass culture products did not always maintain absolute control over their productions. Nevertheless, as the history of another mass cultural medium, the dime novel, makes clear, it would be a mistake to ignore the scripts themselves.

BOOKS FOR THE MILLIONS

The revolution in printing technology that resulted in steam-driven cylinder presses capable of printing mass circulation newspapers for a growing urban working-class readership opened possibilities for low-cost book and magazine publication as well. Beginning in the 1840s, entrepreneurs seized the opportunity to test "story papers," weekly newspapers and pamphlets that contained serialized fiction and miscellaneous advice features.

Their success—the *Flag of Our Union* circulated to about 80,000 readers in the 1850s—inspired two brothers, Erastus and Irwin Beadle, to join forces with Robert, William, and David Adams to cash in on this market. They tried their hand at periodicals, books, and song books before publishing Ann Stephens's *Malaeska: The Indian Wife of the White Hunter*, their first dime novel. Its stupendous success—its sales would eventually reach over a half million—led them to publish several other novels, including *Seth Jones; or, The Captives of the Frontier*, by Edward Ellis. Unlike Stephens, who had an established reputation as a writer of magazine fiction, Ellis was an unheralded schoolteacher not yet twenty years old. *Seth Jones* secured the fortunes of the House of Beadle and Adams, and Ellis's career as a dime novelist. He would write nearly 150 dime novels for the firm over the course of his career. Along with writer Metta Victor, who wrote over 100 dime novels, and her husband Orville, who served as chief editor of the firm, these authors helped transform the House of Beadle and Adams into what literary historian Henry Nash Smith called one of the "industrial giants" of the era.[31] By setting up and controlling its own distribution network centering on urban newsstands, especially in railroad stations, Beadle and Adams had standing orders of 60,000 copies for their novels, making them, according to Smith, the counterparts in the publishing world to steel magnate Andrew Carnegie and oil baron John D. Rockefeller. This was no exaggeration. As Alexander Saxton has calculated, by converting the production of fiction to an industrial enterprise, Beadle and Adams—a veritable "fiction factory," in the words of another historian—sold over 250 million copies of their dime novels over the course of their firm's thirty-eight-year existence.[32]

Clever production, marketing, and distribution strategies, while important reasons for the success of dime novels, cannot by themselves account for the popularity of the novels among their overwhelmingly working-class readership. The content of the novels was appealing as well, especially frontier adventure stories that can more accurately be described as fictional recreations of the Jacksonian ethos of racial equality among white Americans through the means of violence directed at Native Americans. This thematic emphasis was so pervasive that it could hardly have been accidental or coincidental. Rather, it was formulaic, consciously created to match a set of ideological suppositions that insisted race, or more precisely, racism, could blur class distinctions among whites, giving them a shared consciousness of racial equality regardless of sharp differences in class position. Dime novels, in other words, played the same role in the late nineteenth century that minstrel shows played in the antebellum period, but with one notable difference. Minstrel shows had served the interests of the Democratic Party; dime novels functioned to advance the nationalizing and industrializing agenda of the Republican Party by masking class strife and locating the rebirth of a new, postwar American identity in racial warfare in the Far West.[33]

Not all Americans were pleased by the stunning success of dime novels and cheap magazines, especially those featuring stories of urban crime. In the 1870s, moral reformer Anthony Comstock launched a crusade condemning dime novels and story papers for sapping the moral fiber of America's young people. Calling much of this literature pornographic, Comstock mounted a crusade against "vice" that led to the passage of a law—the so-called Comstock Law—banning material deemed obscene and in poor taste from the mails and that continued into the early twentieth century when he led opposition to Margaret Sanger's efforts to educate the public about birth control.[34] Often dismissed as idiosyncratic, Comstock is better remembered as a brevet-general in the battle for control of American culture. He certainly helped set the stage for two authors, Horatio Alger and Owen Wister, who turned the dime novel medium into a weapon to reform and hasten the reconfiguration of American culture.

Horatio Alger was well equipped for the task. Born in 1832 into a family dominated by a Unitarian minister, Alger attended Harvard to study for the ministry but left with a taste for writing. After a short career as a minister, he devoted his time and energy to writing stories for boys that preached the Protestant work ethic and the possibility of rising from rags to a modicum of affluence. As John G. Cawelti points out, Alger's stories were not primarily about rising from rags to riches. His heroes rarely made great fortunes. Rather, they attained something that, at least in Alger's opinion, was worth even more—respectability.[35]

Alger's novels sold in the hundreds of thousands, but not primarily among real-life working-class children put to work in urban factories. His audience was largely middle class, and strongest, many historians have noted, among adults living in rural America seeking validation for bourgeois values through nostalgic fantasies about success in an economic world that preceded the advent of rigid corporate hierarchies. Horatio Alger stories, in a word, fortified middle-class values by transforming the Jacksonian ideal of the self-made individual into a weapon that could function both as carrot and stick in the hands of self-appointed cultural gatekeepers.

No less important than Alger in stocking the middle-class ideological arsenal for the struggle to give new definition to the meaning of American culture was Owen Wister. *The Virginian*, published in 1902, became a national bestseller within a year and complemented efforts by Wister's friends, painter Frederic Remington and President Theodore Roosevelt, to redraw the imaginative boundaries of the American West. Born in 1860, Wister was the grandson of actress Fanny Kemble and at an early age demonstrated a gift for musical composition. At Harvard, he studied law and graduated with Roosevelt but, like Alger, decided against entering an established profession to take his chances with a literary career. He too drank from the trough of dime novels and saw in the western formula novel a genre that, with some important modifications, could appeal to a middle-class readership.

Unlike the authors of dime novels who reinvented the egalitarian themes of Jacksonian Democracy and put them to use building popular support for the nationalizing agenda of the Republican Party, Wister reinvented the idea of the West itself. For Wister, whose conservative friends shared Roosevelt's passion for the American West as a source for revitalizing the body and soul of the nation, the West held the best hope for providing America with an elite body of men who could lead America forward toward a fitter, masculine, and racially exclusive future. Wister, as Saxton explains, especially in *The Virginian*, shifted the basis of white supremacist convictions away from older arguments rooted in religious convictions to more recent rationalizations grounded in social-Darwinian notions of "survival of the fittest." The American West, for Wister, represented the birthplace of a reconstructed America run by a new aristocracy—the southern roots of the character called only the Virginian and his marriage to a northern woman were hardly coincidental—less concerned with killing Indians than with managing property and defending the interests of corporate capital from ruffians deemed socially and racially unfit.[36] Furthermore, as Jane Tompkins has pointed out, *The Virginian* represented a concerted assault on the authority of the "scribbling women" writers who had been the bane of Nathaniel Hawthorne. With its emphasis on violence as opposed to values associated with Christian nurture and the cult of domesticity, *The Virginian* and Wister's subsequent novels turned the western into a genre that helped middle-class men regenerate their identity through a code of violence that at its core devalued women.[37]

The Virginian made the western novel respectable for a male middle-class readership. No less than other leisure-time pursuits, it may have encouraged fantasies as escape routes from social reality, but more importantly it mapped that reality from a particular class and gender perspective. For Wister, the West was the place where "true democracy and true aristocracy are the same thing," where heroic action and corporate capitalism complemented one another, and where women did not compete against men. Wister's imaginative and ideological rewriting of history captured a national audience of middle-class male readers. Within a year of its release, *The Virginian* became a national best seller. Over the course of the twentieth century it would sell over two million copies, serve as the basis for several films, and inspire a television series. By successfully reinventing the American West as synonymous with America itself, Wister, along with artists like Frederic Remington, provided Americans with a powerful nationalizing message that perfectly complemented the rise of the Republican Party to prominence between the end of the Civil War and through the First World War—a period, it is worth remembering, that between the presidencies of Abraham Lincoln and Woodrow Wilson saw the Republican lock on the White House cracked only twice, on two separate occasions by Democrat Grover Cleveland. By the close of the nineteenth century, in the hands of writers like Owen Wister and performers like William F. Cody, "the western" had become central to the set of beliefs that undergirded the triumph of the Republican Party.

But how widely shared were these beliefs in American political culture? Drawing on the insights of literary historian Janice Radway and cultural critic Ien Ang into the way late twentieth-century audiences read romance literature and view television soap operas, some historians have suggested that turn-of-the-century working-class readers appropriated the messages of dime novels and used them to suit their interests. Historian Michael Denning, for instance, demurs from the notion that the "fiction factories" were wholly successful in inscribing working-class readers with the ideological meanings intended by their authors. The braking, or reality-checking, mechanism lay in the way workers read these novels—a way of reading rooted in the artisan culture of the antebellum period. Workers, Denning argues, did not read books in the same way as the Victorian middle classes, that is, "novelistically." Rather, workers continued to read "allegorically," to use the novels "to situate oneself in the world, to name the characters and map the terrain of the social world." This is particularly clear in the way routine and formulaic happy endings could be read. Novelist Henry James may have scorned conclusions that resulted in the triumph of workers and working-class heroines over the forces of evil as "a distribution at the last of prizes, pensions, husbands, wives, babies, millions, appended paragraphs, and cheerful remarks." But, as Denning points out, endings like these represented an ideological reordering of cultural meanings from a working-class perspective. In the hands of workers, the dime-novel products of a mass culture industry, themselves an appropriation of working-class literature, were at least partially re-claimed by their audience. As Denning so tellingly puts it: "And the 'distribution at the last of prizes, pensions, husbands, wives, babies, millions, appended paragraphs, and cheerful remarks' that James objected to is usually, in dime novels, a *redistribution*, an expropriation of the expropriators." The lesson that Denning draws is clear. However powerful they may have been, the industries of mass culture could not erase earlier traditions of popular culture or preclude "alternative" readings of mass-produced "texts"—whether in the form of literature, wild west shows, or circuses.[38]

This is an important argument to bear in mind. But it is also important to remember that what made vaudeville, circuses, wild west shows, and dime novels such powerful disseminators of sometimes subtle, sometimes blatant, ideological messages about white supremacy and national progress was their cumulative effect within a culture that increasingly lived by the dictum that seeing is believing.

PHOTOGRAPHY AND THE DAWN OF A "CHROMO-CIVILIZATION"

Central to the development of America's visual culture was a series of European innovations in "writing with light" that culminated in Louis J. M. Daguerre's 1839 invention of a process of capturing images on copper plates treated with a silver coating and developed with mercury vapors. The "daguerreotype" process may have been invented in Europe, but it took America by storm. In less than ten years, according to historians Mick Gidley and David E. Nye, "a veritable photographic *industry* was under way and, in this sphere at least the United States would not need to look overmuch to Europe again." Indeed, by 1851, according to the *New York Daily Tribune*, American studios were producing three million daguerreotypes.[39] That same year, when American photographers Mathew Brady, Martin Lawrence, and John Whipple received the highest awards for their work at London's Crystal Palace Exhibition, the power and prestige of this new medium was clear. A decade later, President Abraham Lincoln confirmed the place of photography in American political culture when he declared that a Brady portrait taken on the occasion of his speech at the Cooper Union in New York City, and distributed nationally, had played a major role in helping him win the presidency. In Washington, at the very outset of the Civil War, it was again Mathew Brady, having just photographed Lincoln's inauguration, who made *cartes de visite* for hundreds of departing soldiers, both fostering and satisfying a photographic desire, a desire for the photograph, which, given the number of troops in the city, can be understood, as Bill Brown points out, as a desire of the masses.[40] Photography had sufficiently established itself in the public mind as a unique tool of memory—or mnemonic device—to satisfy the interest in keeping absent loved ones pictorially present.

Yet it was the Civil War itself that would establish photography as a medium affecting the way in which the general public would henceforth be able to imagine such momentous historical events as war. Mathew Brady and his team of war photographers for the first time in history confronted audiences with images of the war as a machine producing corpses, thus radically changing their views of battlefields as fields of glory and heroism. His "Incidents of War" exhibit in New York led the *New York Times* to award Brady "honorable recognition for mak[ing] Photography the Clio of the war," proclaiming the exhibit to be "nearly as interesting as the war itself."[41] Alexander Gardner's photographs, displayed in the Brady exhibit, relentlessly foreground dead soldiers' faces, and their mangled, strangely contorted bodies. The pictures fascinated the crowds in Brady's studio. Drawn by a longing to see, they were participating in a new ritual of morbid fixation, where, according to the account in the *New York Times*, "groups [were] standing around these weird copies of carnage," or in Stephen Crane's words, "bending down to look in the pale faces of the dead, chained by the strange spell that dwells in dead men's eyes." As the writer for the *Times* put it, the "terrible fascination" of the battlefield "draws one near these pictures, and makes him loath to leave them."[42]

By the time Crane re-evoked this morbid fascination in his 1895 novel *The Red Badge of Courage*, using the words that we just quoted, the impact of Civil War photographs was already undergoing an ideological containment, as Alan Trachtenberg, among others, has argued.[43] The containment aimed at a nationalist memory of the Civil War as testing ground. "The war as we see it now," John Robes argued in 1891, was an "exhibition of the Anglo-Saxon race on trial," serving "to bring out [the] resolute and unyielding traits belonging to our race," its "unconquerable determination."[44] Yet, as Bill Brown argues, the act of re-imagining the nation depended on "forgetting the photographic archive—or on remembering it, transforming it, within a different medium."[45] And that medium was the traditional wood engraving. In fact, at the time, photographic images could only be mass produced by rendering them as woodcuts. Popular as Civil War images were in the 1890s, what most people, including Stephen Crane, beheld were imitations of photographs, taking away photography's disturbing immediacy, while mediating its message.

Thus, for well over half a century following its invention, photographs had not truly entered the emerging world of the mass circulation of images. For a direct confrontation with the new medium, people still had to flock to individual photographers' studios. But even in its early years, photography's radically modern nature could still be contained within cultural conventions that saw the individual photograph essentially in the light of painterly productions, produced in studios and displayed in portrait galleries.

There is one major exception to this story. Relentless technical development of the new medium would soon make for the reproducibility of photographic images on a massive scale and for their commercial distribution among a mass audience.

This first mass cultural form of photography was the stereograph, which provided viewers with three-dimensional pictures of places and people they would never likely see with their own eyes. The marvel of this medium was that it not only froze time, as do all photographs, but also caught space in a time warp. Viewers were confronted with a virtual space of uncanny realism where the eye could wander, yet as inaccessible as the past itself. In the years before yet further technical developments such as rotogravure allowed for the reproduction of photographs in newspapers and illustrated magazines like the *National Geographic*, stereograph companies produced a vast visual inventory of the world. Stereographs were produced as early as the 1850s, but not until the development of gelatin emulsions and mass production techniques in the 1880s did they become as ubiquitous as television today. In its early days stereographs were produced in virtually every country that had commercial photographers. The first major producer was the London Stereoscopic Company, established in 1854. Intent on making its advertising slogan, "No home without a stereoscope," a reality, it sold over a million views in 1862. The Parisian company of Ferrier almost equaled that sales figure in the same year. But by the late nineteenth century stereographs had become primarily an American phenomenon, exported from its mass market to the smaller national markets of Europe.

By 1900, 6,000 publishers of stereographic images existed in the United States (contrasted with 1,500 in Europe). "The American publishers," one historian writes, "issued an estimated 5 to 7 million *different* images before the last company stopped manufacturing them in the late 1930s. If one speculates that only 100 copies were made from each of these different negatives, then the industry published more than 700 million images." Put in different terms, by the 1880s, home viewing of boxed stereograph sets of landscape scenes, famous battles, and European monumental architecture became the Victorian-era equivalent of watching television.[46]

In the 1880s, the drive to capture the mass market for photographic images took a new twist when George Eastman, through a series of shrewd investments, partnerships, and technological innovations, developed the first film system and a new negative film. In 1888, he patented a new lightweight box camera—he called it a "Kodak"—that individuals could use to take their own photos. He simultaneously concentrated his efforts on film processing and marketing and set up a system whereby customers could mail exposed film to his factory in Rochester, New York, for speedy development. By the 1890s, Eastman had become one of America's leading industrial capitalists and Kodak had become a household word.

In the eyes of Europeans, the Kodak was typically American in a number of ways. It combined production techniques using replaceable parts with a design intended to be user friendly, and, most importantly, it aimed at democratizing the tool of photography. Everyone could henceforth be his or her own photographer. Press the button and Kodak would do the rest. Or, as the French slogan had it: "Click, clack, merci Kodak." On a mass scale, photography would henceforth allow people to record their own individual lives, catching highly private moments with a view to producing visual archives of individual memories, "family albums." All the way from production to consumption, photography had now entered the realm of the private and domestic. As for the mass dissemination of this new tool, one further element struck Europeans as typically American: the marketing acumen through advertising that Americans displayed in creating a demand for the Kodak camera, in the United States as well as in Europe.

Entire areas of human communication, across generations, within families when they wished to relive their own histories, or across geographic distance as in the case of immigrants informing those that had stayed behind, had henceforth become connected to visual exchanges through the miracle of photography.[47] Millions of photographic images, taken by individuals for individual consumption, came to constitute a vast archive of visual memories. It offers dramatic testimony to the way in which photography has affected the human need to remember. It testifies to an almost magical exercise: to prevent time from eroding the visual features of a past that once was our present.

Much as photography may have entered the private sphere as a memory tool, its role in the public sphere was undiminished. In the mass circulation of public images, photography reached a new stage when technical developments such as the halftone screen, breaking down photographic images into tiny dots and, somewhat later, the advent of the wire services, made for the instant transmission of images across the globe. It meant a sea change in the way people now conceived of current events. The writing press would henceforth have to make room for colleagues wielding a camera rather than a pen. As a result a new genre of journalism emerged, known as photojournalism. In both Europe and the United States, the illustrated press got a new lease on life, replacing older forms of visual representation such as engravings with photographs, hoping to satisfy a public need for visual realism. A new form of reportage emerged, known as the photo essay, wherein photographs combined to tell a story and such text as remained served only as a verbal guide to the correct "reading" of the images.

Paralleling these developments in photography were innovations in the field of chromolithography. Like photography, chromolithography was invented in Europe before it traveled to the United States. Unlike early photography, though, its mechanics and purpose were never shrouded in mystery. It aimed at the simple, straightforward reproduction, in color, of man-made images. From its incipience it was practical, down to earth, and openly showed its colors as a tool aiming at a mass market. Thus, more than photography, it directly addressed elite concerns about the hallowed aura of high art, and prompted an elite discourse defending and defining the kind of educated public that could properly appreciate artistic renditions of the world.

Between 1840 and 1900 original paintings were being reproduced lithographically in color and sold in America by the millions. At the peak of America's Victorian age, the mass-produced color lithograph waved unchallenged as the flag of popular culture. Its pervasiveness, as Peter Marzio points out, has led some historians to see the fifty-year period following the Civil War as the "chromo-civilization." Marzio goes on to say that "[t]he most compelling aspect of this story . . . is that the chromo civilization was marked by a faith in fine art, a belief in the power of art to enrich the life of anyone. This attitude embraced the notion, heretical to some, that fine art should be reproduced, packaged, and offered to the masses. The chromo embodied this attitude—it was the democratic art of the post–Civil War decades."[48] As we shall see in a subsequent chapter, there were those, public intellectuals among them, who begged to differ.

DEPARTMENT STORES

The proliferation of Kodaks and chromolithographs bore witness to the rise of a consumer civilization. But the institution chiefly responsible for cementing the transformation of customers into consumers was the department store—a new feature of late nineteenth-century American life that institutionalized preexisting patterns of commercial behavior and simultaneously revolutionized them. Prior to the Civil War, the closest entity resembling a department store was the Bon Marché in Paris, founded in 1852. While there were large dry-goods operations, like Alexander T. Stewart's Marble Palace in New York City, these were wholesale not retail businesses. By the turn of the century, enormous retail shopping emporiums had opened, bearing the names of Marshall Field in Chicago, John Wanamaker in Philadelphia, Roland Macy and Isaac Gimbel in New York City, and I. Magnin in San Francisco. These merchant princes—some of whose operations were bought out by rivals—learned much from strategies of centralization that other business leaders were pursuing and applied them to the retail trade. In effect, they consolidated the specialized functions of numerous small shops under one roof, giving them enormous advantages in their purchasing power and inventory. Added to this were innovations in display techniques and marketing that turned department stores into palatial dream factories of mass—not "pious"—consumption.[49]

The prototype of the modern department store was developed by Philadelphia merchant John Wanamaker, who, in 1876, the year of Philadelphia's Centennial Exposition, turned an old railroad depot into the Grand Depot. By the 1890s department stores were fast becoming dominant and fiercely competitive institutions in the downtowns of most American cities. As historians Stuart and Elizabeth Ewen describe Wanamaker's Chicago store:

> 129 counters totalling two-thirds of a mile in length, with fourteen hundred stools in front of them. Lighting was supplied by leaded glass skylights by day, gas chandeliers by night. In 1896, Wanamaker built a nearly life-sized replica of the Rue de la Paix in his store—'a consolation for Americans who could not go to Paris.' In 1911, Wanamaker opened a new twelve-story structure featuring a Grand Court, and the second largest organ in the world, the latter punctuating the shopping day with sacredness.[50]

Coupled with the development of the mail-order catalog business that Richard Sears and Montgomery Ward carried to heights its originator, Benjamin Franklin, could never have imagined, department stores refashioned American tastes and values in ways that lent a utopian dimension to consumption as a way of life.

In *Land of Desire: Merchants, Power, and the Rise of a New American Culture*, William Leach describes the world of goods available for purchase by the close of the nineteenth century: "Siegel-Cooper's sold ... not only staples, yard goods, notions, ready-made clothing, machine-made furnishings, and hundreds of name-brand pianos but also photographic equipment in the largest photographic gallery anywhere, and monkeys, dogs, cats, birds, lion and panther cubs, and tropical fish in its huge pet department."[51] Other stores expanded even further horizontally into the grocery and restaurant busi-

Fig. 1-6. Wanamaker's Philadelphia department store. 1896. Courtesy of the Library of Congress.

nesses, offering foods and wines at prices local merchants could hardly match. Some offered banking and barber services. Like other industries, notably steel, department stores quickly sought to control the supply of goods by integrating vertically. Marshall Field's, for instance, controlled many of its own factories and mills, while Bloomingdale's owned piano-building and garment factories.

Department stores not only sold goods on a scale antebellum merchants could scarcely have imagined but conjured up and packaged dreams about the meaning of the good life in ways that lent new meaning to Thomas Jefferson's concept of the "pursuit of happiness." Crucial to the success of this new way of thinking about the meaning of happiness were new strategies of exhibition and display, centering on the use of store windows, mannequins, and electricity to dramatize and lend a dreamlike quality to the accumulation of goods. Through their artful narratives of consumer desire, department stores were well on their way to becoming secular cathedrals that suffused the act of consumption with religious meaning and the promise of salvation, especially for women—and not only middle-class women—who found in the

shopping experience and the employment afforded by department stores
what Leach terms "a culture that seemed to offer everyone access to an un-
limited supply of goods and that promised a lifetime of security, well-being,
and happiness."[52]

Although they may have lacked the spendable—it was certainly not dis-
posable—income of their middle-class counterparts, working-class women
were also engaged with new institutions of mass culture and tried to make
the intersecting worlds of mass consumption and mass entertainment work
to their advantage. Whether through fashions, where working-class women
could literally re-fashion their identities by manipulating mass-produced
clothing items, or dancing, which young women carried from saloons to commercialized dance halls and where boundaries of acceptable sexual behavior
could be tested and redrawn, working-class women negotiated for greater
power within their own families and for greater inclusion in the broader society. That process of negotiation, however, as historian Kathy Peiss has insisted, was not exactly between economic equals. Since working-class women
remained economically subordinate to men, the pleasures of commercial culture, while real and liberating in some respects, did little to alter prevailing
power relations between genders.[53]

Owing in no small measure to the efforts of America's merchant princes,
the post–Civil War United States was becoming a new nation with a new set
of values. Where antebellum Americans living at the beginning of the nineteenth century in a producer-centered economy had prized thrift and valued

Fig 1-7. Sears shoe factory, Littleton, New Hampshire. Courtesy of the Library of Congress.

character, postbellum Americans increasingly valued consumer spending and personality (outward appearance) as signs of inner grace and worldly success.[54] A writer like Edward J. Bellamy, descendant of a long line of New England ministers, could find redemptive and utopian possibilities in these transformations. In his best-selling novel *Looking Backward* (1888), he envisioned department stores evolving into great public buildings, characterized by "a majestic life-size group of statuary" standing above their portals, "the central figure of which was a female ideal of Plenty, with her cornucopia."[55] Money, Bellamy forecast, would give way to credit cards, and the nation-state would resemble nothing so much as an enormous corporation with every citizen having equal shares. Prescient in some respects, Bellamy's novel injected America's rapidly emerging consumer culture with utopian dimensions and launched a nationwide movement of Nationalist—or Bellamy—clubs that sought to bring about the realization of Bellamy's vision of America's future. Bellamy, of course, was not alone in thinking about the future. At precisely the same moment he was constructing a literary utopia, some of America's foremost business leaders, scientists, and politicians had even more ambitious plans. Where Bellamy merely imagined a utopia, they set out to construct a series of utopian cities in the form of world's fairs. Intended as arbiters of Culture, they became harbingers of mass culture.

HARBINGERS OF MASS CULTURE:
WORLD'S FAIRS

After the Civil War, the *u*nited States became the *U*nited States. Exactly when this happened is a source of debate; exactly how this happened is a subject that deserves more study.[1] One thing is certain. The reconstruction of the United States was not automatic or natural. How could it have been? The fact that six hundred thousand Americans died in the Civil War guaranteed that divisive memories would linger. True, political reunification between North and South was accomplished in 1877 when the Republican Party won control of the U.S. presidency in the bitterly disputed 1876 election by agreeing to the withdrawal of federal troops from the South. This so-called Compromise of 1877 restored political unity among white Americans at the expense of recently liberated African American slaves and unleashed the full force of the United States government on American Indians in the aftermath of Custer's death a year earlier. The Compromise of 1877 certainly paved the way for the advance of industrial capitalism, but it could not negate the effects of the Panic of 1873, the first in a series of industrial depressions that would plague the American economy well into the twentieth century. In 1877, railroad workers went out on strike and were met with brutal force from the newly effected alliance between industrial capitalists and America's political leaders. Economic instability and industrial violence remained the keynotes of American life throughout the rest of the century and led not a few Americans—and Europeans, like Karl Marx, for instance—to wonder if a war between sections had only served as prelude to a more ominous war—a war between social classes.

These concerns led America's political leaders and economic elites to redouble their efforts to win popular support for their nationalizing agenda. One medium they chose to build this support was the world's fair. Their decision to invest in world's fairs made perfect sense. In the aftermath of London's 1851 Crystal Palace Exhibition, world's fairs had spread to the Euro-

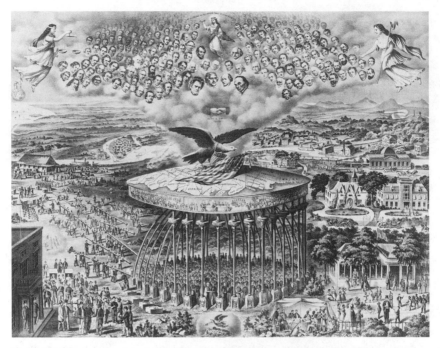

Fig. 2-1. The Library of Congress description of this illustration bears repeating: "A grand allegory of the reconciliation of North and South through the federal program of Reconstruction. Visionary in its breadth and scale, the work is a remarkable combination of religious and patriotic ideology . . . [T]he government is represented as a colossal pavilion-like structure. It has a broad, flattened dome or canopy, on which is drawn a map of the United States, with a shallow drum with a frieze showing the Senate, House of Representatives, Supreme Court, and cabinet. The drum is supported by two systems of slender columns—the straight, outer ones representing the state governments, and the curved inner ones the people. Atop the dome is an eagle with flag and shield. The structure is literally undergoing 'reconstruction.' The bases of the columns of the former Confederate states are being replaced with new ones. The old bases are called 'Foundations of Slavery.' The new ones represent Justice, Liberty, and Education. Under the watchful supervision of the military, civilians carry the new columns and put them into place. The scene is teeming with other symbols and figures. The sky is filled with a multitude of faces—American statesman, public figures, and other historical characters (among others, Joan of Arc and John Milton). Daniel Webster and John Calhoun are prominently featured. The aerial host surrounds the figure of Christ, who says, 'Do to others as you would have them do to you.' Flanking the group are Justice (left) and Liberty (right). Below, beneath the canopy, representatives of the North are reconciled with their Southern counterparts. Union generals Benjamin Butler and Ulysses S. Grant clasp hands with Confederates P. T. Beauregard and Robert E. Lee, respectively, and Horace Greeley embraces Jefferson Davis. Below in a small vignette two infants—one black and one white—lie sleeping in their baskets. Above them flies an eagle with a streamer reading 'All men are born free and equal.'" Engraving, J. L. Giles, 1867. Courtesy of the Library of Congress.

pean continent and become primary weapons in the cultural arsenals of emerging nation-states, like France, that were threatened with internal division and radical political challenges from socialists, communists, and anarchists on the Left, and royalists on the Right.[2] In 1876, the centenary of American political independence from England, the world's fair movement took off in the United States when Philadelphia civic leaders and the U.S. government teamed up to organize the Centennial International Exposition. By the time the era of Victorian fairs ended forty years later, in 1916, with expositions in San Francisco and San Diego, nearly 100 million Americans had visited these extravaganzas of imperial abundance. Held in every region of the country, the fairs organized in New Orleans (1884–85), Chicago (1893), Atlanta (1895), Nashville (1897), Omaha (1898), Buffalo (1901), St. Louis (1904), Portland (1905), Jamestown (1907), and Seattle (1909) acted as powerful nationalizing forces in American life. Just when American society was becoming increasingly turbulent, world's fairs promised material progress well into the future and laid down a blueprint for a racially exclusive technological utopia. Over time, they lent increasing legitimacy to mass entertainment and, as much as any other Victorian-era cultural institution, facilitated the triumph of mass culture in American life. At the same time, they were also a bitterly contested terrain over the meaning and future of American society and culture.[3]

In addition to being popular events—one in five Americans attended the Centennial Exhibition, while some twenty million visited the 1893 World's Columbian Exposition during its six-month run—world's fairs were also products of an economy that was shifting its base from entrepreneurial to corporate-capitalist. Fairs were intended to be run as model corporations. They were financed by stock issues controlled by locally and nationally prominent corporate elites and by funds provided by the federal government. While boards of directors selected managers who set up enormous bureaucracies to oversee the daily operations of the fairs, state legislatures set up world's fair commissions to organize popular support and displays. Like the corporations they were modeled on, world's fairs moved vertically and horizontally in American culture, integrating that culture in the process around commercial and racial values that were intended to stabilize the United States and blunt the edge of class conflict. Put in slightly different terms, the fairs were ideological constructs intended to secure the faith of Americans in the roadmap to the future projected at the expositions. But the fairs also had unintended consequences, as historian James Gilbert has pointed out, fostering the triumph of commercial values over the claims by exposition sponsors to be the rightful inheritors of the mantle of European high culture and civilization. World's fairs, in short, open a revealing window on the complex forces that shaped the social construction of mass culture in turn-of-the-century America.[4]

THE CENTENNIAL EXHIBITION

For its organizers, the 1876 Centennial Exhibition represented an enormous gamble. Just twenty-three years earlier, America's only other effort to emu-

late London's 1851 Crystal Palace Exhibition had turned into a financial de-
bacle, despite the best efforts of newspaper publisher Horace Greeley and
showman P. T. Barnum to keep the 1853 New York Crystal Palace Exhibition
afloat. Then, with the mounting sectional tensions culminating in civil war,
Americans turned inward and lost interest in the exposition fever that had
seized European capitals after London's success. But once the Civil War
ended and it became obvious that national reconstruction would require a
cultural component, national elites pinned their hopes to the world's fair
medium that had been used with such success by European governments to
foster nationalistic sentiments among their citizens.

In the late 1860s, several individuals, including prominent Smithsonian
Institution scientists, began promoting the idea that the occasion of the
centennial of the American War for Independence would be the perfect focal
point for an outpouring of national sentiment. Drawing on their experience
with sanitary fairs during the war and with a series of postwar industrial fairs,
especially in Cincinnati, prominent members of Congress and civic and business leaders in Philadelphia determined to organize a world's fair that would
outshine London's Crystal Palace Exhibition and put to rest the sneering
comments of European commentators who had heaped scorn on American
artistic displays at the 1851 spectacle.

In size, the Philadelphia exposition certainly overshadowed European
precedents. Machinery Hall was the largest building that had ever been
constructed anywhere and featured the Corliss engine, the world's largest
steam engine. Other signs of America's technological and scientific progress
abounded, including Alexander Graham Bell's telephone, but not to the exclusion of the fine arts. The exposition boasted a gallery of fine arts which is
still standing in Philadelphia's Fairmount Park.

Widely hailed as a defining moment for American "civilization," the fair
engendered no small amount of controversy when the exposition's male di-
rectorate determined to keep women out of the decision-making process. By
way of showing their displeasure, middle-class white women demanded and
ultimately won the right to construct a Woman's Building on the exposition
grounds. For the most part, the women who organized the pavilion embraced
the reigning Victorian ideology of domesticity—the belief system that simultaneously prized women's allegedly superior moral attributes and denied
them basic political and economic rights. But they gave this ideology a particular twist and used it as a vehicle for challenging the value system of a rapidly industrializing America. Far from expressing scorn at the examples of
material plenitude and technological advances that stuffed the palatial buildings on the exhibition grounds, Centennial women organizers embraced the
signs of visible material growth to get across the message that new technol-

THE GRAND CENTENNIAL WEDDING,
Of Uncle Sam and Liberty.

Fig. 2-2. Philadelphia Centennial Exhibition of 1876 treated as the "wedding" day of a new post–Civil War republic. Courtesy of the Library of Congress.

ogies would make women even better household managers and that new consumer goods would give women more time to devote to their roles as moral trustees for society as a whole. For them, the world of goods on display at the Centennial meant that women could at long last be free to fulfill their true destiny to secure "havens in a heartless world" for their men.

Despite the fact that racial, ethnic, and class differences between women were ignored on the exposition grounds—nowhere, for instance, was there any treatment of the abysmal conditions facing working-class women—the pavilion represented a notable effort by middle-class women to demand for themselves a right to occupy public space and to give meaning to their lives apart from the exclusionary vision of men.

Exposition managers were more charitable in their response to the challenge presented by women of their own class than to the cultural challenge presented by the "lower sorts." To the chagrin of exposition sponsors, visitors to the Centennial Exposition had to run a veritable gauntlet of popular shows that sprang to life outside the official fairgrounds, just across from the

Main Building. This "Centennial City," as it was popularly called, sported most of the bawdy shows and entertainments associated with urban cultures on both sides of the Atlantic. In addition to ramshackle hotels, constructed, it seemed, overnight, were "pea-nut stands, pie-stalls, the applemen and women, Bologna sausage-vendors, dealers in cakes and lemonade, and the inevitable balloon-man." According to local newspapers, there was also another hold-over from antebellum popular culture, a dime museum that exhibited "the wild men of Borneo, and the wild children of Australia, the fat woman . . . heavy enough to entitle her to a place in Machinery Hall, and a collection of 'Feejees,' who were vouched for by the exhibitors as 'pure and unadulterated man-eaters.'" With its parade of disabled people displayed as "freaks" and its growing number of prostitutes, the Centennial City stood in marked contrast to the cultural vision contained in the Centennial Exhibition and represented a carryover of earlier urban popular cultural forms that American elites had increasingly defined as a threat. Just as elites had tried to gain control over the "pit" in theaters of the Jacksonian period and at performances of Shakespeare, so they set their sights on the Centennial City, convinced that it was utterly out of step with the uplifting visions of national progress on display in the main exposition grounds. In the contest over the prerogative to reconstruct and define the meaning of American culture, Philadelphia civic authorities pulled no punches. They labeled the tenderloin impresarios "pests and nuisances" and, following an oyster house blaze that destroyed adjacent brothels as well, proceeded to burn nearly thirty Centennial City structures to the ground.[5]

Whence this fear and loathing of typical urban amusements? It originated in the process that Lawrence Levine has termed the "sacralization of American culture" whereby elites affixed hierarchical categories of "high" and "low" to cultural practices and institutions.[6] In 1876, the message was clear: traditionally practiced forms and expressions of popular culture would not be tolerated if they impinged on the sacred spaces increasingly being reserved for manifestations of high Culture with a capital C.

If Philadelphia elites thought they needed any justification for burning the Centennial City, that justification came ten years later when English critic Matthew Arnold published *Culture and Anarchy*. An immediate sensation in the United States, *Culture and Anarchy* confirmed American elites' conviction that Culture could be defined as "the best that has been thought and known in the world . . . the study and pursuit of perfection." Culture, according to Arnold, stood in marked contrast to the anarchy of popular culture. Yet, if this was so, then Culture, as conceived by Arnold and his American adherents, was also fundamentally countercultural, a weapon essentially intended to check, if not crush, popular entertainments like those that had been associated with the chaotic amusements afforded by the Centennial City.

THE WORKING-CLASS EXPERIENCE OF MASS CULTURE

To take the full measure of this conflict, it is useful to realize that between 1860 and 1920, many American workers fought for, and obtained, a reduction in the number of hours in their work weeks. As labor historians have reminded us, the struggle for control of time extended far beyond the workplace. This struggle intensified in the late nineteenth century as an increasing number of Americans became accustomed to thinking in terms of leisure and leisure-time pursuits. Exactly what leisure meant and what workers should do with it was the subject of intense discussion, debate, and conflict. At issue were the colliding values of a preindustrial and industrializing world— collisions that intensified between 1860 and 1920 because of the upsurge in immigration from pre-industrialized European and Asian countries.

Preindustrial cultures, as historians E. P. Thompson and Herbert G. Gutman have demonstrated, did not separate work from life. The pace of work was determined not so much by the clock as by the sun, and the workplace was characterized by informal relationships between workers and shop owners that allowed time for storytelling, singing, and no small measure of drinking. With industrialization, these customs were assaulted on a series of fronts. The imposition of standardized time schedules routinized work; the use of heavy machinery led to sanctions against drinking on the job. Through time— and it is important to emphasize that these struggles continued through and beyond the First World War—these economic shifts changed the nature and practice of working-class life, especially in forcing the separation of leisure from the workplace. As several historians have recently made clear, workers' decisions about whether to resist or accommodate to these changes not only set the stage for the drama of mass culture's rise and triumph in American society, but were central to the plot.

In his brilliant *Eight Hours for What We Will: Workers and Leisure in an Industrial City, 1870–1920*, historian Roy Rosenzweig notes the complex pattern of social and cultural changes that swept the city of Worcester, Massachusetts, as it was transformed into an industrial center. As was the case in other industrial communities, employers and civic reformers wasted little time trying to control workers' lives both on and off the job. Through temperance crusades, the establishment of public parks and playgrounds, and ritualistic Fourth of July celebrations, industrialists and their middle-class allies made a concerted effort to influence the way workers experienced their time away from work. But despite these intensive and extensive efforts, Rosenzweig concludes, male "employees managed to retain a significant amount of control over their lives outside the job and within their ethnic communities."[7]

The degrees to which workers exercised control over their lives was apparent especially in the saloon culture that was well entrenched by the late nineteenth century. With its drinking rituals, especially the practice of treating fellow saloon patrons, working-class saloon culture expressed values of "mutuality and reciprocity" that stood in marked contrast to those of the impersonal market mechanisms that characterized economic relations in the broader society.[8]

Just as many Worcester workers carved out a preserve of traditional values in the saloon, so too did they take advantage of official Fourth of July celebrations and public recreational sites to reaffirm ethnic loyalties. Parades and picnics allowed immigrant groups to display the importance they attached to their countries of origin. In sharp contrast to the disciplined world of the factory, picnics became occasions for revelry, and through public expressions of drunkenness workers could thumb their noses at the values of their employers. Similarly, despite employers' best efforts to create playgrounds that would permit the supervision of children, these recreational grounds became sites for re-creating and reaffirming ethnic loyalties and for defying authority. Children of particular immigrant groups claimed particular parks for themselves, and some children, complaining that the parks were no longer any fun, chose to stay away. However small, such acts of resistance to the encroaching values of industrial employers reflected the intention of workers to set their own terms and define for themselves the meaning of time away from work.

How were these traditional habits of selective accommodation and resistance affected by the rapid rise of mass culture industries and their growing permeation of working-class leisure time? Based on the limited number of studies that have addressed this question, there is reason to doubt that workers were suddenly shaped into passive consumers. As Rosenzweig, Lizabeth Cohen, and Mary Murphy have shown, the spread of commercialized leisure did not happen overnight and workers were not converted into a homogeneous mass audience.[9] There were two constraining factors. First, commercial amusements cost money and a significant number of working-class families lived in poverty—as late as 1929, Rosenzweig notes, fully one-fifth of Americans lived in poverty. Second, ethnic loyalties persisted and fostered the continuation of traditional working-class festivals and holidays.

To counter the first problem, namely that American workers just did not have the money to attend world's fairs, American world's fair organizers and the corporate sponsors paid for workers' excursions to the fairs. To address the second problem, namely that of working-class cultural traditions, world's fair authorities set aside special days for fairgoers to celebrate their ethnic contributions to American national progress. Did these actions by world's fair builders mean that they successfully destroyed working-class cultural practices? Not in the short term. But, by sometimes incorporating selective elements of those cultures into their own productions, and sometimes destroying them, as in the case of the Centennial City, world's fairs and other mass culture institutions would contribute to the gradual erosion of many working-class cultural institutions.

A RITUAL OF NATION-BUILDING: THE 1893 CHICAGO WORLD'S COLUMBIAN EXPOSITION

The promoters of the next major American world's fair to follow the Centennial Exhibition, the 1893 Chicago World's Columbian Exposition, knew their Matthew Arnold well and set out to inscribe their understanding of Culture on the American public. As plans unfolded for their celebration of the 400th anniversary of Columbus's landfall in the New World, they saw themselves giving visible form to Arnold's conception of Culture as synonymous with civilization generally and American civilization specifically. Drawing on an array of talented artists and architects led by Daniel Burnham, Chicago's civic leaders superintended the creation of a gleaming White City studded with monumental plaster-of-paris neoclassical exhibition palaces that, in their eyes, cinched their claim to have equaled the achievements of European civilization in a city hitherto known for its Great Fire, its soot, and its stockyards. As if to underscore the national significance of this event—and the turbulent social context in which it took place—exposition authorities gave their backing to plans by the editors of *The Youth's Companion* to involve millions of schoolchildren around the country in the 1892 dedication ceremonies of the fair. Those plans culminated in an idea conceived by Francis J. Bellamy.

Were Americans uncertain about the future of the country? Were the re-United States united in name only? What better way to nurture sentiments of nationalism than to make the flag an object of reverence and emotional attachment among the nation's schoolchildren? The nationalizing thrust of the exposition became clear a full eight months before the fair's official opening when ceremonies were held in October 1892 to dedicate the exposition. It was the intensive planning for these ceremonies, held in conjunction with the first celebration of Columbus Day, that stirred Francis J. Bellamy's imagination. The result was a mass ritual that would outlast the fair—the Pledge of Allegiance.

Born in 1855 in Mt. Morris, New York, Francis Bellamy was the product of a long line of Baptist ministers descended from Joseph Bellamy, one of Jonathan Edwards's disciples during the Great Awakening of the 1730s. To say that his family had a predisposition to thinking in redemptive terms would be an understatement. His first cousin, Edward, carried this propensity into the secular arena and gained national fame in 1888 as the author of the utopian novel *Looking Backward.* Unlike Edward, who had studied law, Francis never set out with any intention of wavering from his familial vocation. After graduation from the Rochester Theological Seminary, Francis worked as a minister in Little Falls, New York. Then he moved to Boston, where he took the pulpit at the Dearborn Street Church and where his concerns about America's social fragmentation only deepened. To redeem the nation from the threat of class and ethnic warfare, Francis joined forces with his more famous cousin and sought to usher in a Christian Socialist utopia that would follow the blueprint of economic nationalism laid down in *Looking Backward.*[10]

Because of his seemingly radical ideas, Bellamy lost his pulpit, but not before gaining the notice of one of his parishioners, Daniel Ford, publisher of *The Youth's Companion,* one of the most widely read magazines of its time. Ford hired Bellamy as his special assistant and assigned him to work with one of his editors, James Upham, who was already hard at work on a project to involve public schools around the United States in commemorating America's first Columbus Day in October 1892 with a broad range of programs that would center on flag-raising ceremonies.[11]

Flag-raising ceremonies, like Columbus Day itself, were very recent innovations in the nation's schools and, like world's fairs, were direct responses to the social and political struggles of the Gilded Age. Prior to the 1880s, displays of the American flag had generally been limited to patriotic occasions and military or governmental functions. But in the mid-1880s, a movement began to place American flags in every public schoolroom across the United States and to organize flag-raising ceremonies in the nation's schoolyards. In the long run, this movement would lead to the creation of the American Flag Association, in 1897, and eventually to the proclamation in 1916 of a national Flag Day. In the short run, this movement to turn the flag into an object of veneration by schoolchildren inspired a New York City school principal and former Union colonel in the Civil War, George T. Balch, to craft a "salute to the flag" for his largely immigrant pupils to recite: "I give my hand and my heart to my country—one nation, one language, one flag."[12] It also inspired Upham to use *The Youth's Companion* sponsorship of the flags-in-the-schools campaign to make money for the Perry Mason Company, parent company of his magazine, by selling flags—and lots of them—to school districts around the country. Upham was a patriot; he was also a marketing genius. As John W. Baer explains, Upham ran ads in his magazine encouraging students to buy shares for ten cents apiece in flags for their schools. At the same time, he made clear that the burden of paying for a flagpole should be borne by local school boards. His strategy worked. In a brief four-year span between 1888 and 1892, thousands of schools purchased flags—in 1891 alone some 25,000 schools bought flags.[13]

Upham did not stop there. With the 400th anniversary of Columbus's arrival in the New World looming on the horizon, Upham concocted a new scheme for promoting the veneration of the flag—one that would historicize the roots of the modern American nation, not in the recent and divisive memories of the Civil War, but in the distant past, in the moment of Columbus's "discovery" of the New World. In his dreams, Upham may well have fantasized about rewinding history and giving Columbus the U.S. flag to plant on the shores of the New World. That clearly was not possible. But there was nothing to stop him from giving the American flag to a later generation of American schoolchildren who could raise it in their schoolyards in Columbus's name. And that is precisely what Upham set out to do.

Meanwhile, plans were well under way for the massive world's fair in Chicago to honor Columbus's arrival in the New World. Sponsored by the federal government and underwritten by Chicago's corporate capitalists, the World's Columbian Exposition, with its monumental white buildings and demeaning exhibits of American Indians, Africans, and people deemed "other" than Anglo-Saxon, attacked the class cleavages besetting America by unfolding a highly visible narrative of national progress leading to the triumph of civilization in the United States—if only Americans would put their trust in the hands of the men and women who created the fair. Since its inception in 1890, the exposition's promoters had sought ways to build public support for their enterprise. In early 1892, Charles C. Bonney, a world's fair official, proposed nationwide involvement in the fair's dedication ceremonies, scheduled for October 21, 1892. "The day of the Finding of America should be celebrated everywhere in America," Bonney declared, with public schools becoming sites for the celebration. "Let it also be suggested," Bonney argued, "that a desirable note of unity would be given if at least one feature of the exercises be identical, both in the Exposition dedication, and in all local celebrations."[14]

Not surprisingly, given his search for unity between the dedication celebrations in Chicago and in communities around the country, Bonney got wind of Upham's work at *The Youth's Companion*. When contacted by world's fair officials, Ford, the publisher of the magazine, threw the resources of the Perry Mason Company into the effort to link fair and flag. He pulled his new special assistant, Francis Bellamy, from the flag-in-the-schoolhouse campaign to work with Upham to devise a way to link the public school ceremonies with the dedication festivities that would launch the fair.

Upham and Bellamy proved to be a perfect match. While Upham mobilized support between educators and their students for a National Columbian Public School Celebration, Bellamy became a lobbyist for a presidential proclamation declaring the nation's first Columbus Day. More than that, after meeting with congressmen and state department officials, and even enlisting former president Grover Cleveland in the campaign, Bellamy actually drafted the wording for the proclamation that President Benjamin Harrison issued on July 21, 1892. "Let the flag float over every school house in the country," Bellamy wrote, "and the exercises be such as shall impress upon our youth the patriotic duties of American citizenship."[15]

Having secured the presidential proclamation declaring October 21 as Columbus Day, Bellamy and Upham turned their talents to wedding school ceremonies celebrating Columbus's arrival in the New World with the dedication exercises of the Chicago World's Columbian Exposition. Upham was insistent that some kind of flag salute would be the best way to join the events, but he and Bellamy agreed that the so-called "Balch salute" was "too juvenile, lacking in dignity and comprehensiveness for this occasion."[16]

But how to improve upon it? Upham confessed that he was at wit's end and told Bellamy that he "would have to do the thing if it was done at all." With various deadlines looming, Upham and Bellamy agreed to have dinner and brainstorm about a new salute. As they talked matters over, Bellamy's own thoughts began to crystallize. "It had become apparent to me," he recalled, "that so long as we arrived merely at some improved 'Salute to the Flag' we were bound to be hazy; we would be likely to formulate some sonorous speech which might prove less popular than the Balch Salute. Accordingly, I suggested a new trail, in which the general notion of a flag salute would be subordinate to a vow of loyalty, or allegiance, to the flag based on what the flag definitely stood for." "I argued long and earnestly," Bellamy emphasized, "for this *fundamental distinction*. I pointed out that the word 'allegiance' had for everybody a Civil War familiarity; that it had a grip which everybody could sense; and that if we should build up the formula on that idea of *pledging allegiance* it would stand by itself as a thing vastly more than any mere 'Salute to the Flag,' and would rapidly supersede the Balch formula."[17]

After dinner, Bellamy and Upham returned to the *Youth's Companion* building. Bellamy asked Upham to wait outside his office and shut the door. Then, in a burst of creative energy that lasted about two hours, Bellamy transformed the Balch salute into a national pledge of allegiance. Thirty years later, he vividly remembered "how the sequence of the ideas grew and how the words were found." His account is worth quoting at length:

> Beginning with the new word *allegiance* I first decided that *pledge* was a better school word than "vow" or "swear" and that the first person singular should be used, and that *my* Flag was preferable to "the."

When those first words, *I pledge allegiance to my Flag* looked up at me from the scratch-paper the start appeared promising. Then for the further reach: should it be "country," "nation" or "Republic"? That was hard. *Republic* won because it distinguished the form of government chosen by the fathers and established by the Revolution. The true reason for allegiance to the flag is the *Republic for which it stands.*

Now how should the vista be widened so as to teach the National fundamentals? I laid down my pencil and tried to pass our history in review. It took in the sayings of Washington, the arguments of Hamilton, the Webster-Hayne debate, the speeches of Seward and Lincoln, the Civil War. After many attempts all that pictured struggle reduced itself to three words, *One Nation, indivisible.* To reach that compact brevity, conveying the facts of a single nationality and of an indivisibility both of States and of common interests, was, as I recall, the most arduous phase of the task, and the discarded experiments at phrasing overflowed the scrap basket.

But what of the present and future of this indivisible Nation here presented for allegiance? What were the old and fought-out issues which always will be issues to be fought for? Especially, what were the basic national doctrines bearing upon the acute questions already agitating the public mind? Here was a temptation to repeat the historic slogan of the French Revolution, imported by Jefferson, "liberty, fraternity, equality." But that was rather quickly rejected, as fraternity was too remote of realization, and as equality was a dubious word. What doctrines, then, would everybody agree upon as the basis of Americanism? *Liberty and Justice* were surely basic, were undebatable, and were all that any one Nation could handle. If they were exercised *for all* they involved the spirit of equality and fraternity. So that final line came with a cheering rush. As a clincher it seemed to assemble the past and to promise the future.[18]

In one epiphanic moment, Bellamy had constructed a vow of allegiance to an *indivisible* nation (imagine how that concept registered only twenty-eight years after the Civil War and in the midst of the era's class violence!) that, in exchange for an oath of fealty, promised "liberty and justice for all." This was a masterstroke of nationalist ideological innovation that closed the door on potentially subversive concepts like "equality" and "fraternity."

Bellamy was positively euphoric about his accomplishment. By his own account, when he penned the final words to the Pledge, he threw open his office door and read the text to Upham, who stood transfixed by what he heard. Rapture quickly gave way to reflex, and the editor of *The Youth's Companion* "snapped his heels together" and rhapsodized: "Now up there is the flag. I come to salute; then when I get to the words 'My Flag,' I stretch out my hand and keep it raised while I say the rest."[19]

Word and gesture were joined.[20] Both men were ecstatic. At a time of immense social and political strain, Bellamy and Upham had combined their talents and hit upon a nationalizing ritual that would discipline the American body politic by literally disciplining the minds and bodies of a future generation of Americans.

This was no small accomplishment, but there was still much to do before the Columbus Day festivities. Because the national salute was meant to be recited *and* performed in less than two months, Bellamy and Upham organized what Bellamy would later call America's first public relations campaign. They made full use of *The Youth's Companion* to explain to teachers and students how the Pledge should be implemented:

> At a signal from the Principal the pupils, in ordered ranks, hands to the side, face the Flag. Another signal is given; every pupil give the Flag the military salute—right hand lifted, palm downward, to a line with the forehead and close to it. Standing thus, all repeat together, slowly: "I pledge allegiance to my Flag and the Republic for which it stands: one Nation, indivisible, with Liberty and Justice for all." At the words, "to my Flag," the right hand is extended gracefully, palm upward, towards the Flag, and remains in this gesture till the end of the affirmation; whereupon all hands immediately drop to the side. Then, still standing, as the instruments strike a chord, all will sing "America, My Country 'tis of Thee."[21]

With these instructions in hand, public school teachers carefully prepared their charges. As they did so, teachers no doubt made abundant references to the other component of Columbus Day—the vast cultural undertaking unfolding in Chicago.

Like Bellamy and Upham, world's fair sponsors had been working feverishly to prepare for the Dedication Day ceremonies. They had also been blanketing the United States—and, indeed, much of the world—with press releases about the fair and encouraging teachers to incorporate elements of the fair into their lesson plans. Exposition sponsors were thrilled with Bellamy's and Upham's achievement, and immediately made the Pledge part of ceremonies that kicked off the three days of festivities that led up to Dedication Day. On October 19, at exactly 1:30 p.m., schoolchildren across Chicago were organized in assemblies that started with a reading of President Harrison's Columbus Day proclamation. Then came a flag-raising ceremony during which "the pupils saluted the colors" and "pledged their allegiance to the flag."[22] By the close of the dedication ceremonies in Chicago, which were

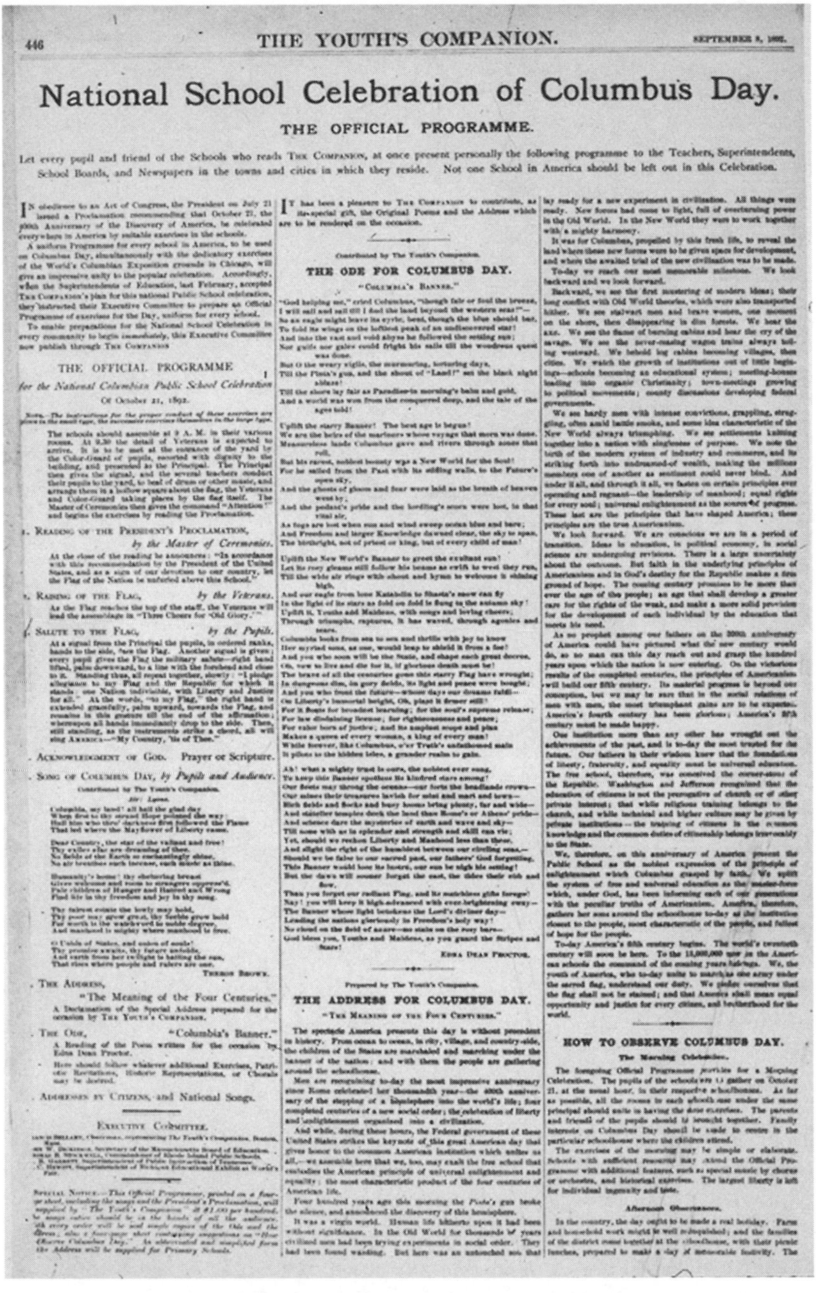

446 THE YOUTH'S COMPANION. SEPTEMBER 8, 1892.

National School Celebration of Columbus Day.

THE OFFICIAL PROGRAMME.

Let every pupil and friend of the Schools who reads THE COMPANION, at once present personally the following programme to the Teachers, Superintendents, School Boards, and Newspapers in the towns and cities in which they reside. Not one School in America should be left out in this Celebration.

THE OFFICIAL PROGRAMME

for the National Columbian Public School Celebration

Of October 21, 1892.

1. READING OF THE PRESIDENT'S PROCLAMATION, *by the Master of Ceremonies.*

2. RAISING OF THE FLAG, *by the Veterans.*

As the Flag reaches the top of the staff, the Veterans will lead the assemblage in "Three Cheers for 'Old Glory.'"

3. SALUTE TO THE FLAG, *by the Pupils.*

ACKNOWLEDGMENT OF GOD. Prayer or Scripture.

SONG OF COLUMBUS DAY, *by Pupils and Audience.*

THE ADDRESS, "The Meaning of the Four Centuries."

THE ODE, "Columbia's Banner."

ADDRESSES BY CITIZENS, and National Songs.

EXECUTIVE COMMITTEE.

THE ODE FOR COLUMBUS DAY.

"COLUMBIA'S BANNER."

EDNA DEAN PROCTOR.

THE ADDRESS FOR COLUMBUS DAY.

"THE MEANING OF THE FOUR CENTURIES."

HOW TO OBSERVE COLUMBUS DAY.

Fig. 2-3. Text for "Salute to the Flag by the Pupils," in "The Official Programme for the National School Celebration of the Columbus Day," *The Youth's Companion* 65 (8 September 1892), p. 466. This becomes the basis for the Pledge of Allegiance.

Fig. 2-4. Schoolchildren in Hampton, Virginia, performing the Pledge of Allegiance, ca. 1900. Photograph by Frances Benjamin Johnston. Courtesy of the Library of Congress.

witnessed by between one and two million people, it was clear that in the course of dedicating a fair, the UNITED States had been rededicated through a participatory ritual that, through word and deed, required citizens to pledge their allegiance to the chief emblem of the newly reconstructed modern American nation-state.

The Pledge, in short, was a major victory for American nationalists who had no doubt that the Americanization of the world began at home. But, as important as it was for uniting Americans into a mass ritual, the pledge only hints at the power of the fair for defining American culture. Shortly before the fair opened to the public, Chicago's mercantile and corporate elite made a decision that would have consequences no less momentous. Instead of excluding popular amusements from the fairgrounds or burning them to the ground, fair managers decided to include a range of popular shows as an appendage to the fair. At a right angle to the White City, they organized the Midway Plaisance, a mile-long avenue that combined urban pleasures with anthropological instruction. The story of the relationship between the White City and the Midway Plaisance reveals in a microcosm the shifting and contested boundaries of American culture and sheds light on how mass culture gained legitimacy as a vital component of American culture by nurturing public support for the growing imperial ambitions that propelled the United States into competition with European colonial powers at the turn of the century.[23]

True to Arnold's litmus test for determining what Culture really was, exposition authorities initially envisioned the World's Columbian Exposition as a sacred site where the greatest artistic and technological achievements of the human intellect could be worshiped. There was no room in this vision for amusements that were characterized as vulgar by Victorian-era newspapers and magazines. But, as often happens, economic necessities forced Chicago's cultural barons to modify their best-laid plans. Simply put, the fair's board of directors became increasingly concerned about the exposition's financial solvency. Particularly troubling was the knowledge that, despite the fate of the Centennial City in Philadelphia, enterprising showmen in Chicago would set up hurdy-gurdy shows outside the White City that would pick the pockets of fairgoers before they ever arrived at the fair. Here was a dilemma. Could exposition builders have Culture and commercial success too? Their answer was affirmative and inspired by the French colonial shows that lay at the base of the centerpiece of the 1889 Paris Universal Exposition—the Eiffel Tower.

For the Paris fair, French government officials enlisted the support of leading French anthropologists, who turned villages representing French colonists from Africa and Asia into ethnological field stations that would buttress

Fig. 2-5. The White City and Midway Plaisance of the 1893 Chicago World's Columbian Exposition. Courtesy of the Library of Congress.

public support for French imperial policy. The possibilities of such shows for popularizing the emerging discipline of anthropology were not lost on American anthropologists who attended a world's congress of anthropology held in conjunction with the 1889 fair. Neither were the possibilities of such shows lost on Chicago's fair planners, who saw in the opportunity to blend entertainment with serious anthropological instruction a way out of their Arnoldian conundrum.

By the time the World's Columbian Exposition opened to the public, the Midway Plaisance had been listed in the official fair directory as "Department M" and placed under the charge of Harvard ethnology professor Frederic Ward Putnam, who also headed the exposition's anthropology department. Presented to the public as a living ethnological museum, complete with villages of Africans, Native Americans, Japanese, Chinese, Irish, Germans, and Middle Easterners, the Midway struck some visitors as a Darwinian laboratory for applying evolutionary ideas about racial hierarchy to society. "What an opportunity was here afforded to the scientific mind to descend the spiral of evolution, tracing humanity in its highest phases down almost to its animalistic origins," the *Chicago Tribune* explained.[24] With its "anthropology live" shows fundamentally degrading many of the people put on display, the Midway lent scientific legitimation to categories of "savagery" and "civilization," reinforced dominant American perceptions of underdevelopment in the Third World, and had the effect of making the White City seem all the more cultured and refined—at least to white Americans.

The latter caveat is important because, while it is true that the products of America's mass culture industries were deeply embedded with racist messages that had the effect of providing the ideological glue that unified white Americans during an era of enormous class tension and upheaval, to assume that these messages went unchallenged is simply wrong.

For instance, from the vantage point of many white Americans, the 1893 Chicago World's Columbian Exposition seemed proof positive that American "civilization" had come of age and could compare favorably with the best that Europe had to offer. From the perspective of some white women and most African Americans, however, the fair came to represent what was wrong with American society.

The role of women in the fair was complex. Not all middle-class women agreed with the strategy developed for advancing women's rights at the Centennial Exhibition. Some feminists, notably suffragist Susan B. Anthony, determined to seize the occasion of the World's Columbian Exposition to advance a broader political and economic agenda for women. When plans for the fair were announced, Anthony and her allies organized a Queen Isabella Society and carried a petition to Congress demanding that women be included on the exposition's board of directors, to guarantee that "there will be in the exhibition a presentation of the share taken by women in the industrial, artistic, intellectual, and religious progress of the nation." But the Congress rejected Anthony's petition and established a separate Board of Lady Managers with Bertha Palmer, wife of exposition manager and mercantilist Potter Palmer, at its head.

As was the case in Philadelphia, women in 1893 had to overcome opposition from men who preferred that women restrict their involvement in the fair to fundraising activities. To Palmer's credit, she gained support for a Woman's Building, but her initial pleas to integrate women's and men's exhibits in appropriate exposition halls devoted to transportation, agriculture, and so forth fell on deaf ears. In Chicago, as in Philadelphia, women were represented at and used by the fair to advance a social reform agenda rooted in the ideology of domesticity. And the separate-but-equal nature of their representation in the fair conveyed the message that women were still second-class citizens in the American republic.

Constrained by the nature of their representation at these fountainheads of American mass culture, some middle-class women, notably Anthony and other suffragists, had some success in turning the fairs into platforms to advance their views. Others saw in the technologies on display possibilities for relieving women of household drudgery. And, in the case of the World's Columbian Exposition, the fair included a Congress of Women drawn from a variety of professions and interests to address social and economic problems confronting women that the displays in the Woman's Building tended to mask.

Through their involvement in world's fairs, many middle-class women, by emphasizing their traditional roles as producers of Culture and guardians of Civilization, consciously sought to enlarge their involvement in the public sphere. For some, the path led directly to suffrage; for others it led to social reform; for yet others, both. In any case, because of their presumed cultural authority and, because of their race, white middle-class women had a modicum of power and influence in shaping the Chicago fair that distinguished them from other groups, notably African Americans.

When the idea was first proposed for a fair to commemorate Columbus's arrival in the New World and to celebrate the progress the United States had made on the pathway of civilization since its founding, African Americans hoped to use the fair to demonstrate their achievements since emancipation from slavery. They were bitterly disappointed. The only African American to serve in any executive decision-making capacity was appointed to serve as an alternate delegate to the national commission, and only after bitter protests from African Americans across the country. No less galling was the decision by exposition managers that all exhibits in state buildings would have to be approved by state committees. Since whites controlled these committees almost exclusively, African Americans rightly believed that their exhibit proposals would be refused. The only concession that African Americans wrung from world's fair managers was to set aside a special "Colored People's Day" at the fair that would follow the precedent for special days at the fair accorded European American ethnic groups.[25]

For many African Americans, the latter gesture smacked of the worst sort of tokenism. Led by anti-lynching advocate Ida Wells, they urged African Americans to boycott the fair. Renowned African American leader Frederick Douglass counseled a different tack. A former slave, who had advised presidents and fought for social and economic justice in American society, Douglass had been appointed by the Haitian government to serve as its representative at the fair. A boycott, Douglass argued, would play into the hands of white racists and allow them to brand African Americans with a negative label. It would be far better, in Douglass's view, to use the occasion of the day and the fair to condemn social injustice at the fair and in American society generally.

With African Americans divided about how best to respond to the fair's explicit racism, "Colored People's Day" took place on August 25, 1893. Those advocating a boycott found much support for their position among African Americans and much in evidence at the fair to vindicate their stance. Only about one thousand African Americans visited the fair and had to run a gamut of watermelon stands set up by entrepreneurs eager to demean African American visitors. Douglass was sickened by what he saw, but determined to give the speech he had prepared for delivery even in the face of white hecklers. "Men talk of the Negro problem," Douglass sneered. "There is no Negro problem. The problem is whether the American people have loyalty enough, honor enough, patriotism enough to live up to their own Constitution." Why, he asked, should African Americans be treated worse than former Confederates? "We fought for your country, we ask that we be treated as well as those who fought against your country. We love your country. We ask that you treat us as well as you do those who only love a part of it." The White City, he concluded, while not a "whited sepulcher," came awfully close.

One member of the audience was so impressed by Douglass's remarks that she declared his speech "had done more to bring our cause to the attention of the American people than anything else which had happened during the fair." Ida Wells did more than mend fences with Douglass. She teamed up with Douglass and several other prominent African Americans to write a noteworthy pamphlet that attacked the ideological premises of the fair. "Theoretically open to all Americans," one contributor wrote, the exposition was "literally and figuratively, a 'White City,' in the building of which the Colored American was allowed no helping hand, and in its glorious success he has no share."[26]

The response of African Americans to the World's Columbian Exposition provides one of the clearest indications that ordinary people in positions of relative powerlessness did not simply regard mass entertainments as sources of amusement or respond passively to them. In the case of the Chicago fair, African Americans tried to convert a mass cultural medium to their own purposes, to turn a vehicle of dominant, white supremacist ideology into a weapon to fight a war of position to advance their own social and political agenda. Measured in absolute terms, their success was small, but small successes added up. Forty years later at the 1933–34 Chicago Century of Progress Exposition, building on the moral victory scored at the 1893 fair, African Americans successfully turned another world's fair into a laboratory for developing tactics that would influence the Civil Rights Movement of the 1950s and 1960s.

If, as is sometimes said, history is filled with unintended consequences, the same certainly holds true for mass culture. Additional evidence for that proposition comes from ethnological performances along the Midway Plaisance.

Along the Midway, that mile-long avenue of mass culture and consumption that ran perpendicular to the White City, ethnological villages, featuring live displays of predominantly nonwhite people, were intended to give living and visible proof to the proposition that human beings could be divided into categories of civilization and savagery—categories that neatly rationalized the imperialistic calculations of exposition sponsors and reinforced values associated with social Darwinism, especially the belief in the naturalness of social hierarchy, competition, and the survival of the fittest.

The intentions of exposition sponsors, however, were imperfectly realized, at least insofar as the people on display were concerned. Of all the so-called Midway Types, none were subjected to more ridicule and scorn than the seventy Dahomeans brought to the fair by the French explorer and labor contractor Xavier Pené. According to one souvenir guidebook: "The habits of these people are repulsive; they eat like animals and have the characteristics of the very lowest order of the human family." To keep his charges under control, Pené provided plenty of alcohol and actually encouraged the Dahomeans to perform their "authentic" dances with pint bottles in their hands. But the Dahomeans were anything but pliant subjects. As one European described the reactions of Dahomean women who were forced to parade up and down the Midway: "A good many people imagine, I suppose, [that the African women] are sounding the praises of the Exposition or at least voicing their own wonder at the marvels they have seen since coming to this country. But the fact is that if the words of their chants were translated into English they would read something like this: 'We have come from a far country to a land

where all men are white. If you will come to our country we will take pleasure in cutting your throats.'"[27]

The Dahomeans were not the only ones who found ways of subverting
the intentions of exposition sponsors. When the Inuits, organized into an Eskimo Village, were told they would not receive food unless they wore their
fur skins in the heat of Chicago's summer, one of the Inuits seized the village
manager by the throat and threatened his life. Ultimately, several Inuits
took the concessionaire to court and won release from their contract. Other
people put on display as ethnological specimens also made small gains, which
were important, given their positions of relative powerless in American society. Native Americans, for instance, received recognition of their right to
negotiate contracts with showmen and thereby won some modicum of control over the conditions of their performances.

The complexities and contradictions of the performative dimension of
American mass culture also came to light in the so-called Oriental villages
which featured displays of people from the Middle East. Villages of people
from Egypt, Algeria, and Turkey were vital to the "orientalist" strategy of
exposition sponsors whereby some people were displayed as "other." Especially important to conveying this structure of feeling were performances of
the "belly dance," generally referred to as the *danse-du-ventre* because, as one
newspaper put it, the translation would offend prevailing Victorian sensibilities. The performance featured a woman dancer who, according to a contemporary account, "revels in all the glory of oriental colors and barbaric jewelry
and . . . displays her charms, dimly hidden by a gauze nothing; a narrow zone
of gauze silk through which the warm flesh tints are distinctly visible." Intended to reinforce impressions of the backwardness of the Middle East, the
effect of the belly dance cut in another, unanticipated direction. In the Palace
of Eros, the dancer concluded her performance by doing the splits, evoking
lewd comments from the overwhelmingly male and college-age audience. The
performance also attracted the attention of local moral reformers and clergy.
The latter, together with the exposition's Board of Lady Managers, tried to
close the theaters, but since the shows' profitability was crucial to the exposition's financial success, they were allowed to continue. The Palace of Eros, in
other words, doubled back on the plaster-of-paris palaces of the White City,
and threatened the very existence of Culture with erotic pleasure.[28]

The import of the World's Columbian Exposition for the future of American culture was not lost on many of the nation's clergy who tried to block
exposition officials from running the fair on Sundays. For at least a decade,
control of Sundays had been an issue in America. According to James Carey,
Sunday had long been "a region free from control of the state and commerce
where another dimension of life could be experienced and where altered

forms of social relationship could occur." "As such," Carey argues, "the sabbath [had] always been a major resistance to state and market power." Beginning with the standardization of time zones to accommodate railroad schedules and continuing with the efforts of William Randolph Hearst to market a Sunday edition of his newspaper, America's corporate elites had tried to "infiltrate into the practical consciousness of ordinary men and women and uproot older notions of rhythm and temporality." The drive to keep the World's Columbian Exposition open on Sunday was part of this strategy. Those opposed to Sunday opening argued that to "corrupt the Sabbath is to debauch the morality of the masses." Supporters, on the other hand, asked how it could be "a desecration of the Sabbath to give to the masses a grand object lesson in all the arts and sciences?" In the end, after prolonged litigation, the courts sided with the directors, allowing the exposition proper to remain open with the understanding that Midway shows would be closed.[29]

Ambivalence is probably the best word to characterize the relationship between the Midway Plaisance and the White City, at least in the minds of exposition directors. If the directors did not fully embrace the Midway, neither did they emulate Philadelphia's example and torch popular amusements. By making some effort to package Midway entertainments as instructive, they made the Midway into an adjunct, not an adversary, of the White City. The effect was momentous. At precisely the moment some Americans were starting to force culture into categories of "high" and "low," the World's Columbian Exposition, by encouraging millions of fairgoers to travel freely between the Midway Plaisance and White City as part of their exposition experience, had the effect of loosening those categories and making mass culture seem quintessentially American.

The nationalizing effects of the Chicago fair did not go unnoticed. Steel magnate Andrew Carnegie, for one, liked what he saw. From his commanding position high atop America's socioeconomic pyramid, Carnegie responded to the widening fault lines of class conflict and lingering feelings of sectionalism by extolling the value of the fair for promoting feelings of "intense Americanism." He took immense satisfaction from the behavior of the crowds at the fair:

> The impression made by the people *en masse* was highly complimentary to the American. I never heard a foreigner give his impression who failed to extol the remarkable behavior of the crowd, its good manners, temperance, kindliness, and the total absence of rude selfish pushing for advantage which is usual in corresponding gatherings abroad. The self-governing capacity of the people shone forth resplendently.[30]

Long before cultural theorist Michel Foucault advanced his theories about the power of cultural institutions to regulate behavior and long before sociol-

Fig. 2-6. The Midway at the 1915 San Francisco Panama-Pacific International Exposition. Courtesy of the Library of Congress.

ogist Tony Bennett described the role of Victorian-era universal expositions in "winning the hearts and minds" of the masses, Carnegie lent his prestige to advancing the cause of America's "exhibitionary complex."[31] As Carnegie put it, "the seventeen years that passed between the Philadelphia exhibition and that at Chicago was a period quite long enough." "At least once every twenty years," he declared, there should be "a national reunion" similar to the World's Columbian Exposition held in every section of the country.[32]

Carnegie would get his wish—in spades. The 1893 fair launched a full-blown world's fair movement in the United States. Following Chicago's triumph, major international fairs were held in San Francisco (1894), Atlanta (1895), Nashville (1897), Omaha (1898), Buffalo (1901), St. Louis (1904), Portland (1905), Jamestown (1907), Seattle (1909), San Francisco (1915–16), and San Diego (1915–16). What made this movement possible was the recognition that the Chicago fair had been, in essence, a modular construct that, as cultural historian John G. Blair explains, could be "added to, substituted for, or perhaps even rearranged."[33] This lesson was certainly learned by Michel de Young, a San Francisco newspaper publisher and California's commissioner to the 1893 fair. Before the Chicago fair closed, de Young determined to hold a Midwinter Exposition in San Francisco that would reproduce on a smaller scale the essential features of the 1893 spectacle. When it opened in 1894, the Midwinter fair "assumed something of the character of an inner circle of purely exposition buildings with an outer concentric circle of concessional features." As was the case at Chicago, those concessions included commercial amusements and ethnological displays of nonwhites. The exposition form changed—midway concessions were now firmly considered central to American world's fairs and would remain so into the future—but the ideological message that abundance at home required an empire abroad remained substantively intact.

This message, apparent at all the fairs held between 1893 and 1916, came into sharpest relief at the 1904 St. Louis Louisiana Purchase Exposition, another in the chain of monumental "white cities" forged in the wake of the 1893 exposition. The St. Louis fair—still remembered for its Tin Pan Alley theme song, "Meet Me In St. Louis, Louis"—was, according to one of its sponsors, better remembered as "the greatest colonial exhibition in the history of the world." Exposition authorities had reason to boast. With the assistance of the U.S. War Department and government anthropologists, exposition backers secured 1,200 Filipinos for display at the fair's "Philippine's Reservation," where they were expected to be living advertisements for the government's colonial policy for the Philippines, which the United States had acquired from Spain in the Spanish American War of 1898. No less impor-

Fig. 2-7. More than one thousand Filipinos were displayed at the 1904 St. Louis Louisiana Purchase Exposition as part of the U.S. government's effort to win popular support for the recent acquisition of the Philippine Islands in the war with Spain. Courtesy of the Library of Congress.

tant, St. Louis world's fair builders effected a notable transformation in the relationship between Midway and White City. Far from torching the commercial entertainments as had happened in Philadelphia, or treating them as an annex to the world's fair, as had been the case in Chicago in 1893, St. Louis exposition authorities incorporated the midway for the 1904 fair into the main exposition grounds, thus revealing the growing centrality of midway-based mass cultural formations to modern American life.

By the turn of the century, world's fair promoters had molded mass entertainment, academic anthropology, and Arnoldian beliefs about Culture into a veritable world's fair culture industry capable of promoting dreams of empire and consumerism. They inspired and in turn drew inspiration from an army of midway showmen who, in reversing the arrangement of the World's Columbian Exposition and making Culture the adjunct of commercial entertainment, remapped the cultural landscape of the United States, dotting it with amusement parks, motion picture palaces, Tin Pan Alley music and many other complex and contradictory forms of mass culture that proliferated in the wake of the great Chicago fair. To be sure, the frontiers of American mass culture were rapidly expanding both at home and abroad.

THE EXPANDING FRONTIERS
OF AMERICAN MASS CULTURE

In 1893, with the Chicago fair in full swing, the bottom fell out of the American economy. Just one year later, in response to deep wage cuts, railroad workers in George Pullman's company town, right outside of Chicago, went on strike and were met with crushing force by company agents and U.S. troops. With the Civil War still a living memory and signs of class conflict everywhere to be seen, there was cause for additional worry in the form of the 1890 census, which had concluded that the frontier period in American history had ended. In his famous paper on "The Significance of the Frontier in American History," read to a group of historians meeting in conjunction with the 1893 fair, American historian Frederick Jackson Turner interpreted the census to mean that there was no more frontier "safety valve" to release the pent-up social pressures resulting from immigration, urbanization, and industrialization. But, Turner hastened to add, the search for new frontiers would continue to characterize the American experience well into the future.

There is no evidence that Turner took time from his reflections on the American frontier to visit the White City or the Midway Plaisance. But if he had, he would have found evidence of another new frontier in the commercialized pleasures of the fair. That was certainly the way a number of cultural entrepreneurs, including George Tilyou and Sol Bloom, responded to the fair. Indeed, the Chicago fair fired dreams for creating whole new culture industries like amusement parks and accelerated the development of others, like motion pictures. It left its mark on the development of popular music, reconfigured American theater, and introduced America to a new medium of mass communication—the picture postcard. After the Chicago World's Columbian Exposition, American culture would never be the same. The development of amusement parks helps explain why.

AMUSEMENT PARKS

American amusement parks owe their origins to several sources that con-
verged in the Chicago fair. Chief among those were Europe's famous pleasure
gardens—London's Vauxhall, Copenhagen's Tivoli, and Vienna's Prater—
and American urban parks that had been created over the course of the nineteenth century to provide pleasurable antidotes to the social consequences of
the industrial revolution and to give urban and especially middle-class residents a controlled form of recreation. The Chicago fair, with its park-like setting and popular Midway Plaisance, seemed to combine the best features of
both traditions and opened the eyes of several entrepreneurs to the possibility of making their fortunes from perpetuating the legacy of commercialized
pleasures found at the fair.

The initial site for implementing such plans was Coney Island, a five-
mile-long area of Atlantic Ocean beach separated from Brooklyn by a creek.
Close enough to Manhattan to attract the attention and money of many social
groups interested in leaving New York City for varying periods of time, Coney
Island developed multiple identities over the nineteenth century. Initially, it
served as a resort area for Manhattan's privileged classes, but, with the opening of improved mass transportation links with the city, Coney Island quickly
developed popular amusement areas that resembled the urban entertainments
established on the outskirts of the 1876 Philadelphia Centennial Exhibition.
By the early 1890s, pressures increased to reform Coney Island entertainments and make them "wholesome." Fire again did the trick. Between 1893
and the close of the century, numerous fires destroyed tenderloin shows and
concessions, making it easier for reformers and show business entrepreneurs
to reinvent Coney Island as a series of linked Midway Plaisances—Sea Lion
Park (established in 1895), Steeplechase (1897), Luna Park (1903), and Dreamland (1904)—offering abundant opportunities for working- and middle-class
Americans to find socially acceptable pleasures.

As historian John Kasson has made clear, each park had a distinctive character. Steeplechase was created by George Tilyou, whose father had worked
in vaudeville and operated a hotel on Coney Island. In 1893, the younger
Tilyou traveled to Chicago and left that city's fair ablaze with thoughts of
fun and profit. "We Americans," Tilyou wrote, "want either to be thrilled or
amused, and we are ready to pay well for either sensation." Captivated by
George Ferris's revolving wheel on the Midway, he cut its dimensions by half
and made it one of the leading attractions of his Coney Island venture, which
was named for another featured amusement, a mechanical steeplechase race.
No less popular were shows that loosened the restraints of prevailing Victorian sexual attitudes. The "Barrel of Love," a gigantic, revolving cylinder,
threw complete strangers together in compromising positions. The steeple-

Fig. 3-1. Coney Island Bathing Pavilion, ca. 1905. Courtesy of Robert W. Rydell.

chase ride offered more explicit entertainment. Young lovers could ride their double-saddled mounts around the track but had to exit through a public gallery, where audiences would double over with laughter as compressed air jets blew women's skirts toward their heads and a clown zapped men on their thighs with a low-voltage electronic prod. After overcoming this ordeal, the couple could and generally did join the audience to await the passage of the next riders.[1]

Over the course of Steeplechase's operation, Tilyou traveled to other fairs and returned with additional world's fair midway–inspired mechanical amusements and shows. In 1902, he incorporated one of the leading midway attractions from the 1901 Buffalo Pan-American Exposition, the "Trip to the Moon" illusion. Ironically, Tilyou's decision had the unintended consequence of spurring the owners of that concession, Frederic A. Thompson and Elmer "Skip" Dundy, to set up their own rival Coney Island amusement.

Thompson and Dundy's Luna Park, which replaced the financially troubled Sea Lion Park, bore a closer resemblance than Steeplechase to the "anthropology live" shows on the Midway Plaisance. In addition to its featured attraction, "A Trip to the Moon," Luna Park included an Eskimo Village, a Chinese theater, and various European ethnic attractions. No less popular were re-creations of disasters. Crowds thronged to reenactments of the Johnstown and Galveston floods and to the "Fire and Flames" spectacle, which featured flames consuming an apartment building and rescuers trying to save desperate residents. Thompson and Dundy, following the Buffalo expo-

Ah there! Coney Island.
Copyright 1897 by Strohmeyer & Wyman.

Fig. 3-2. Coney Island pleasure seekers. Stereograph, 1897. Courtesy of the Library of Congress.

sition's recipe for success, emphasized the importance of wrapping amusements in architecturally distinctive casings—the predominant architectural accent at Luna Park was a Middle Eastern exoticism dubbed "oriental"—and relied on electrical illumination to keep the entertainments open well into the evening.

Like Luna Park, and unlike Steeplechase, which appealed to a primarily working-class clientele, Dreamland appealed to middle-class thrill seekers. Created by politicians, not showmen (though the boundaries between politics and show business, as the careers of P. T. Barnum and Sol Bloom made clear, were not always distinct), Dreamland featured a 375-foot electrical tower inspired by a similar erection at the Buffalo fair, as well as a partially nude female form over its main entrance, a massive dance hall, and shows featuring persons with physical disabilities—called "freaks"—along with mechanical amusements and displays purporting to represent foreign countries.[2]

Coney Island's popularity was overwhelming. As Judith A. Adams notes,

Luna Park alone attracted four million visitors during its second year of operation, and by 1910 Sunday crowds alone could number around a million. Not surprisingly, Coney Island inspired the creation of similar amusement parks around the country—about 1,500 of them by 1919—among them Olympic Park in Irvington, New Jersey; Riverview Park in Chicago; Cedar Point in Sandusky, Ohio; Kennywood, near Pittsburgh; and Columbia Gardens in Butte, Montana. All featured mechanical rides—carousels, roller coasters, and the like. Most exhibited "freaks" and variants of world's fair ethnological concessions. Filipinos displayed at the 1905 Portland fair, for instance, were exhibited at amusement parks around the country for the next several years. Some of the parks, like Riverview, specialized in thrill rides; others, like Olympic Park, set a different tone and resembled European pleasure gardens. Columbia Gardens tried to have it both ways, and therein lies an important story about the social function of amusement parks at the close of the century.[3]

Located just outside the mining city of Butte, the site that would become Columbia Gardens was developed initially as a recreational site for Butte's working classes. By the early 1890s, it featured a growing number of urban amusements. In 1899, the site was purchased by copper king and former Montana commissioner to the World's Columbian Exposition William A. Clark, who transformed it into an amusement park for Butte's immigrant workforce and their children. Clark's timing was exquisite. He was running a hotly contested race for the U.S. Senate and certainly needed the support of Butte's working class. In Butte's highly charged atmosphere of class and ethnic tensions, Clark may well have been interested in running a classic bread-and-circus operation whereby he thought he could win the hearts and minds of workers by entertaining them and their families. But it is also possible that Clark, who invested more than $100,000 a year in Columbia Gardens for several years, saw the amusement park as a source of revenue and as another way to influence the values of his workers. In an era marked by massive strife between labor and capital, Clark, by controlling how workers spent their time away from their jobs, may well have viewed his amusement park as a safety valve and as a chance to foster a set of consumerist values. Precedents for both possibilities certainly existed in the world of Coney Island's amusements.[4]

The exact reasons for the appeal of amusement parks and their overall significance have been debated by historians. Adams argues that amusement parks "turned engines of work into joy machines" and afforded Americans opportunities to escape from the oppression associated with their nation's rapid rise to industrial prominence and the repression associated with its Victorian culture. Kathy Peiss similarly notes how Coney Island became a vehicle for making "heterosexual expressiveness not only respectable but a privilege for which women and men gladly paid." Kasson, while not denying that one source of Coney Island's popularity lay in its carnivalesque subversion of Victorian values, emphasizes that it "offered 'fun' in a managed celebration for commercial ends." "Dispensing standardized amusement," Kasson writes, "it demanded standardized responses" that were "profoundly conformist" and "fundamentally manipulative." Furthermore, the emphasis at Coney Island on entertainment speeded the advance of consumerism in American culture and transformed amusement into "the new opiate of the people." According to Woody Register, Coney Island and its clones were less opiates than elixirs that advanced a concept of "Peter Pan manhood," whereby "men would be liberated from the duties, responsibilities, and toil of adulthood." Functioning as ritualistic and liminal exercises and as safety valves that enabled masses of Americans to find release from the pressures of industrialized and urbanized life, amusement parks joined fairs and wild west shows and circuses in carrying a nationwide audience across an important threshold toward a new cultural experience where consumerism and leisure became hallmarks of a new national identity. Over the course of the twentieth century, this process would continue to evolve and find expression in several direct offshoots of Coney Island, like Disney corporation theme parks and resorts as well as amusement parks like Six Flags Over Georgia, Busch Gardens, Universal Studios, and Knotts Berry Farm. One might also fast forward to the transformation of Las Vegas into a "themed city" which, by the close of the twentieth century, could boast hotels that "take inspiration from ancient Egypt, old Hollywood, and Oz." Like Coney Island and its turn-of-the-century contemporary operations, these latter-day theme parks and themed cities were also influenced by the cumulative commercialization of American culture and Americans' growing demand for entertainment. Central to this process was the rise of the motion picture industry.[5]

MOTION PICTURES

As was the case with so much else having to do with early twentieth-century American culture, the Chicago World's Columbian Exposition served as catalyst. Along with Ferris wheels, Dr. Welch's grape juice, and internal combustion engines, this fair introduced Americans to William Dickson's kinetoscope. Dickson saw the commercial possibilities of the motion picture medium even when his boss, Thomas Edison, in one of his few lapses of judgment about the commercial possibilities of a new technology, failed to do so. Over the next three years, with rapid improvements in motion picture projection technology (the Lumière brothers in France developed the cinematograph, Dickson developed the biograph, and Thomas Armat won an endorsement from Edison for his vitagraph), minute-length films joined the world of urban entertainments, "chasing" audiences from vaudeville theaters between shows. As many historians have noted, the novelty of these "flickers" quickly wore off, but the entrepreneurial dreams of improving upon the medium did not. As Daniel Czitrom observes, two crucial developments occurred almost in tandem. First, Edwin S. Porter, in *The Great Train Robbery* (1903), pioneered new editing techniques that made it possible to tell a story via the film medium instead of simply recording events. Second, vaudeville and arcade owners began to open small storefront theaters devoted exclusively to motion pictures, especially "story" films. These nickelodeons, so-called because of their five-cent admission charge, spread like wildfire—from a handful in 1905 to several thousand three years later. Attendance figures are difficult to determine, but it seems evident that by 1908 about twenty-five million Americans a week went to nickelodeon performances. Within six years, attendance soared to seven million a day. By the start of the First World War, motion pictures had become the super nova in the expanding galaxy of American mass entertainments and among the most extensively incorporated.[6]

To control markets and patents, the major producers of motion picture equipment and films, following the precedent of vaudeville managers, combined to form the Motion Picture Patents Company—a veritable corporate "trust" and paradigmatic culture industry all rolled into one. But the efforts of the major film producers and distributors to control the industry backfired, culminating in a 1915 court decision that, in an era remembered more for its rhetoric than reality of "trust busting," found the so-called Patents Trust guilty of unfair trade practices. Even before this decision, independent producers, especially Carl Laemmle, sought to undercut the power of the Trust by luring away its most talented performers—including stars Florence Lawrence and Mary Pickford. With its tremendous capitalization, Hollywood's motion picture industry stood poised to effect a revolution in the way people saw the world. The major roadblock lay in overcoming the disdain that middle-class Victorian audiences held for a form of entertainment that had hitherto seemed positively un-American because of its popularity with immigrants and the urban working classes.

As many film historians have documented, motion pictures initially gained popularity among the immigrant working classes of America's cities. Not only were nickelodeons inexpensive, costing the proverbial nickel to enter, but they showed films produced abroad. "Over half of the 4,000 films released annually came from France, Germany, and Italy," historian Lary May notes, and these productions, far from extolling Victorian values of thrift, hard work, and upward mobility, challenged Victorian values. In sharp contrast to middle-class Protestant beliefs, the films highlighted the alternative values of the working classes. As May writes: "Generally the backdrop was made up of the Virgin Mary or the Catholic Church. Unlike American themes of sexual restraint, these tales depicted premarital sex and even adultery as human weaknesses or even as something to be enjoyed. Rarely was sex condemned outright. Interracial love affairs also received a sympathetic portrayal. Often heroes and heroines were overwhelmed by circumstances or fate, culminating in tragic or pessimistic endings rather than triumphing over obstacles."[7] The content of the early films, especially their political content, seems to have cut at a right angle to prevailing Victorian norms about proper social decorum.

The production of alternative meanings, however, did not stop with the process of consuming mass cultural forms. In an intriguing challenge to those who argue that the ideological messages of mass culture products trickled down and were passively absorbed by the working classes, historian Steven J. Ross has called attention to working-class film producers who tried to counter the growing hegemony of major Hollywood studios. According to Ross, some members of the political Left "used the newest medium of mass culture, the movies, as a political weapon in their struggles for greater justice and power." Exactly what motivated workers and political radicals to turn to film as an educational and entertainment vehicle was clear. By the early years of the twentieth century, industrialists were sponsoring films that vilified organized labor generally and strikes specifically. At first, working-class audiences marched out of theaters showing such films. By 1911, the American Federation of Labor (AFL) was taking the lead in producing films intended to counter the negative imagery of organized labor. With films like *A Martyr to His Cause* (1911), the AFL's defense of John McNamara, accused of bombing the *Los Angeles Times* building, and *From Dusk to Dawn* (1913), a Socialist Party production that advocated the orderly overthrow of capitalism, working-class cinematic critiques of prevailing power relations in American society gained a large following among workers. Importantly, as Ross emphasizes, working-class films were multidimensional and polysemic in their ideological content. Some films, those produced by the AFL, stressed unionization as the vehicle for reforming American capitalism; others, those produced by some socialists, sought "to utilize moving pictures as a permanent feature of Socialist propaganda."[8]

Further distinguishing working-class films was the way the working classes experienced moviegoing. At the very moment the process of sacralization was drawing borders between "high" and "low" forms of culture, workers continued their early traditions of being actively involved with performances. Unlike middle-class theaters, where seating was hierarchically based depending on the price one paid for a seat, working-class cinemas were more egalitarian and informal. Since films were short, lasting only a few minutes on average, workers could come and go as they wished. Once inside, the atmosphere was anything but quiet. Families and friends used the cinemas as social gathering places and could be every bit as engaged in performances as their counterparts who had attended live theater a generation before.[9]

In the early twentieth century, it was precisely this working-class valence attached to motion picture-going that posed a dilemma for early Hollywood filmmakers, who were trying to broaden film audiences—and widen profits—by appealing to the middle class. The solution came from a producer of melodramatic one-reelers for working-class audiences, David Wark Griffith. Born in Kentucky in 1875, Griffith pursued a career on stage before turning to film. Once involved with the movies, he helped pioneer a style of flashback and cutback editing that enabled him to shatter barriers of time and space and claim the mantle of realism for his productions. At the same time, Griffith began using his productions for Biograph studios as conscious instruments of middle-class reform, arguing that the film medium could uplift and instruct the lower classes while reaffirming the rightness of the Victorian social and moral order. In 1915, he yoked these convictions to the effort following the Civil War to reconstruct and reunite the nation at the expense of African Americans and produced his feature-length *The Birth of a Nation*, a "silent" film that involved full orchestral accompaniment. With its explicitly white-supremacist interpretation of history, *Birth*, the subject of our next chapter, helped the fledgling motion picture industry gain legitimacy in precisely the same way that many other mass culture industries had won approval—by lending legitimacy to dominant racist presuppositions.

As movie theaters—often called "palaces"—replaced vaudeville theaters in the wake of *Birth*'s triumph, they bore witness to the power of motion pictures to effect fundamental changes in the American cultural landscape while simultaneously serving as conduits for perpetuating ideologically laden messages about white supremacy that had been central to the reconstruction of the United States after the Civil War. The rise of motion pictures to a place of respectability—indeed, centrality—within modern American culture capped the broader development and consolidation of mass culture industries as promoters and beneficiaries of a set of practices and values associated with the rise of mass consumption and leisure. By the end of the First World War, mass culture had become synonymous with the American way of life, but its triumph was hardly automatic. As the unfolding history of the American theater makes clear, it was the result of a great deal of struggle, compromise, and negotiation within and between dominant and subordinate groups in American society.

NEW DEVELOPMENTS IN AMERICAN THEATER

Changes in American popular theater owed a great deal to the 1893 Chicago fair. For theater producers, performers, and audiences alike, the "hootchy-kootchy" shows along the Midway Plaisance at the World's Columbian Exposition were a revelation and led to the reconfiguration of an already existing form of American theater, the burlesque show.

With its mixture of parody and bawdy humor, the burlesque show was as multilayered and embedded in the history of Europe as was the circus. But beginning in the 1860s, burlesque took a distinctive American turn when the manager of a beer garden took a troupe of French ballerinas, stranded in New York City, and put them on stage in an impromptu rendition of the popular melodrama *The Black Crook*. They became an instant sensation, had a run of over a year, and probably grossed a million dollars. What happened was simple. As Russel Nye puts it: "*The Black Crook* introduced the popular theater for the first time to the display of the female figure for its own sake, something which had little relationship to plot, theme, characterization, or any other dramatic element." In short, the "girlie show" had been born. Following its success, parades of similar shows, like the British Blondes, proliferated across urban America, attracting male audiences, usually in honky-tonk settings, often saloons, complete with curtained rooms where women performers and female impersonators titillated patrons and sold them drinks.[10]

What the World's Columbian Exposition did, through its Midway shows, was suggest the possibility that burlesque shows, if kept in check, could gain the same kind of legitimacy that Midway performances of the belly dance had inadvertently received by virtue of their association with the world's fair. And that is exactly what happened. In the decades following the fair, burlesque entertainments featuring risqué women performers like Fanny Brice and comedians like W. C. Fields became increasingly popular in legitimate theater and made inroads in vaudeville, a development that subtly loosened vaudeville from its moorings to Victorian sexual standards.

By the turn of the century, a number of so-called "hot" female performers, including Eva Tanguay, who was billed as "The Queen of Perpetual Motion," had eroticized their vaudeville acts, heralding the revolution in sexual behavior that would transform American values in the 1920s. The success of these vaudeville performances with both male and female audiences inspired aspiring theater impresarios like Florenz Ziegfeld, who once worked briefly for Buffalo Bill and operated a dime museum, to sell female sexuality to a broader public. Ziegfeld's innovation, the "revue" of women dancers, with its dazzling parade of women dressed in costumes that ranged from bathing suits to spangled American flags with battleship hats, became a fixture in American culture beginning in 1907. By the 1920s, his "Ziegfeld Girls" had set a standard for female beauty, but that standard was conspicuously racist inasmuch as all of his thousands of women performers were white.[11]

As powerful and popular as they were, burlesque and vaudeville did not completely overshadow other forms of theatrical entertainment. Indeed, the monopolistic practices of theatrical syndicates produced a backlash and, ironically, helped breathe new life into an older form of popular theater—the tent show. Traveling tent shows had been fixtures in American culture since the early nineteenth century when religious groups found the portable tent conducive for holding revival meetings. With the rise of theater syndicates, some actors and former theater managers, influenced by the uses circuses made of tents, turned to the tent show as a way to circumvent the restrictions placed on their repertoire and bookings. By the 1890s, a thriving tent-show business had penetrated rural markets with a mixture of melodrama, opera, and variety acts. Comfortable with one-night stands that made enforcement of recently enacted copyright restrictions difficult, tent show companies, which featured a "stock" character called Toby who voiced the frustrations of rural Americans over their declining social status, effectively thumbed their noses at the larger syndicates and gained an enormous popularity in the Midwest and South in the early years of the twentieth century. Their success, however, was only temporary. With the penetration of motion pictures and radio into rural markets by the 1920s, tent shows lost their audience and receded from the cultural landscape by the middle of the twentieth century.[12]

PICTURE POSTCARDS, MAIL-ORDER
CATALOGS, AND ADVERTISING

It is sometimes difficult to remember that something as ordinary as a picture postcard has a history. Their origin can be traced directly to Europe and the efforts by European merchants to promote products. In the 1870s, the potential of cards as conveyors of correspondence led to numerous efforts on both sides of the Atlantic to persuade postal services to afford lower rates. In the United States, this happened in 1872. The next year, the picture postcard was introduced, but postcards did not really catch on as a popular form of correspondence until the 1893 Chicago fair, when postcards conveyed both images and written messages from fairgoers to the folks back home. After the fair, the postcard industry took off, and postcards became the calling cards of the burgeoning tourist industry. Postcards proved a boon to the tourist industry and helped usher in a culture that increasingly lived by the slogan "To see is to know," as one Smithsonian Institution scientist put it.[13]

Postcards, whether regarded as trophies or as pieces of the true cross, revolutionized the way Americans communicated. In similar fashion, the rise of the mail-order business helped transform commercial relations in both rural and urban America. By the beginning of the twentieth century, leading re-tailers like Wanamaker and Sears had long since prevailed upon the U.S. Post Office to facilitate the distribution of advertising materials and commodities themselves through the creation of one-cent advertisers' postcards, Rural Free Delivery, and rural parcel post delivery. By 1920, according to one lead-ing historian of the mail-order system, the Midwestern family, on average, was receiving catalog shipments every three weeks. The effects were stun-ning. As Thomas Schlereth explains: "Chicago-based mail-order houses ho-mogenized the nomenclature of much of American material culture," giving uniform names to farm implements like weed-cutters, which in different re-gions of the country had previously been referred to as "sling-blades" or "slam-bangs." Just as they standardized the spoken and written word and popular-ized the practice of installment buying, mail-order catalogs, which Sears in 1894 titled "Consumer Guides," standardized American architecture. By the early twentieth century, small-town America was increasingly characterized by single-family houses supplied by mail-order companies that made it pos-sible for rural Americans to build and furnish their homes according to the latest standards of convenience and style set by department stores.[14]

Accompanying the rise of the mail-order business was another hallmark of America's burgeoning consumer culture, advertising. Merchants, not to men-tion cultural entrepreneurs like Barnum, had long advertised their products. But as Roland Marchand points out, advertisements "largely featured the product itself; most gave little attention to the psychic byproducts of owning it." Right around the First World War, the nature of advertising changed, and advertisers began thinking of themselves as social healers, selling not only products to use but images that would help Americans shape their per-sonal identities within a fluid American society. By the 1920s, advertising agencies like J. Walter Thompson Company and N. W. Ayer & Son had caught up with the marketing revolution pioneered by department stores and made New York's Madison Avenue synonymous with their profession.[15]

THE COMIC STRIP

The importance of images for the development of American mass culture was underscored by the development of another medium in the late nineteenth century—the comic strip. In a relatively short span of time, comic strips be-came a distinctive art form and a primary means for framing popular con-cerns about issues as divisive as immigration restriction and women's rights. While they often perpetrated dominant racial, ethnic, and gender stereo-types through pictorial and verbal caricature, cartoonists could also turn their artistic talents toward ridiculing prevailing values and suggesting alternative ways of seeing, thus underscoring the complex and often contradictory nature of mass culture.

The precise origins of the comic strip are not clear, but historian David Kunzle makes this telling observation with respect to the development of comic art in Great Britain: "The comic strip, with its fast, irregular pace, its frequent stops and starts (publication in installments), and its physical freneticism—which often escalated into bizarre and terrible accidents and extreme violence between people—mirrored the (feared) railway experience, which was a metaphor for life." "The comic strip," he continues, "both paralleled and cemented the railway experience: read en route, and especially at stops and changes, when there was nothing new to look at, it posited and connected life as a series of junctures."[16] Cartoon art, especially in the form of political cartoons, had a long history in America and Europe. Then, in 1893, the publishers of the humor magazine *Puck* set up a separate pavilion at the Chicago fair to boost the sales of their publication. For that occasion, they generated a series of color cartoons, some of which poked fun at world's fair visitors and world's fair organizers, while others lampooned the people put on display with degrading racist and ethnic stereotypes. *Puck* and the *Puck* pavilion were inspirations, but the newspaper comic strip may have had to wait for another day were it not for the competition between two newspaper publishers to capture a mass market. The market in question consisted of readers of two rival newspapers, Joseph Pulitzer's *New York World* and William Randolph Hearst's *New York Journal.* To capture Hearst's share of the market, Pulitzer determined to make the *World* more visually exciting. To accomplish this goal, he first tried to introduce color reproductions of established artistic masterpieces in his Sunday editions. When this effort backfired because of technical problems with his four-color rotary press, he hit upon the idea of using the vehicle of comic art to comment on the pressing social concerns of the day. In 1894, he employed Richard Outcault, an American-educated and Paris-trained artist, to come up with a comic art form that would appeal to readers. Outcault had little trouble settling on a thematic focus for his art and devised a series called "Hogan's Alley," which lampooned immigrant life in American cities. He had more difficulty settling on a character to build his narrative around, but was helped in that endeavor when a pressman determined to color the gown of one of Outcault's comic figures a bright yellow. When the February 16, 1896, edition of the *World* appeared, "The Yellow Kid" was an immediate eye-catcher and newspaper seller.[17]

There was more to the "Yellow Kid" than the color of his gown. Outcault's kid, with his bald head, nearly toothless grin, and oversized ears, sometimes

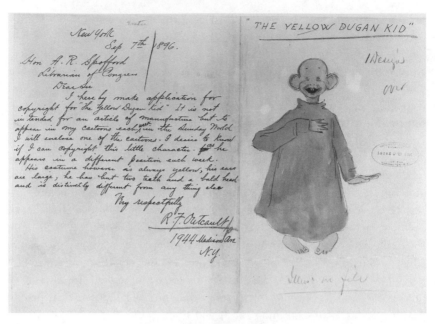

Fig. 3-3. Richard Outcault's "Yellow Kid" wore an eye-catching yellow gown. 1896. Courtesy of the Library of Congress.

resembled caricatures of Asians that had been used to build popular support to restrict Asian immigration to the United States. As was the case with other major innovators of mass cultural forms ranging from the Beadle Brothers and Buffalo Bill to Harry Von Tilzer and Florenz Ziegfeld, Outcault's central innovation was to devise a new medium, a mass-produced art form, for conveying variations of ethnic and racial stereotypes to a mass audience.

Outcault's success registered in two ways. First, there was the competition for his services. Second, there was the proliferation of the comic strip medium itself—a medium that by the close of the twentieth century would rivet some 86 million adults and 26 million children to newspapers every day.

Competition for Outcault's talents followed quickly on the heels of the success of the "Yellow Kid." Hearst evidently bribed him to jump ship and join the *Journal*'s staff. But Pulitzer, not to be outbid, persuaded Outcault to return. This bidding war between the newspaper magnates became so tantalizing that journalists, trying to decide what to call this new brand of journalism, with its roaring headlines and emphasis on making news instead of reporting it, let the comic strip be their guide. "The Yellow Kid" gave rise to the expression "yellow journalism"—a form of journalism that beat an incessant drum to build public support for America's acquisition of an overseas empire and the 1898 war with Spain.[18]

As if to demonstrate the proposition that the sincerest form of flattery is imitation, newspaper publishers and artists tumbled over each other to capitalize on Outcault's achievement of blending ideology with art. In 1897, Hearst's *Journal* began running Rudolph Dirks's thickly accented "The Katzenjammer Kids," which, with its not-so-distant echo of vaudeville comic routines, blended ethnic stereotyping with a strong dose of rebelliousness against established institutions like family and school. By 1900, the *World* told its readers that it would expand its comics section, called "The Funny Side," to eight pages. Over the next two decades, Americans, who only a few decades before had scorned Sunday newspapers as violation of the Sabbath, would be reading a host of "funnies," most of which relied on ethnic and racial humor to deliver whatever social criticism they might offer.

Perhaps no cartoonist was more talented in this latter respect than George Herriman, whose "Krazy Kat" debuted in 1911. In an era when the women's suffrage movement was challenging many presuppositions about gender relations and Victorian sexual values were increasingly ridiculed by a younger generation, Herriman's strip, which featured an androgynous cat's affections for a brick-throwing, married mouse, raised troubling issues about fundamental matters of sexual identity. By the First World War, a growing num-

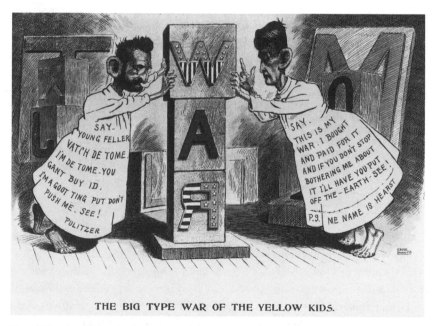

THE BIG TYPE WAR OF THE YELLOW KIDS.

Fig. 3-4. This 1898 lithograph calls attention to the "yellow" journalism that surrounded America's War with Spain. Newspaper publishers William Randolph Hearst and Joseph Pulitzer are each portrayed as "The Yellow Kid." Courtesy of the Library of Congress.

ber of cartoonists, like Rube Goldberg and George McManus, were developing the comic strip medium into a form of social satire and a fount for a host of new American slang expressions. By the First World War, because of the new vocabulary they acquired from comic strips, Americans could "zoom" to work and express their incredulity at anyone by telling them that their ideas were "baloney."[19]

But comic strips were anything but nonsense. They were a commercial art form that advanced, even while occasionally criticizing, the values of America's developing consumer culture. The evolving creations of cartoonist Richard Outcault were a case in point. With scores of talented artists threatening to steal his thunder, and with "The Yellow Kid" declining in popularity at the turn of the century, Outcault turned his talents to developing a new cartoon strip. After his "Lil Mose," cast right out of the mold of the minstrel show, failed to catch on, he created a strip called "Buster Brown" that appeared in 1902 and featured the adventures of a sometimes naughty but fundamentally good-hearted blond and curly-haired American boy and his dog Tige. In ways that would have made P. T. Barnum proud, Outcault then decided to capitalize on Buster Brown's distinctive shoes and clothing. At the 1904 St. Louis fair, he sold the commercial rights to Buster Brown to shoe manufacturers, whiskey distillers, and cigar makers, all of whom built Buster Brown into their advertising, thus setting in motion a commercial phenomenon that would only gain momentum over the course of the twentieth century as cartoon characters, including those that expressed ambivalence about American consumerism, would be used to endorse a dazzling array of consumer products.

By the time of Outcault's death in 1928, the comics had long since epitomized the triumph of American mass culture, outfitting Americans with shared images, a new vocabulary, and an opportunity to laugh at others as well as themselves. Their full power, however, would not be felt until the 1930s, when they introduced a stunning array of superheroes to rescue the United States from the throes of the Depression.[20]

SOUNDS OF THE CITY

The triumph of mass culture was certainly a visible one; it was also audible. Before the 1890s, sentimental ballads like the ones composed by Stephen Foster for minstrel shows—"Swanee River" and "Old Black Joe," for instance—dominated American popular music. But with the mass production of pianos and other musical instruments, together with fundamental transformations in the writing and marketing of music, music fell to the same economic pressures that affected other components of American mass culture.

The World's Columbian Exposition again was a catalyst. The exposition's

music director was Theodore Thomas, America's premier symphonic conductor and the individual chiefly responsible for making symphonic music
the province of elites in American society. Not surprisingly, given the exposition's obeisance to Arnoldian cultural ideals, the exposition's official musical program included an ambitious series of performances heavily weighted
toward Strauss and Wagner. But exposition authorities also recognized the
need to fill the void left by the cordoning off of symphonic music as the cultural property of affluent elites. To satisfy popular tastes, they included open-
air band recitals featuring performances of music by John Philip Sousa. Sousa
was no less interested in educating audiences than Theodore Thomas, but
never shunned entertainment as a medium for uplift. To accomplish his twin
goals of entertaining and educating audiences, Sousa dipped into the participatory well of American music and turned his performances into festive sing-
alongs that set the stage for the dramatic encores that became his trademark.

In contrast to the sobering and uplifting harmonies of the White City,
music along the Midway jarred the senses and reinforced perceptions of
the exposition's central message about the contrast between "savagery" and
"civilization." Guidebooks warned visitors about the "most awful cacophony"
emanating from bands in the Chinese, Turkish, and Egyptian theaters and
urged them to enjoy the "civilized music" in the German and Austrian villages. But warnings only made the forbidden seem more desirable—a phenomenon that showman Sol Bloom was quick to capitalize on. Bloom, whose
career would lead him from blackface minstrelsy and the Midway through
Tin Pan Alley and Broadway theater to the U.S. Congress, where he became
one of that institution's most powerful members and one of the prime movers
behind the creation of the United Nations, managed the Algerian and Tunisian
villages at the Chicago fair and wrote the melody for what became one of the
most popular tunes in America in 1893—the "Hootchy-Kootchy."[21]

Just as the Midway's "hootchy-kootchy" dances cut against the grain of
Victorian morality, so some of the Midway's syncopated music forced a rede-
finition of American music. In particular, the musical performances in the Dahomean village may well have inspired the creation of a distinctive American
musical form—ragtime. As one exposition-goer recorded, one of the Dahomean performers "sang little descending melodies in a faint high voice . . .
To his gentle singing he strummed an unvarying accompaniment upon a tiny
harp . . . With his right hand he played over and over again a descending passage of dotted crotchets and quavers in thirds; with his left hand he syncopated ingeniously on the two highest strings." While it is impossible to prove
that ragtime originated on the Midway, the presence of so many future ragtime performers on the Midway, including Scott Joplin and Ben Harney, in-
creases the probability that the Midway, quite contrary to the intentions of

Fig. 3-5. Impresario Sol Bloom poses with Minnie Reynolds, registrar of real estate instruments for New York County, after closing a large real estate transaction. Photograph 1928. Courtesy of the Library of Congress.

exposition organizers, nurtured its growth and popularity by hinting at its commercial possibilities.

By 1893, the market revolution that had so affected other aspects of American culture was transforming the character of American music. The year before the fair opened, a minstrel show performer and aspiring songwriter, Charles K. Harris, had composed a song, "After the Ball," and persuaded "the peerless baritone," James Aldrich Libbey, to include it as part of his performance in "A Trip to Chinatown." Audiences loved it, and orders for sheet music poured into Harris's company. When Sousa made it part of his world's fair repertoire the next year, the song became America's first multimillion-selling hit.[22]

There was more to Harris's success than can be accounted for by either the arrangement or lyrics of "After the Ball." The key to his success was salesmanship, or song "plugging." As Harris explained it: "I made up my mind that the song was going to be a success and so I conceived the idea that I would have someone in the gallery start the applause. The rest of the audience would surely follow." They did. And Harris did not stop there; he paid as many as fifty different singers to sing the song around the country. As one magazine reported: the song's "popular success carried it to the ends of the earth. Globe trotters heard it hummed by coolies in Hong Kong and by natives on the shores of the Red Sea." The success of "After the Ball" registered immediately with rival music publishers, who in the late 1880s had begun concentrating their operations in New York City. After Harris's hit tune, they redoubled their efforts to produce songs that vaudeville entertainers would then popularize and thereby create a popular market for the publisher's sheet music. The popularity of their music, in other words, did not exactly originate in the spontaneous demand of the public. As one authority on American popular music put it: "To feed the now huge market for songs, publishers began manufacturing them assembly-belt-style." By the turn of the century, a song "was the product of a calculated effort to meet a specific need. To help increase their list, publishers hired a staff that included arrangers to put melodies on paper and harmonize them for illiterate composers, piano demonstrators to exhibit songs to potential clients, staff writers to manufacture songs on order."[23]

The handful of commercial music houses that controlled the production of popular music by the turn of the century also controlled its distribution. In 1907, following the example set in other entertainment industries, Leo Feist, M. Witmark & Sons, F. B. Haviland, F. A. Mills, and Charles K. Harris, owners of the major houses of New York City's fabled Tin Pan Alley—so called because of the tinny din of piano music coming from the open windows of their offices along 28th Street between Broadway and Sixth Avenue—organized their own trust, the American Music Stores, Inc. They successfully fixed the price of sheet music at fifty cents and, in a move no less important, secured an agreement from the major department stores not to undersell each other. In the eyes of some contemporaries, Tin Pan Alley was nothing more than "a popular song factory."[24]

Like the publishers of dime novels, whose techniques they emulated and perhaps bettered, Tin Pan Alley music publishers understood the importance of having a product that would sell. And much of what sold were songs and lyrics that put into music the powerful sentiments about race that permeated other aspects of American mass culture. Beginning in the 1890s, Tin Pan Alley publishers made "coon songs," hitherto a staple of minstrel shows, part of their repertoire. More than five hundred songs with titles like "Coon! Coon! Coon!" and "A Red Hot Member" played on white sexual fantasies and helped pave the way, in the late 1890s, for the music industry's embrace of ragtime music, which, in turn, generated a new dance craze, the cakewalk, which probably owed its origins to the African American dance forms that had been parodied in minstrel shows. As the new century got under way, ragtime domi-

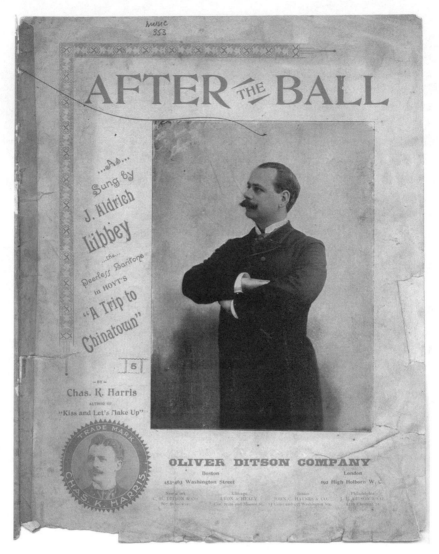

Fig. 3-6. Sheet music cover from "After the Ball," Music-353, Duke University Rare Book, Manuscript, and Special Collections Library.

nated American popular music, but in songs like Irving Berlin's "Alexander's Ragtime Band" (1911), the syncopation that African American composers like Scott Joplin had helped pioneer and write down had largely been commercialized and homogenized for consumption by white middle-class audiences.

Like ragtime, jazz had its origins in African American culture, especially in southern cities like New Orleans where it came of age in tandem with the blues and, by the 1890s, with ragtime. Unlike ragtime, jazz, because it depended so heavily on improvisation and "swing" that defied standard notation, remained a largely African American and southern musical tradition until 1917. What changed in 1917 was America's role in world affairs. America's entry into the First World War resulted in a mass migration of African Americans from the South to the North and West. Following in their wake were the southern white jazz bands, especially the Original Dixieland Jazz Band, that arrived in New York City from New Orleans in 1917 and began capturing white audiences with their music, which was derived from African Americans. As it became apparent that jazz could appeal to white audiences, old questions of marketing an improvisational musical form presented themselves with a new force.[25]

But the solution was already at hand. In 1877, Thomas Edison had invented the phonograph. By the 1890s, recordings were being made of classical music and, by the close of the first decade of the twentieth century, dance music. Recordings seemed like the perfect solution to the problem of capturing and marketing the sounds of jazz, and, in 1917, when the first jazz record was produced, the Jazz Age had begun. When, in 1921, record sales hit nearly one hundred million in a single year, it was clear that the commercialization of American music had become one more piston driving the commercialization of American culture as a whole.

But, as a number of scholars have made clear, the commodification and commercialization of jazz and its antecedents were only parts of a more complicated story about the complexities and contradictions of mass culture. In his landmark *Steppin' Out: New York Nightlife and the Transformation of American Culture, 1890–1930*, Lewis Erenberg calls attention to the emergence, by 1920, of "a new and vital popular culture that offered a way out of many of the limitations and controls of nineteenth-century society, culture, and institutional identity."[26] Standing somewhere near the wellspring of cultural energy stood a range of urban cabarets and nightclubs. By attracting the sons and daughters of affluent Victorian Americans to performances of ragtime music and jazz in settings where alcohol loosened inhibitions about dancing, these night spots, in effect, reversed the process of cultural creation. It no longer flowed from "high" to "low"; it rushed geyser-like from "low" to "high." In cabarets, forerunners of New York's nightclubs of the 1920s, the atmosphere recalled the antebellum theater, where lines between performers and audience often blurred. Performers and cabaret-goers shared the same dance floor and danced to the same bands, thus obliterating traditional theatrical distinctions between performers and audiences. In this world of the urban carnivalesque, where categories of "high" and "low" could be inverted and social norms transgressed, individuals could and did inscribe their own, sometimes quite rebellious, meanings on American culture. Audiences, for instance, could share in Sophie Tucker's open embrace of sexuality through songs like

"I Must Have a Little Liquor When I'm Dry" (1919) or "That Lovin' Soul Kiss" (1910). In the intimate surroundings of the cabarets and clubs it was easy to cut loose from Victorian constraints and to insist on greater personal freedom as one of the rights of citizens living in a consumer republic.

By the 1920s, with the Jazz Age in full swing, it was clear that American mass culture produced both centripetal and centrifugal energies. On the one hand, it generated enormous centralized and bureaucratized culture cartels that produced ideologically laden cultural products that ranged from popular songs to popular literature. On the other hand, audiences and consumers of mass cultural products treated these creations less as finished products than as raw materials with which to make their own cultural meanings. This essential tension, even contradiction, between these two aspects of American mass culture was also apparent in radio—a medium of mass communication that signaled the arrival of a new era of electronically mediated and corporate-controlled mass culture.

RADIO

Radio was the product of a series of scientific and technological breakthroughs made between 1898 and 1900 by Italian Irish inventor Guglielmo Marconi, who produced a wireless telegraph capable of communicating with ships beyond the sight of land. Beginning with his efforts to gain a British patent for his invention and to establish a monopoly controlling its production, there were strong indications that radio would follow the pattern of other communication technologies like telegraphs and telephones and become a corporation-run commodity. But American efforts to improve upon Marconi's invention and business acumen followed a strangely circuitous route that, for a brief period in the early years of the century, concentrated the power of radio communications in the hands of thousands of amateur users. Not unlike latter-day computer hackers, these amateur radio "hams" created a fascinating community of like-minded individuals interested in alternatives to corporate- and government-controlled means of communication.[27]

The technology that radio amateurs had in common owed its origins to the scientific interest in electromagnetic waves on both sides of the Atlantic that preceded Marconi's breakthroughs. In the United States, this research, as well as Marconi's innovations, inspired Reginald Fessenden to carry Marconi's ideas one step further. Between 1900 and 1906, Fessenden carried out a series of experiments that allowed him to broadcast both the human voice and music over a distance of a couple of miles. One year later, he made the first transatlantic radiotelegraphic transmission.

Within six years, thousands of Americans, mostly young men and boys, began building their own radios and using radio technology to communicate with one another. What accounts for the popularity of early radio technology? Historian Susan J. Douglas pinpoints several factors. First, crystal radio sets played on the American male's long-standing romance with technology. In this case, radio technology seemed to empower individuals at precisely the moment other technologies of mass production in the workplace seemed overpowering and alienating. Second, in an era of growing concern over the power of corporate "trusts," radio permitted an end run around corporate-controlled means of mass communication. Put briefly, radio users did not have to pay the phone company or the U.S. Postal Service, for that matter, for the privilege of communicating with each other. Third, in an age of Tarzan-like heroes striding across continents, radio heralded the possibility of heroic action. For instance, wireless operators aboard the doomed luxury liner *Titanic*, which hit an iceberg on its maiden voyage in 1912, found a nearby ship that was able to rescue 710 of the ship's 2,224 passengers. As wireless operators aboard other ships performed similar services in times of emergency, the appeal of radio found expression in popular novels and magazines.[28]

In the fall of 1920, a Pittsburgh department store decided to advertise the broadcasts of Frank Conrad, a local Westinghouse engineer and amateur radio broadcaster, in the hopes of selling radio receivers. Its advertising worked and came to the attention of one of Westinghouse's chief executives, Harry P. Davis, who had a brainstorm. He proposed to convert one of his company's plants, recently idled by the end of the war, to the production of radio receivers and persuaded Conrad to relocate his broadcasting equipment from his garage to the roof of the factory. Westinghouse immediately began promoting its newly created station—KDKA. Then, on November 2, 1920, it made history. That evening, Conrad broadcast the returns of the presidential contest between Warren G. Harding and James M. Cox. This in turn set off a stampede to buy radio receivers. In 1920 there were probably about 1,000 sets that picked up KDKA's election-night broadcast. By the end of 1924, some three million sets had been sold and over 500 stations were on the air.

In retrospect, given the commercial pressures to sell radios, it is easy—and right—to suggest that the next step, namely commercials themselves, followed logically. But they did not automatically become part of radio's repertoire. The steady commercialization of American culture had produced a steady stream of criticism by American intellectual leaders and cultural conservatives, and many Americans were still alive who remembered the battles over the commercialization of Sundays with newspapers and world's fair openings. To offset these critics and to avoid alienating consumers with a constant barrage of commercial advertising, radio executives developed a formula that allowed them to mix business with pleasure—the sponsored radio show. As the 1920s roared into existence, radio shows sponsored by soap companies, grocery stores, and tobacco companies became increasingly common-place and, by the onset of the Second World War, utterly routine.

There was an additional offshoot of radio technology, the so-called wired wireless or multiplex system that allowed telephone wires to transmit multiple messages at the same time. First developed by George Owen Squier, Chief Signal Officer in the U.S. Army and the first army officer ever to obtain a Ph.D., this technological innovation led Squier to develop a way to transmit music from phonographs over the electrical wires. In 1922, he founded a firm called Wired Service that he renamed Muzak—a name he derived from his love for music and his admiration for the Kodak corporation. What he discovered was that ambient music soothed his own workers and even made them more productive. When his company put his system in elevators to calm nervous riders and learned from studies that the piped-in music had the desired effect, Muzak was well on its way toward becoming a staple of American—and global—consumer culture. By 1998, the Muzak corporation boasted 2,000 employees ("audio architects") and had 80 million listeners worldwide.[29]

With the advent of Muzak, commercial radio, and the discovery that the contents of already existing forms of mass entertainment like vaudeville and popular music could be repackaged for a nationwide listening audience, radio executives furthered the process of national cultural reconstruction and consolidation that followed in the wake of the Civil War. The promoters of radio were technical and cultural innovators. But it is more accurate to think of them as cultural pioneers who, like their forebears who invaded and settled the American West, often followed trails blazed by others. By the time radio was becoming a part of the American scene, American mass culture had already come of age and had made its presence felt in Europe.

"THE AMERICANIZATION OF THE WORLD"?

Long before he died on the *Titanic*'s maiden voyage in 1912, W. T. Stead had established his credentials as one of England's most influential journalists. His 1894 book *If Christ Came to Chicago* built his reputation on both sides of the Atlantic as an astute observer of the contradictions of American life. In 1901, a full generation before American magazine publisher Henry Luce proclaimed the advent of the "American Century," Stead, drawing on his skills as a journalist and as a long-time observer of the United States, wrote *The Americanization of the World; or, The Trend of the Twentieth Century*. Stead's Americanized spelling of "Americanisation" for the American edition of his book reflected more than orthographical conventions; it reflected his conviction that a new economic power stood poised to change the world right down to its use of language. The English, Stead argued, had to recognize that "the world is being Americanized" and understand their "race-unity" with American Anglo-Saxons or face "ultimate reduction to the status of an English-speaking Belgium." This might be a big pill for his countrymen to swallow, Stead recognized, but the "trend of the twentieth century" was already plain in Britain. To make his case, Stead quoted from fellow journalist Fred Mackenzie's *The American Invaders*, which described how a "typical" Englishman began his day at the beginning of the twentieth century:

> In the domestic life we have got to this: The Average man rises in the morning from his New England sheets, he shaves with Williams' soap and a Yankee safety razor, pulls on his Boston boots over his socks from North Carolina, fastens his Connecticut braces, slips his Waltham or Waterbury watch in his pocket, and sits down to breakfast. There he congratulates his wife on the way her Illinois straightfront corset sets off her Massachusetts blouse, and he tackles his breakfast, where he eats bread made from prairie flour (possibly doctored at the special establishments on the lakes), tinned oysters

from Baltimore and a little Kansas City bacon, while his wife plays with a slice of Chicago ox-tongue. The children are given "Quaker" oats. At the same time he reads his morning paper printed by American machines, on American paper, with American ink, and possibly, edited by a smart journalist from New York.[1]

With these words, *The Americanization of the World* sought to convey the sweep of American cultural products in England and Europe at the dawn of the twentieth century. To be sure, some British and European reviewers thought Stead exaggerated his claims about Americanization.[2] For us, however, the crucial question that Stead begs is this: how should we evaluate the influence of American mass culture overseas? Were the products of American culture industries passively absorbed and unthinkingly used? Three American cultural exports—American representations at international expositions, wild west shows, and photographic images—serve as useful starting points for answering these questions.

FROM THE CRYSTAL PALACE TO THE 1900 PARIS UNIVERSAL EXPOSITION

By the beginning of the twentieth century, European and British audiences had been exposed to American exhibits at dozens of international exhibitions that had followed in the wake of London's fabled 1851 Crystal Palace Exhibition. At that fair, American exhibitors knocked British government officials, industrialists, and the broader public back on their collective heels with displays of Colt revolvers and McCormick reapers. Almost overnight, the United States established itself as an industrial and commercial power worthy of note that also gave every appearance of lacking the artistic heft expected of a truly civilized nation. As French statesman Georges Clemenceau put it before his death in 1929: "America is the only nation in history which miraculously has gone directly from barbarism to degeneration without the usual interval of civilization."[3] American representations at England's and Europe's world's fairs between 1851 and 1900 only sharpened that image, especially at the 1900 Paris Universal Exposition.

"Until the Great Exposition of 1900 closed its doors in November, Adams haunted it, aching to absorb knowledge, and helpless to find it." With these words, American historian Henry Adams opened the "Dynamo and the Virgin," the most famous chapter of his autobiography, *The Education of Henry Adams*. Captivated by the Paris exposition's displays of automobiles and dynamos, radium and x-rays, cinematography and chromophotography, Adams reflected on the distance the world had traveled since the Middle Ages. On the Paris exposition grounds, as he described his feelings, he "entered a su-

Fig. 4-1. Illustration depicting the American arrival at the 1851 Crystal Palace Exhibition. Over the course of the nineteenth century, American exhibits at world's fairs in Europe conveyed the material facts about mechanization and modernization that would awe many Europeans and provide the support for the theorizations of European cultural critics discussed in chapter 6. Currier and Ives lithograph, 1851. Courtesy of the Library of Congress.

persensual world, in which he could measure nothing except by chance collisions of movements . . ." Awestruck by "physics stark mad in metaphysics," he proceeded to reflect on the symbols of power on view at the fair and concluded: "All the steam in the world could not, like the Virgin, build Chartres."[4]

Whether Adams was right about steam and Chartres, or about dynamos and virgins for that matter, he certainly captured the lure that the Paris Universal Exposition held for anyone interested in the meaning of modernity. And Adams was not alone. Some fifty million people visited this fair, making it the most highly attended event of its kind since the world's fair movement had begun with London's 1851 Crystal Palace Exhibition.[5] To be sure, not all of these visitors "felt the forty-foot dynamos as a moral force" and most, while fatigued, probably derived more pleasure than anguish from the stunning array of exhibits divided between the Trocadero, the banks of the Seine, and the Bois de Vincennes. But Adams's account, while exceptional, should not be discounted. He did, after all, recognize the Paris Universal Exposition for what it was—a cultural powerhouse.[6]

In late 1899, a U.S. ship arrived in France carrying the bulk of the American displays for the fair. Full of cargo, the *U.S.S. Prairie* bore a name that was full of meaning. Nine years earlier, the U.S. Census had proclaimed the end of the frontier period in American life; three years after that, at the 1893 Chicago fair, historian Frederick Jackson Turner had read his famous paper on the significance of the frontier in American life, in which he had cautioned: "He would be a rash prophet who should assert that the expansive character of American life has now entirely ceased."[7] The *Prairie* and its Paris-bound stores bore out Turner's prediction.

When they arrived in Paris, the nearly 7,000 exhibits, which had already been fit into the exposition's classification scheme, were dispersed to pavilions and annexes spread around the exposition's various sites. Unlike many world's fairs that had a central site, the Paris Universal Exposition, like many European universities both then and now, occupied diverse sites around the city. The arrangement was complicated, but not beyond human understanding, as the U.S. assistant commissioner-general, B. D. Woodward, tried to explain:

> From the domain of Pure Art on the Champs Elysées one is led, on the Esplanade des Invalides, to the home of Art applied to Industries; thence to the Champ-de-Mars, where the raw products of the earth are viewed side by side with achievements wrought by human intelligence and ingenuity; and, finally, to the Trocadero, where, amid exotic surroundings, the remote races of the earth strive to enter into competition with the elements of advanced civilization.

The core ideas of the exposition, in other words, were saturated with ideas of racial hierarchy and the deep-seated conviction that "civilization" had triumphed over "savagery."[8]

These broad racialized zones of the exposition were linked by exhibition avenues that ran along both sides of the Seine. On the Left Bank, foreign pavilions joined the Champ-de-Mars (site of the tower Gustave Eiffel had erected for the 1889 exposition) and the Esplanade des Invalides. On the Right Bank, a mélange of commercialized entertainments and official exposition structures stretched between the Trocadero and the Champs Elysées. Even with these exhibition areas, French exposition officials had concluded long before the fair opened that additional space would be required to accommodate the quantity of domestic and foreign exhibit material. Consequently, exposition planners had leapt six miles across the city to the east and established an exposition annex in the Bois de Vincennes—future site of the 1931 Paris Colonial Exposition.

Even this expansion of the exposition grounds left American officials wanting more. A year and a half before the fair opened, the French director-general had tried to put a stop to U.S. demands by reminding the U.S. commissioner-general, Ferdinand Peck: "You know the old saying, 'The prettiest girl in the world can only give what she has.'" But American officials refused to take the hint. By the time the fair opened, they had persuaded French authorities to accommodate the desires of several American corporations, including the McCormick Harvester and Southern Railway companies, to build their own pavilions and to provide additional annexes to major exposition palaces to satisfy the demands of American business and agricultural interests.[9]

Exactly why French authorities conceded so much to the American commission is not hard to explain. The Paris Universal Exposition, like all world's fairs, reflected the intrigues of international politics. Increasing the exhibit space of the United States to the levels enjoyed by Britain and Germany had the not-so-subtle effect of diminishing the stature of France's European rivals at the Universal Exposition. But the decision to inflate the American presence at the fair had this unintended consequence: it gave the United States a commanding port of entry to French and European markets.

In retrospect, it might seem as if the strength of the U.S. presence at the Paris fair was diluted because American exhibits were scattered around various exposition sites. But the breadth of the U.S. presence across the fair's expanses made it difficult to find a sector of the fair without an American element.

For instance, in the major exhibition palaces near the Eiffel Tower that were dedicated to outfitting visitors with lasting lessons about the meaning of "civilization," the United States developed displays devoted to mining and metallurgy, education and liberal arts, civil engineering and transportation, chemical industries, and textiles. Exhibits included a replica of an American surgical theater, a ten-foot-tall model of a modern American office building, and numerous models devoted to improving river transportation systems. For visitors who may have wondered about the natural resources of the United States, U.S. displays of mining processes and products in the Palace of Mines occupied half of the ground-floor exhibit space. Of all the American exhibits in this zone of the fair, perhaps the most captivating was the "moving stairway," forerunner of the modern escalator, that was installed to convey visitors between the floors of the textile building. As one exposition official explained: "If in a hurry you can run upstairs; if you wish to come down your speed in descent must exceed that of the stairway's ascending motion."[10] Clearly, this was a device befitting a nation that thought of itself as moving only in an upward direction.

Across from the Champ-de-Mars, in the area of the exposition set aside for colonial exhibits, the U.S. government, despite its formal denials of having colonies, requested and received space in the Trocadero Palace for exhibits from Cuba and Hawaii. Because of an outbreak of plague in Hawaii, the Hawaiian displays were relatively small. But the Cuban exhibit, housed in a Renaissance-style pavilion built within the Trocadero Palace, more than made up for the limited Hawaiian showing. For these displays, the U.S. War Department allocated $25,000 and detailed its military liaison to the U.S.

Fig. 4-2. Otis escalator installed at the 1900 Paris Universal Exposition. The rise of American corporations and their role in promoting American products overseas should not be underestimated. For Europeans, exhibits of American technology came to be seen as synonymous with American culture. Courtesy of Otis Elevator Co.

Commission to Cuba to help Gonzalo de Quesada, Cuba's future minister to Washington, D.C., assemble displays of natural resources from more than 400 exhibitors that would "illustrate the opportunities that capital now has in the development of the island."[11]

As vital as they were to the American representation in Paris, the Cuban exhibits also posed a dilemma. As Peck explained the situation to U.S. secretary of state John Hay, French exposition authorities had decided that, since Cuba was not technically a colony or an independent nation, exhibits from Cuba "would have to be received from Cuban exhibitors as American citizens" thus granting "recognition on the part of the Commission that Cubans are American citizens." Given the divisive debates in the U.S. Congress over the annexation of Cuba, the secretary of state was unwilling to open a back door to Cubans wanting to claim U.S. citizenship on a technicality. Conse-quently, Peck had to persuade French exposition authorities to make an ex-ception to their rules of classification to allow the Cuban exhibits to appear in a niche by themselves. But having negotiated this concession, the question came up as to whether the United States flag could be flown over the Cuban exhibits. This too required delicate diplomacy and apparently was resolved with a decision to drape the Cuban pavilion in red, white, and blue bunting.[12]

The American presence at the fair was also in evidence along the Right Bank of the Seine, in the area allocated to the commercial amusements, where American dancer Loie Fuller's private theater became one of the hits of the fair. Fuller, clad in layers of revealing gauze, danced in the light of green spotlights and became a one-woman living tableaux and the personification of the exposition's Art Nouveau style. Her modern dance performances made the neoclassically designed U.S. National Pavilion, which stood across the river scrunched between the Austrian and Turkish pavilions, seem utterly out of step with modern times.[13]

But beneath its neoclassical facade, signs of a modern American mass culture abounded. As one senior U.S. official wrote of the building's interior: Here "the American will be at home with his friends, his newspapers, his guides, his facilities for stenography and typewriting, his post-office and his telegraph station, his money exchange, his bureau of public comfort and even his ice-water. He may consult his 'ticker,' where from four to six each after-noon he can receive direct from the New York and Chicago Stock Markets the latest quotations of the busy forenoon hours at home."[14]

Ironically, although it was intended to demonstrate the strength and sta-bility of America's commercial present and future, the building's structural stability was always in doubt. Indeed, one *New York World* reporter leaked engineering reports that warned the pavilion was so poorly designed that, if it were ever filled to capacity, "the whole structure would inevitably collapse toward the centre, and the great dome would fall on top of that heap." These reports struck nerves already frayed by a steady barrage of criticism about the building's structural and aesthetic features. Morin Gustiaux, one of the pavilion's assistant architects, actually challenged the *World* reporter to a duel. Not to be intimidated, the *New York Times* ran a blunt editorial, con-demning the pavilion as "a bad imitation of European work . . . which seems to have been modeled after that Venetian church which is known to flippant tourists as 'Santa Maria della Volute.'"[15]

Where American architects failed to project a distinctive American na-tional identity, U.S. artists and sculptors succeeded, but in a vein that often reinforced European ideas that America's industrial progress had come at the expense of its civilization. As Diane P. Fischer has argued, American art was carefully packaged for the fair to convey a sense that the United States had both the economic resources and talent to merit consideration for full membership in that elite club of "civilized" nations dominated by Europe's colonial powers, especially France. As Fischer puts it, representations of American art were selected "to demonstrate not only America's new cultural status, but also its economic, technological, imperial, and agrarian riches."[16] These messages were clear from the decorations and sculpture on view inside the U.S. National Pavilion and in the sections of the Grand Palais given to American oil painting. Far from simply occupying an independent, aesthetic realm at the fair, American art, more than anything, provided visual reinforcement for assertions of America's new role as an imperial power—one that could afford to leave European ideas about "civilization" in the dust.

One of the primary underpinnings of this new civilization was on view across the Alexander Bridge from the Grand Palais in the U.S. Publisher's Building. Inside this building, it was not so much Culture as the commercialization of Culture—what cultural critic Walter Benjamin would term "art in the age of mechanical reproduction"[17]—that was on view. The centerpiece of the exhibit was the enormous Goss Press that, each hour, printed and folded 50,000 copies of the sixteen-page Paris edition of the *New York Times*. As one foreign commentator wrote: "These Americans introduced us to a machine far more formidable than their revolving cannon—the machine which produces and automatically disgorges a newspaper by a single operation. A man, or—in default of a man—a boy, plays upon a key-board for a few minutes, and lo! the type has been selected and set up, and the characters printed upon a revolving cylinder. It is as rapid and complete as the transformation of a pig into pork, in the great factories of Chicago."[18] While not exactly laudatory, this commentary captured an important European perception about American "civilization" at the dawn of the new century—namely that, since mass production and mass culture had already become its defining features, American culture really could be reduced to its technology and mechanical reproducibility.

Further examples of America's industrially and technologically based culture were on view at the Vincennes Annex of the fair, where displays of automobiles, bicycles, railroads, elevators, revolvers, and machine tools were featured in the American sections of Machinery Hall and where the McCormick Company erected its own separate exhibition hall. Inaugurated with ceremonies that featured John Philip Sousa's band, these exhibits lent visible support to the proposition offered by the American exhibit as a whole that "the Republic is rapidly developing a highly perfected as well as a soundly organized civilization, and particularly that it promises fair to solve, to the satisfaction of all, that problem which has so long annoyed Europe and the world and all ages, viz., the practical and satisfying combination of the artistic with

20589 Paris Exposition 1900
Enthusiastic Frenchman Saluting the
American Flag
Copyrighted 1900 by William H. Rau

Fig. 4-3. "Enthusiastic Frenchman Saluting the American Flag" was the caption placed on this photograph of the American Pavilion at the 1900 Paris Universal Exposition. Courtesy of the Library of Congress.

the utilitarian, the aesthetic with the enduring, the beautiful and graceful with the progressive and strong."[19] This was a heady proposition and one, as our final chapter makes clear, that not all Europeans agreed with. To be sure, there were grounds for confusion, since expositions were not the only way American mass cultural forms infiltrated Europe. Europeans also gained insights into American "civilization" from the multiple treks of Buffalo Bill's Wild West performers across England and the Continent.

BUFFALO BILL'S WILD WEST IN EUROPE

In 1886, William Cody received an offer that seemed too good to be true. Thanks to the skill of his manager, Nate Salsbury, Buffalo Bill received an invitation from the organizers of London's American Exhibition to perform as part of their show in the Earls Court exhibition complex. To be honest, the English promoters of the American Exhibition were desperate. They had sought to capitalize on growing interest in the United States in England by organizing an event in 1886 that would be sponsored by British royalty and the U.S. government, including President Cleveland himself. Initially, they had some success gaining support from prominent individuals on both sides of the Atlantic but overreached when they began listing supporters, like the president and the Prince of Wales, without their consent. With supporters falling by the wayside and with the British government insisting that the American Exhibition not compete with the government-sponsored 1886 Colonial and India Exposition, the exhibition's organizers decided to postpone their event for a year. As they scrambled to keep their plans afloat, the show's promoters, while on a trip to Washington, D.C., had the good luck to cross paths with Salsbury. This master impresario, who had first encouraged Cody to shift his attention from the stage to outdoor entertainment, was as interested in lining up a European tour for Buffalo Bill's show as a way of giving it greater legitimacy in the eyes of the American public as the promoters of the American Exhibition were interested in reclaiming credibility in the eyes of the British public for their shaky enterprise. Over dinner and drinks, they struck a deal that gave the Wild West star billing in the American Exhibition. The results were simply incredible. Not since P. T. Barnum had paraded General Tom Thumb around the sitting rooms of British aristocracy had there been a comparable American production in England.[20]

The scale of Cody's undertaking amazed the press on both shores of the Atlantic. When the show's company boarded the *State of Nebraska* steamship for London, its entourage included "83 saloon passengers, 38 steerage passengers, 97 Indians, 180 horses, 18 buffalo, 10 elk, 5 Texan steers, 4 donkeys, and 2 deer." As the ship steamed across the ocean, Major John Burke (one of the show's managers) and an advance party plastered London with posters and drummed up anticipation in the press. As one London newspaper described the scene:

> I may walk it, or bus it, or hansom it: still
> I am faced by the features of Buffalo Bill.
> Every hoarding is plastered, from East-end to West,
> With his hat, coat, and countenance,
> lovelocks and vest.

Despite a recent hoof-and-mouth outbreak, British officials turned a blind eye to the government's quarantine regulations and, after the ship docked at Gravesend, allowed the troupe to board three trains and head immediately to

Fig. 4–4. Drawing of Buffalo Bill and members of his show in the Vatican, 1890. Buffalo Bill Scrapbook. Courtesy of the Buffalo Bill Historical Center, Cody, Wyoming, MS6.IX.6.1.

the arena that was part of the twenty-three-acre American Exhibition site that would serve as the staging ground for the show.[21]

Several weeks prior to the show's opening, Buffalo Bill's encampment became a veritable Mecca for England's upper crust. Among the many notables to visit the site was the former prime minister, William Gladstone, who toured the grounds in the company of the American consul general and, amidst great fanfare, met the Indian chief Red Shirt. Over lunch, Gladstone lifted a glass to the future of Anglo-American relations. Then, on May 5, just four days before the show opened to the public, the Prince of Wales, the future King Edward VII and a notable rake, accepted an invitation from Cody to bring his wife and daughters to attend a special preview of the Wild West performance. Afterwards, he met all of the performers, including Annie Oakley, who, in an episode widely reported in the press, ignored proper etiquette and shook hands with the Princess of Wales, whom she later described as a "wonderful little girl." Neither the prince nor princess took offense; to the contrary, the prince made a point of telling his mother, Queen Victoria, about the performance and urged her to attend one. With remarkable speed, proper arrangements were made for a command performance of the Wild West on May 11, and, for the first time since her husband's death a quarter of a century before, Queen Victoria appeared in person at a public performance.[22]

Her attendance at the Wild West show was news everywhere in the English-speaking world, and the fact that she made her appearance in the context of the celebrations that marked the Jubilee Year of her reign only added more weight to the occasion. And what an occasion it was. When the show began and a rider entered the arena carrying the American flag, Queen Victoria stood and bowed. The rest of the audience followed suit, while British soldiers and officers saluted. As Cody described the moment:

> All present were constrained to feel that here was an outward and visible sign of the extinction of that mutual prejudice, amounting sometimes almost to race hatred, that had severed two nations from the times of Washington and George the Third to the present day. We felt that the hatchet was buried at last and the Wild West had been at the funeral.

Over the course of the next century, it would become fairly routine practice for American mass cultural exports to serve as weapons for accomplishing specific U.S. foreign policy objectives. In the Victorian era, this use of mass culture was still being nurtured and the Wild West was one of the key incubators.[23]

That the Wild West also held enormous potential for domestic politics was equally clear, especially when Queen Victoria asked for another command performance of the Wild West show on the eve of her Jubilee Day festivities. For this occasion, the kings of Belgium, Greece, Saxony, and Denmark, as well as an assortment of Europe's princes and princesses, including the future German kaiser William II, joined England's royal family to take in the Wild West performance and show their subjects that they too could delight in ordinary pleasures. The highlight of the show came when several monarchs, including the Prince of Wales and the kings of Denmark, Greece, Belgium, and Saxony, hopped aboard the Deadwood Stagecoach with Buffalo Bill in the driver's seat and rode around the arena while the assembled Indians engaged in a mock attack. As they left the stagecoach, the prince, renowned for his love of poker, which American diplomats had introduced to English aristocracy only a decade before, supposedly said to Cody: "Colonel, you never held four kings like these." To this, Cody retorted: "I've held four kings, but four kings and the Prince of Wales makes a royal flush such as no man has ever held before." In another version of Cody's reply, Buffalo Bill allegedly said that he held "four kings and a royal joker." Whatever the truth, in both accounts it is the leveling effects of American mass entertainment that shine through the repartee.[24]

During the Wild West's run at the American Exhibition, Cody's managers rarely missed a beat. They organized twice-a-day performances that played to crowds that averaged around 30,000. This meant that, since the grandstand could seat about 20,000, the show played to standing-room only crowds who thrilled to the performances based on "The Drama of Civilization" and to the stage effects, which included sweeping painted backdrops of the American West illuminated by electricity. They also kept careful track of the distinguished guests who visited the show and published their portraits around Buffalo Bill to serve as endorsements of the production. By the time the American Exhibition closed in October 1887, well over a million people had witnessed Buffalo Bill's performances, making him every bit as popular in London as Benjamin Franklin had been in Paris a century earlier.

Capitalizing on their triumph in London, Burke and Salsbury shrewdly extended the Wild West's tour of England by booking twice-a-day performances in the industrial cities of Birmingham and Manchester, where Cody's crew devised spectacular special effects in the form of cyclones and prairie fires and even featured a six-day race between two cowboys riding horses and two bicyclists. When the cowboys won, it seemed additional evidence of the vitality and virility of the American frontier as represented in the Wild West show.[25]

By all accounts, Cody's tour of England was a smashing triumph. It was so successful that, before the troupe returned to the United States, the show's managers had laid plans for a return engagement—this time to the European continent. In April 1889, Cody's Wild West headed for Paris and the 1889 Paris Universal Exposition. For this engagement, Cody refashioned the show to include, among other novelties, the Cowboy Band playing the French national anthem and several performers dressed as fur trappers, who represented the French influence in Canada. But the essential message of the show remained unchanged: in the United States white, Anglo-Saxon "civilization" had tamed "savagery," rendering "savages" a source of amusement, ethnographic study, and inspiration for a shared racial consciousness among whites that held the potential for blurring class distinctions.[26]

Cody's commanding reputation, inflated by his advance team's publicity blitz, triggered an overwhelming response. More than 10,000 people, including French president Sadi Carnot, turned out for the opening performance. On almost a daily basis, French newspapers were filled with accounts of the Wild West and its performers, especially the American Indians, who attracted attention wherever they went, especially when they climbed the Eiffel Tower. Touching the Indians became a popular sport among young French couples, who, newspapers reported, thought such contact would assure fertility! Some children were inspired by the show as well; they set up their own wild west encampment in the Bois de Boulogne. And Rosa Bonheur, the famous French artist, went so far in her adulation of Cody as to paint several portraits of Buffalo Bill and to ask for (and receive) the head of Buffalo Bill's horse for her studio after the animal died. Throughout the summer, as Buffalo Bill memorabilia vied with exposition souvenirs as popular keepsakes, there was good reason to believe that the main event in town was

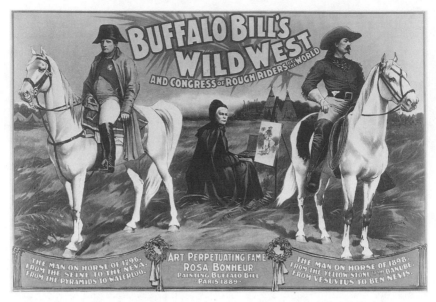

Fig. 4-5. Poster putting Buffalo Bill in the company of Napoleon. 1896. Courtesy of the Library of Congress.

not the fair, but the Wild West. Never immodest, Cody got caught up in the adulation he received and, in a show of bravado, if not bad taste, tried to present the French president with a special gift—a nine-foot-tall lamp, topped off with a preserved bison head and a scarlet red lampshade. When President Carnot politely declined the gift, there was reason to believe that, for all of the synergy associated with "Americanization," it was sometimes possible for Europeans to just say no.[27]

From Paris, the Wild West traveled to southern France and Spain. Then, in early 1890, Cody's show traveled across Italy with performances in major cities, including Rome, where Pope Leo XIII singled out the performers for a special blessing. In Bologna, the Wild West played for eight days, made a huge profit, and left the Bolognese with stirring impressions of the American West, and vivid memories of congested streets and oversold arenas (see frontispiece). In Bologna and elsewhere, Wild West concessionaires introduced audiences to popcorn, giving them a lasting taste of American mass culture.

After blazing a trail across Italy, Cody's show headed north to Germany, where it was refashioned into an imperial circus billed as "Buffalo Bill's Wild West and Congress of Rough Riders of the World." The show expanded to include representatives of foreign troops, including Arabian and Syrian horsemen. By the time Cody returned to England for another command performance for Queen Victoria, his show had earned a reputation on both sides of the Atlantic for its "authentic" representation of the American West and for inspiring dreams of freedom in European societies that seemed locked into class-based social hierarchies.[28]

EUROPEAN RESPONSES TO THE WILD WEST SHOW

Looking at European responses to American mass culture, whether in its early forms like Buffalo Bill's Wild West show touring Europe, or in later forms like Hollywood movies, or advertisements for American consumer products, they have always been of two kinds. Some have been on the level of articulate reflection producing a repertoire of critical views; others have consisted of selective appropriation, redirecting the impact of American cultural exports, sometimes Europeanizing them as well.

To take the example of Buffalo Bill in Europe, we need to answer two questions. First, at the level of articulate, specific responses, the question is what did Europeans choose to read in what they saw? What did they make of it? Did they enjoy it as pure entertainment, a display of American exoticism? Were they impressed by the Wild West's showmanship, its mastery of a form of popular entertainment? And, if so, did they recognize a typical American flair in it, far surpassing anything they had seen so far? Or was it rather a matter of affiliation with a historical narrative of conquest and imperial expansion that they could meaningfully relate to the world they lived in? The intention of Buffalo Bill's staging was certainly to make the story of the American West merge with the story of European expansion at a time when European colonization reached the far frontiers of its own empires. European audiences may have been aware of this larger connection and may have seen the show as confirming views of Western superiority and the White Man's civilizing mission. Yet, when we conceive of response in terms of reception and appropriation, we need to take a longer view. We need to ask ourselves to what extent the Wild West intersected with ideas about the American West that had already been formed by earlier carriers of imagery, in novels by the likes of François René de Châteaubriand and James Fenimore Cooper, through journalism, travelogues, immigrant letters, or visual materials such as paintings, drawings, prints, and photographs. In fact, the European fantasy of the American West had already spawned its own popular authors like Balduin Mollhausen and Karl May in Germany, Gustave Aymard in France, and Mayne Reid in England. The American West had already been appropriated and made to serve as a projection screen for European fantasies, for instance of White-Indian male bonding in a setting reminiscent of German dreams of pristine nature, as in May's romances, or in the guise of a quasi-anthropological exoticism, as in Aymard's stories. To put it in slightly different terms, the Wild West made a splash in a pond already filled with images of the American West.[29]

Equally important to remember is that Europe was never just one homogeneous setting for the reception of Buffalo Bill's Wild West show as an accomplished form of American mass culture. Each European country had at the time its own specific history in fictionalizing the American West. For instance, among European countries, Germany offers the clearest case of a longtime infatuation with the American Indian. This may have had to do with a romantic, if not nostalgic, affiliation with peoples threatened by the onward march of civilization, an affiliation that had the marks of a projection of feelings of loss of cultural bearings prevalent in a Germany undergoing rapid modernization itself. As Hans Rudolf Rieder, translator and editor of Buffalo Child Long Lance's book *Longlance: A Selfportrait of the Last Indian (Langspeer: Eine Selbstdarstellung des letzten Indianers)*, would put it in 1929: "The Indian is closer to the German than to any other European. This may be due to our stronger leaning for that which is close to nature." Karl May, the single most important molder of German views of the American Indian, viewed the Native Americans as being essentially good. Their great advantage over white people consisted in the ability to understand nature and harmonize with it. As Heribert von Feilitzsch puts it: May "captured in this portrayal the sentiment of Germans living in a rapidly industrializing country. The traditional German attraction to nature and romanticism increased in a world which seemed to evolve into an increasingly sterile and cold environment. In May's novels the reader could identify with the Native American who also faced the destruction of his living space, and for similar reasons: ruthless materialism." In 1876, the year of the Battle of the Little Big Horn, May himself wrote this passage in his *Geografische Predigten (Geographical Sermons):* "the site of that desperate fight in which the Indian lets fly his last arrow against the exponent of a bloodthirsty and reckless 'civilization.' . . . At the beginning of the 19th century the 'Redskin' was still master of the vast plains . . . But then came the 'Paleface,' the White man, drove the 'Red brother' from his hunting grounds . . . but traditions will weave their golden gleam around the vanished warrior of the savanna, and the memory of the mortal sin committed against the brother will continue to live in the song of the poet."[30]

Exotic and intriguing the Indians may have been to Europeans. Yet, at the same time, there was the sense that, here on display, reenacting their historical defeat at the hands of whites, were literally the last of the Mohicans, the representatives of a vanishing race. Such, white Europeans and Americans agreed, was the course of history. This tragic dimension may have actually heightened interest in Buffalo Bill's Indians as living representatives of a different race. Much of the European press gave equal if not more space to the Indian living quarters, with their tipis pitched on the show's grounds, than to the historical drama that made up the Wild West show. As one Italian newspaper put it: "their eyes are good and proud, they have the gentleness of a dying race." Yet, their image as bloodthirsty savages, well established in Europe at the time, also permeated much of the press reports. It was further disseminated by European equivalents of American dime novels and pulp magazines with names like *Buffalo Bill, the Wild West Hero.* The show did nothing to alter these impressions, with its central drama always portraying the Indians as savage aggressors who were eventually defeated by Buffalo Bill and other such heroes.[31]

Infatuation with the Indian, though, was not the only romance that engaged Europeans. Before Buffalo Bill appeared in Europe, Europeans had also become fascinated by the cowboy. The appeal of Buffalo Bill's Wild West lay as much in the heroism of the pioneer and frontiersman—tales that Cody restaged through his performers' stunning mastery of everything having to do with horses. As a result of the Wild West, the two romances became interlinked, and children growing up in Europe would play Cowboys *and* Indians for generations to come.

Buffalo Bill, then, clearly encountered in Europe a world already alive with images of the American West. While Cody may have been more catching than others in his showmanship, in other words more "American," it is important to ask, did European audiences notice this difference? Or was the Wild West just another touring show, turning the American West into a pageant, only better than rival shows? As it turns out, there were clear moments in the European response that spoke of an awareness of the Americanness of Buffalo Bill's Wild West. Billed in 1883 as "America's National Entertainment," the Wild West show captured what was fresh and original—what was least bound by tradition and imitative of European models—in American life. Mark Twain certainly sensed this when he wrote to Buffalo Bill after seeing the Wild West show in 1886 before its first European visit: "It is often said on the other side of the water that none of the exhibitions which we send to England are purely and distinctively American. If you take the Wild West show over there you can remove that reproach."

But, as historian John Sears has pointed out in a perceptive essay, as much as the show may have succeeded in embodying the "wildness" of the West, the show was as much a display of the products of nineteenth-century industrial civilization as it was of the savage life of the frontier.[32] The key to the whole affair was not the wild men and animals, the Indians, the frontier types, the bucking broncos and buffalo, but the revolver and the repeating rifles, two of the most innovative products of nineteenth-century industrial civilization in the United States. They were products of what Americans proudly—and Europeans admiringly and enviously—had come to call the "American System of Manufactures," whereby machine tools had made it in-

CHAPTER FOUR | 114

creasingly possible to produce precise, interchangeable parts. Both types of
firearms, as used in the show, were seen as mediators between a world of increasing technological precision and the freewheeling life of the frontier.
The heart of the show was a display of shooting which ritualized the practical and symbolic role of guns in American culture. In Europe, for a number
of historical reasons, the gun had never become a significant symbol in popular culture and folklore.

Two of the most famous firearms produced by the technological revolution in America were the Colt revolver, invented by Samuel Colt in 1835, and
the Winchester repeating rifle. They were the principal weapons used by
Buffalo Bill, Annie Oakley, Johnny Baker, and the other sharpshooters in the
Wild West show. Without such rapid firing and accurate weapons, neither
the Wild West show nor the conquest of the West, which the show reenacted,
would have been possible. As one program for the Wild West explained: "The
bullet is a kind of pioneer of civilization. Although its mission is often deadly,
it is useful and necessary. Without the bullet, America would not be a great,
free, united, and powerful country."[33]

The exhibitions of shooting were not the only way in which the Wild
West showed off American know-how. The methods of publicizing the show
by blanketing cities with posters also captured international interest. The
production of the show was itself a demonstration of the rapidly evolving
technologies of printing, the reproduction of images, and advertising. As
Cuban nationalist and poet José Martí explained to readers of several Spanish-
language newspapers: "'BUFFALO BILL' we read printed in large colored
letters on every corner, wooden fence, sign post, dead end wall in New York.
Sandwich-men—that is what they are called—walk along the streets, stuffed
between two large boards which fall front and back, and sway as does the un-
troubled fellow who carries them, while the crowds laugh and read the bright
letters shining in the sun: 'The Great Buffalo Bill.'"[34] Effective posters preceded the show as it traveled about Europe. Moreover, the way the show was
moved from place to place provided part of its cultural message, of its "Americanness." In its first ten years the show committed about half of its performances to European audiences. As time went on there were, in the logic of
touring, fewer long stays at major centers and more short stands. The resulting logistical problems were solved with such skill that during the extensive German tours, according to Annie Oakley:

We never moved without at least forty officers of the Prussian Guard standing all about with notebooks, taking down every detail of the performance.
They made minute notes on how we pitched camp—the exact number of
men needed, every man's position, how long it took, how we boarded the

trains and packed the horses and broke camp; every rope and bundle and kit was inspected and mapped.[35]

The secret for efficient loading, which may have been invented by the Wild West show, was to link railroad flatcars together with planks so that the wagons would come off in a continuous line, already in parade order for passing through the center of town en route to the fair grounds. Clearly, what struck the German military as worth copying was an example of American organizational and logistical acumen.

But not always was the perception of the show's Americanness this positive. Given the popularity of Buffalo Bill's show in Germany, a great demand remained for equivalent events. Thus two famous men in the evolution of German mass culture, Carl Hagenbeck and Hans Stosch-Sarrasani, took their cues from the American example. Carl Hagenbeck, who founded the Stellingen Zoological Garden near Hamburg in 1907, not only displayed animals but human beings as well. His *Völkerschaustellungen* (exhibitions of peoples) were also ethnologically oriented as previous such shows in Germany had been. In the summer of 1910 he had an entire Indian agency set up at his zoo, in which a group of Sioux Indians under Chief Spotted Weasel could be observed by the visitors. The exhibition included a program that was similar to Buffalo Bill's, with Indian attacks on a log cabin and on a stagecoach, and horse stealing thrown in for good measure.[36] In 1912, circus director Sarrasani refused to inaugurate his Circus-Theater in Dresden without exotic Indians, so he contracted a group of twenty-two Sioux from the Pine Ridge reservation to perform. Since 1901 Sarrasani had built an impressive company whose outstanding artistic achievements were given utmost effect by unconventional ideas, and which made best use of modern advertising. As a man of practical life, he was always keen on professional competence. Until about 1932, seven issues of *Sarrasani* were published, documenting the work of his circus and expressing the intentions of Stosch-Sarrasani. As one issue put it, with characteristic modesty: "What Bayreuth is for the lover of operas, Sarrasani is for the enthusiast of the circus." As Rudolf Conrad tells it, Sarrasani's attempts to give a certain image to his company were, of course, accompanied by polemics against everything questioning his claim to exclusiveness, even though he adopted and imitated some of his competitors' ideas. With respect to the Wild West, Sarrasani wished to draw a clear line between the American show and what he himself offered the public:

> The Americans who had then moved across Europe, sucking in the golden money, were no models, were almost repelling. With their system of three stages they bluffed the German need for quality and beauty. As soon as the bluff is over, the American department store system, the method of whole-

sale junk is rejected by the Germans ... The old Colonel Cody, himself a
fighter in the last Indian wars, had formed around himself a body guard of
subjugated redskins, they followed him to Europe and they disappeared with
him. In his horse operas they had remained almost unnoticed.[37]

There is more than a little *pique* and *jalousie de métier* in this statement. Yet
the choice of words is telling. Sarrasani is out to point to the inherent Americanness of Buffalo Bill and other features of American life coming to Europe,
only, as Sarrasani says, to be rejected after a while. Ironically, though, while
trying to call the Americans' bluff, he missed one crucial ingredient. The
Americans may have bluffed their way across Europe, but they certainly
satisfied a German, and more generally European, need for authenticity. The
"Wild West fever" caused by Buffalo Bill's show in Europe had centrally to
do with the show's claim to represent "the real thing" that people in Europe
had read about and dreamed about for years. The Wild West show was fast,
exciting entertainment that competed with the big circuses that emerged at
about the same time in the United States and a little later in Europe as well,
but offered something the circuses did not: authenticity. As the *Liverpool
Mercury* put it in 1891, it is "a piece of the Wild West bodily transported to
our midst ... It is not a show in the ordinary acceptance of the term, because
the actors are each and all real characters—men who have figured not on the
stage, but in real life." As a reporter from Dortmund, Germany, described the
emotions, desires, and yearnings kindled by the show:

> What would we have given in our childhood days, when we pored over
> [Gabriel] Ferry's "Coureur de Bois" with glowing cheeks, to witness the ro-
> mantic Indian figures in reality. Now that we have settled with our childhood
> dreams, comes this Colonel Cody, called Buffalo Bill, and floods us with all
> that we once so desired ... This show is truly an experience.[38]

Here was an experience of the real thing, of living history that had just
passed. These are critical words when it comes to exploring the appeal of
forms of American mass culture. No sales pitch has more powerfully drawn
publics around the world toward forms of American mass culture than the
claim of authenticity. It was a lesson that others would learn and apply in the
not so distant future. For instance, Coca-Cola would be advertised as being
"the real thing." Levi's jeans would for many years be advertised as being "the
original Levi's," an American original. This is exactly what Buffalo Bill had
promised as well by bringing real Indians, real buffaloes, real cowboys, and
the West as it really was or had been, to Europe. Like their American counterparts, Europeans, for the most part, fell for this ploy. They loved it and
never sat back to call Buffalo Bill's bluff in that respect. Today, a wild west

Fig. 4–6. Winnetou monument, Ruurloo, the Netherlands. Among non-German speaking nations in Europe, the Netherlands was the country where Karl May was most widely read for many generations. From the 1950s to the 1970s annual summer plays were organized in a small town in the Netherlands, based on Karl May's Indian fantasies. To commemorate these summer festivals, a sculpture of the leading Indian character in May's fiction, Chief Winnetou, was commissioned and festively unveiled, as recently as 2002. Here he is, with a Dutch windmill in the background, a fictional character assuming tangible form. Photograph 2004. Courtesy of Rob Kroes.

theme park outside of Munich attracts over one million visitors a year, and a dozen other wild west attractions stretch from Spain to Scandinavia.[39]

AMERICAN PHOTOGRAPHS IN EUROPE

Wild West productions fueled interest in Europe in "authentic" visual representations of the United States, and American stereographic firms happily supplied photographic images. As Judith Babbitts puts it: "For it was not

American music or cinema that first appealed to Europeans looking for something other than the Old World's traditional cultural forms, but a nineteenth-century toy that brought an American-made world into its parlors and classrooms."[40] Thanks to the productive and reproductive capabilities of major American stereographic manufacturers, millions of images of the United States circulated in Europe, and, by 1900, American photography was exciting attention for, of all things, its artistic potential.

As early as the 1867 Paris International Exposition, Europeans were impressed by American landscape photographs. There, Carleton E. Watkins exhibited twenty-eight large prints and three hundred stereographs. There were also California landscapes by Martin Lawrence and Thomas Houseworth, which were praised in the *Illustrated London News*. Subsequently, Watkins received a gold medal and Houseworth a bronze for their achievements. Hermann Vogel, a photography juror representing Prussia for the exposition as well as photographic chemist and scholar and, later, Alfred Stieglitz's photography professor, summarized it nicely: ". . . America is still to us a new world, and anything which gives us a true representation as a photograph, is sure to be looked upon with wondering eyes."[41] His views would be echoed by later Europeans who, with a feeling of astonishment, discovered that America, despite not being a traditional *Kulturnation* like Germany, had something artistically valuable to offer. Thus, on the occasion of the First International Amateur Exhibition of Photography, held in Hamburg, Germany, in 1893, one reviewer expressed himself thus: "Probably nobody would have expected the Americans to be the most noble and refined group—in their artistic expression and their appearance in the whole exhibition. After all there seems to be a strong and original artistic movement in this young *Kulturnation* . . ."[42] The tradition of fine printing, of the photograph as an object of beauty, which has a long history in the United States, was only to be further confirmed through the teaching of grandees like Edward Weston and Ansel Adams, and the manifesto *f.64*.

If America's pioneering role in the emancipation of photography as a new form of art is remarkable, equally striking is the European sense of surprise and amazement. Europe's preconceived ideas of American culture as intrinsically incapable of producing anything artistically worthwhile, at least as measured by European yardsticks, were given the lie. What is strikingly absent from the American debate about photography as art are any self-conscious considerations of an American cultural deficit. Never, in the field of photography, did Americans anxiously follow the European scene, nor did they await cues from Paris or other European cultural capitals, as they have done in so many other areas of artistic production. At least in this new area of the mechanical arts they were unburdened by any sense of cultural inferiority.

How remarkable then that in another similar area, that of film, developments took a different course. Again, in the years following World War I, America took the lead. But it did so in ways that in the eyes of Europeans seemed to confirm rather than upset their stereotyped views of American culture. Film production in America unabashedly geared itself to the mass market with production techniques that seemed to follow an industrial rather than an artistic logic. In the European attempts at saving film as another potential art form from the pressures of the mass market, intellectuals and cultural critics were quick to conceive of films coming from America as a negative yardstick, a model to be avoided rather than followed. One reason for this difference between the artistic evolution of photography and film may have to do with the economics of film production. Compared to the production of individual fine prints of artistic photographs, the organization of film production involves many people and much money, in conquering markets, domestically and abroad. Americans were never loath to follow the dictates of a mass market. In terms of intellectual debate concerning the status of film as art they were never as quotable as in the area of photography. That they were instrumental in democratizing the new medium at the same time, managing to find a mass audience for film as mass culture, while upsetting established discourses concerning high versus low culture, was a thing that would dawn on European critics only much later.

THE TRIUMPH OF AMERICAN MASS CULTURE

In the late nineteenth century, U.S. exhibits at European world's fairs, wild west shows, and photographs had powered the expansion of American mass culture across the Atlantic. But, at the dawn of the twentieth century, even as the Paris Universal Exposition of 1900 was attracting record crowds, the importance of exhibitions for the export of American culture was about to be eclipsed by a new mass cultural medium, motion pictures. Indeed, the rapid growth of American motion picture exports to Europe is nothing short of phenomenal. At the beginning of the twentieth century, American film producers had concentrated their efforts on capturing the domestic market and securing protective tariff legislation to put the brakes on foreign film producers trying to compete for American markets. Then, in 1909, after leading American filmmakers organized themselves into the Motion Picture Patents Co., they began a concerted effort to capture foreign markets. Measured just in terms of raw footage exported abroad, the results resembled nothing so much as a cascading boulder smashing into a small mountain lake. According to Kristin Thompson, American producers captured 60 percent of film sales in Britain in the short span between 1909 and 1912. Then, with the outbreak of the First World War in Europe, European distribution networks were disrupted and continental trade journals told producers to anticipate an "invasion" of American films. By early 1917, 30 percent of the films in the French market were American products, while in England the percentage had soared to over 73 percent. Even more revealing, and in the eyes of British and European imperialists, absolutely horrifying, was data showing that American films were saturating British and European colonies. Singapore was a case in point. In 1913, less than 1 percent of film imports were American productions; by 1918, fully 26 percent came from the United States. In Latin America, the bottom fell out of European exports. By 1916, for instance, 60 percent of film imports to Argentina came from America. The

Fig. 5 1. Poster advertising Dutch release of Charlie Chaplin's 1921 film *The Kid*. Courtesy of the Amsterdam Film Museum.

"Americanization of the World," as W. T. Stead had put it at the beginning of the century, was in full bloom.[1]

There was no disputing the power of this new, silent, motion picture medium. As early as 1909, as they hoped to offset local and state efforts to ban films because of perceived threats to Victorian-era moral standards, American film producers organized a National Board of Censorship that established guidelines for the voluntary censorship of films that depicted vice or crime. British film producers followed suit. In 1912, they established, with the aid of the Home Office, the British Board of Film Censors. Then, in 1914, with the outbreak of war in Europe, censorship took on new meaning and the categories for banning or editing films expanded dramatically in the United States, England, and across Europe.[2]

What triggered the expansion of censorship was, on the one hand, the war and its expanding horrors and, on the other, the 1914 release of David Wark

Fig. 5-2. Poster advertising the 1922 Danish release of *Under the Yoke* (1918) starring Theda Bara. Courtesy of the Amsterdam Film Museum.

Griffith's *The Clansman*, which, after its debut in Los Angeles, was almost immediately retitled *The Birth of a Nation* and released for its "world premier" at the Liberty Theater in New York City. There is no minimizing this film's importance. In terms of film history, it revolutionized cinematic techniques and helped pave the way for the advent of the feature film, one of Hollywood's innovations that knocked European filmmakers back on their heels. In terms of American social history, the film was even more significant. By applying a racist narrative, derived from Thomas Dixon's play and novel *The Clansman*, to the history of the American Civil War and to the era of reconstruction that followed, *The Birth of a Nation* helped lend legitimacy to the system of racial apartheid that structured U.S. race relations well into the twentieth century. Both the story of this film and its reception in the United States are well known, but both bear retelling here in a transnational context because both the film and the protests that it occasioned informed the cultural politics of the First World War. Specifically, the controversy over this film, and the film medium more generally, helped set in motion a full-blown effort by the U.S. government, through the Committee on Public Information (popularly known as the Creel Committee), to weld the products and forms of American mass culture into weapons of war that the U.S. government claimed would help make both the world and America safe for democracy.

THE BIRTH OF A NATION

The Birth of a Nation was the product of three life stories rooted in the defeat of the South during the Civil War and in the triumphant racism that led to legalized apartheid in the United States and to the lynching of hundreds, if not thousands, of African American males between the 1890s and the Second World War. The three life stories are those of Thomas Dixon, Jr. (1864–1946), an evangelical Baptist minister and novelist; David W. Griffith (1875–1948), an actor turned filmmaker; and Woodrow Wilson (1856–1924), a political scientist turned historian and only the second Democrat elected to the White House since the Civil War. Each was an ideological innovator in his own right; together they provided the structure of thought and feeling that provided the foundation for what historian Ronald Takaki has termed the "iron cage of race."[3]

Dixon, born in rural North Carolina, Griffith, born in Kentucky, and Wilson, born in Virginia, came of age by struggling to come to terms with the South's defeat in the Civil War. Each accepted the finality of military defeat; each, with shades of difference, agreed that slavery had succeeded as a system of racial management but failed as an economic system. But none accepted the legitimacy of northern efforts to reconstruct the South after the war. Indeed, all three pursued career trajectories premised on rewriting history in ways that nationalized and modernized white supremacist arguments that had earlier justified slavery in the minds of whites.

Dixon's early life included the bitter experience of his family's declining economic fortunes, his father's involvement with the Ku Klux Klan, and a burning desire for education. In 1883 he graduated from Wake Forest College and earned a scholarship to the Johns Hopkins University to pursue advanced study in history and political theory. In his first graduate seminar, he sat next to Woodrow Wilson and struck up a friendship that would last a life-time. Unlike Wilson, who was far more focused on his studies, Dixon struggled over his goals, alternating between his growing love of theater and writing and his strong sense that he should be preparing either for the ministry or law. After a semester at Johns Hopkins, Dixon made his decision. He left the university and headed to New York City to pursue a career in acting. The lure of politics, however, sent him rushing back to North Carolina where he was elected to a seat in the state legislature. After serving out his term, he deter-mined to finish law school and enter the legal profession, but he found this career as unfulfilling as politics. Responding to "that inner voice," he followed the call to the ministry, receiving ordination from Wake Forest College. Dixon quickly became an acclaimed minister and orator and, in 1888, received an in-vitation to deliver the commencement address at Wake Forest. For the same occasion, he prevailed on the board of trustees to confer an honorary Doctor of Laws degree on his friend Woodrow Wilson, an honor that Wilson never forgot. In 1889, Dixon was invited to the pulpit at the Twenty-third Street Baptist Church in New York City, where the "meteoric popularity" of his ser-mons captured the fancy of John D. Rockefeller. Over the next decade, Dixon's fame as a minister and lecturer grew. He gave hundreds of coast-to-coast lec-tures to audiences that, all told, numbered around five million. Topics in-cluded "The New Woman," "Municipal Corruption," and "The Anglo-Saxon Alliance." Dixon argued for Cuban independence from Spain and strongly supported Theodore Roosevelt. As a result of his popularity on the lecture circuit, Dixon acquired a modicum of wealth sufficient to enable him to pur-chase a yacht that he tellingly named "Dixie."[4]

At the turn of the century, Dixon had a national reputation that a later generation of American television evangelists could appreciate and would try to emulate. But, in 1901, a theatrical production of *Uncle Tom's Cabin* changed Dixon's life. The performance so enraged him with its depictions of the moral turpitude of the antebellum South that he determined to rush forward with a long-simmering project to write a "true history" of the South, one that would take aim especially at the Reconstruction years. In a matter of sixty days, he transformed fourteen years of research into a novel that he titled *The Leopard's Spots: A Romance of the White Man's Burden—1865–1900* after the question raised in Jeremiah 13:23: "Can the Ethiopian change his skin, or the leopard his spots?" Like Owen Wister, Dixon found in the novel the perfect medium to enlighten a mass audience of middle-class Americans, bringing to them a message of religious and racial redemption.[5]

The United States, Dixon argued, was being threatened by forces of mass immigration, class conflict, and, above all, racial amalgamation. As the Rev-erend John Durham, Dixon's protagonist, explained: "The beginning of Negro equality as a vital fact is the beginning of the end of this nation's life. There is enough negro blood here to make mulatto the whole Republic . . . Can you build, in a Democracy, a nation inside of a nation of two hostile races?" If the United States was a nation in desperate need of social salvation, white southerners, with their long experience of trying to save the Anglo-Saxon race from defilement, offered turn-of-the-century Americans hope for the future. "When," Reverend Durham proclaimed to a Boston church member, "your metropolitan mobs shall knock at the doors of your life and demand the reason of your existence, from these poverty-stricken homes, with their old-fashioned, perhaps mediaeval ideas, will come forth the fierce athletic sons and sweet-voiced daughters in whom the nation will find a new birth."[6]

Exactly what Dixon had in mind became clear in *The Clansman: An Historical Romance of the Ku Klux Klan* (1905). Here Dixon purposefully set out to rewrite the history of the Reconstruction era, by telling the story of two families, one from the North, the other from the South, whose initial friendship, subsequent enmity, and ultimate bonding through shared racial and gender values offered a blueprint for creating a racially pure republic in America's future. The novel opens with a portrayal of Abraham Lincoln as the "Great Heart." "Even his political enemies had come to love him," Dixon wrote. His assassination, however, opened the floodgates of political intrigue and allowed radical Republicans, especially Stoneman, a character modeled on the radical Republican congressional representative Thaddeus Stevens, to gain the upper hand. Bent on revenge and, at least in Stoneman's case, acting under the influence of a mulatto woman, northern Republicans set out to destroy the South. They disfranchised whites, put unqualified blacks into positions of political power, and turned the other cheek when biracial troops raped southern women. To save the South, and more importantly, in Dixon's eyes, to save the white race and the purity of white women, a group of southern males banded together and organized the Ku Klux Klan. As the Klan was rescuing Stoneman's son from certain execution, even the old radical Republican saw the error of his ways. "My will alone," Stoneman confessed, "forged the chains of Negro rule. Three forces moved me—party success, a vicious woman, and the quenchless desire for personal vengeance. When I first fell a victim to the wiles of the yellow vampire who kept my house, I dreamed of lifting her to my level." With burning crosses illuminating the surrounding hilltops, Stoneman's daughter, who had fallen in love with one of the Klan organizers, asked her lover: "What does it mean?" His reply came straight from Dixon's innermost convictions: "That I am a successful revolutionist— that Civilisation has been saved, and the South redeemed from shame."[7]

Like his friend Dixon, Woodrow Wilson was also a "revolutionist." When Dixon and Wilson sat next to each other at Johns Hopkins, Wilson had already determined to become a scholar. By the time *The Clansman* appeared, Wilson had succeeded, becoming not only a respected political scientist and historian but president of Princeton University. A Virginian by birth, Wilson understood the personal and collective weight of the South's military defeat and occupation as well as Dixon and, like Dixon, set out to rewrite its history. In 1901, his multivolume *History of the American People* appeared. For Wilson, if the Civil War had been a tragic necessity, Reconstruction had been a tragedy, period. Calling Reconstruction the "veritable overthrow of civiliza-tion in the South" caused by a "handful" of radical Republicans who deter-mined to "put the white South under the heel of the black South," Wilson argued that Reconstruction had disfranchised "the more capable white men" and given power to African Americans who were unprepared and unfit to exercise it. The results, he implied, were predictable. The rise of the Ku Klux Klan, he stated, could be explained as "[o]ne lawless force [being] in con-test with another." The "mischief of reconstruction," as he put it, would not be corrected until later in the century when southern states began "readjusting their elective suffrage so as to exclude the illiterate negroes" while "the rest of the country withheld its hand from interference."[8]

By the close of the nineteenth century, there had been, Wilson trumpeted, "a return to normal conditions." But great dangers lay in wait. "Immigrants," he noted, "poured steadily in as before, [but] with an alteration of stock . . ." No longer were the immigrants made up of the "sturdy stocks of the north of Europe." Now, the immigrants came from Hungary and Poland; these, he claimed, were composed of "sordid and hapless elements" who lacked "any initiative of quick intelligence" and who ranked as low in the hierarchy of hu-manity as the recently excluded Chinese, who "seemed separated by their very nature from the people among whom they had come to live."[9]

Embedded in Wilson's argument was the same distortion that lay at the root of Dixon's. According to both the scholar-turned-college (and soon to be U.S.) president and evangelist-turned-novelist, the Republican Party had sown the seeds of discord between "old stock" white Americans in the North and South. Just when whites in the North and South should have been em-bracing each other on the basis of common "racial stock," the Reconstruction policies of radical Republicans had driven a wedge between them. To make matters worse, Wilson argued, Republicans actually shaped policies that val-ued biracial social interaction. True, the Reconstruction period in American history formally ended in 1877, but both men believed that recovering from the "mischief" caused by Radical Republicans and their "negro" allies would require a sustained national effort in the twentieth century. Rewriting his-tory, both men were convinced, was a necessary first step in fomenting a rev-olution in the way whites thought about themselves in terms of shared racial identification. But, for Wilson, rewriting national history in racist terms was prelude to a more important task, one that would effect a revolution in the way white Americans thought about each other in terms of empire.

In a remarkable address, entitled "The Ideals of America," delivered in 1901 on the 125th anniversary of the Battle of Trenton, Wilson held out the prospect of a new American revolution, one that would restore national unity by transforming the United States into an imperial power capable of taking up Rudyard Kipling's challenge to Americans to take up "the white man's burden." Indeed, according to Wilson, that new American revolution had already occurred when the United States occupied the Philippine Islands during the Spanish American War. "No war," Wilson declared, "ever transformed us quite as the war with Spain transformed us." As a result, the "nation that was one hundred and twenty-five years in the making has now stepped forth into the open arena of the world." But how could Americans reconcile their devotion to liberty and their brutal occupation of the Philippine Islands? "Liberty," Wilson explained, "is not itself government. In the wrong hands, in hands unpracticed, undisciplined, it is incompatible with government. Discipline must precede it, if necessary, the discipline of being under masters." The Filipinos, he insisted, "can have liberty no cheaper than we got it. They must first take the discipline of law, must first love order and instinctively yield to it." Americans, Wilson announced, "are old in this learning and must be their tutors." By contrast, the Filipinos, he declared, "are children," while "we are men in these deep matters of government and justice." "You cannot," he added by way of response to critics of America's policies in the Philippines, "call a miscellaneous people, unknit, scattered, diverse of race and speech and habit, a nation, a community." "They are," he reiterated, "of many races, of many stages of development, economically, socially, politically disintegrate, without community of feeling ... You may imagine the problem of self-government and of growth for such a people—if ... you have an imagination and are not doctrinaire."[10]

So as not to appear doctrinaire himself, Wilson included a veiled warning in his speech. "There are, unhappily, some indications that we have ourselves yet to learn the things we would teach," he noted. Clearly the very problems that Wilson projected onto the Philippine Islands could be found closer to home. No less than the Philippine Islands, the United States, with its swelling numbers of immigrants, bursts of industrial violence, and mushrooming numbers of political dissidents, evidenced signs of a body politic in need of discipline, especially if the United States was to live up to its "destiny" to become "a great power in the world."[11]

Where would this discipline come from? The future president of the United States already had an important ally in his old friend Thomas Dixon, whose evangelical use of the mass-produced novel represented nothing so much as a sustained effort to rewrite history in order to bring about the rebirth of the Democratic Party that Wilson himself set his sights on leading. It is arguable that Dixon's and Wilson's efforts at ideological innovation through literature would have been sufficient to win over a majority of Americans to their project to link racial apartheid at home to imperial expansion abroad and thereby facilitate the return of the Democratic Party to control of the national government. But thanks to the efforts of another southerner, David Wark Griffith, the power of the word—the words of Dixon and Wilson specifically—was about to be augmented with the power of the screen.

Born in 1875 in Kentucky in circumstances of near poverty to an evangelical-Methodist mother and a father who had been a Confederate soldier and Democratic state legislator, Griffith later recalled how he would "get under the table and listen to my father and his friends talk about the battles and what they'd been through and their struggles." When the economic depressions of the Gilded Age led to the loss of his family's property, Griffith joined a traveling theater company before deciding to act in and direct motion pictures. He made hundreds of one-reel films in an effort that Griffith himself described as "grinding out sausage." As Michael Rogin explains, these shorter films had four themes in common: "the presence of weak or repressive women"; nascent female sexuality; "the presentation of domestic, interior space as claustrophobic"; and "the use of rides to the rescue." The films were modestly successful, but Griffith had long nurtured a dream of making a film about the Civil War. After reading *The Clansman*, which had become a popular Broadway play in 1908, Griffith knew he had the "treatment" for a narrative film that would weld together his interests in cinematography, aesthetics, history, and ideology. For $2,500, he acquired the screen rights to *The Clansman* and agreed to give Dixon one quarter interest in the film. Both men became rich as a result.[12]

What Griffith brought to Wilson's and Dixon's efforts to rewrite American history was his conviction that seeing was believing and that, through the medium of film, mass audiences could see for themselves the "truth" of what Dixon and Wilson were writing. *The Birth of a Nation* opened with scenes that, with the help of paragraph-long captions, claimed to be telling the truth about the past. Slavery, the film suggested, originated with New England merchants and shippers, whose descendants, the abolitionists, caused the Civil War. What was southern life like under slavery? To answer that question, Griffith introduced the fictional characters drawn from Dixon's novel. When, in the film, the Stoneman boys visit their southern chums, the Camerons, they discover an idyllic plantation economy where slaves work

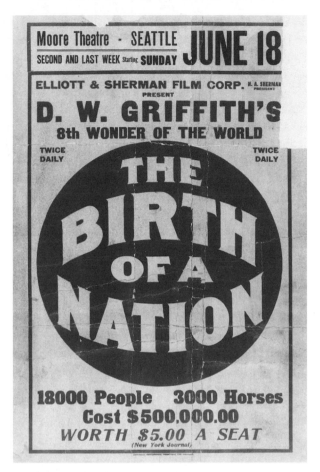

Fig. 5-3. Advertisement for *The Birth of a Nation*, 1915. Note the film is described as "the eighth wonder of the world," the same words that were used to describe the trans-Atlantic cable in Fig. intro.-2. Courtesy of the Library of Congress.

cheerfully under the paternalistic gaze of plantation owners. In this ideal setting for romance, Phil Stoneman falls in love with Ben Cameron's sister, while Ben Cameron is smitten by a photograph that Phil carries of his sister, Elsie (played by Lillian Gish), who stays back in Washington, D.C., with her father, Austin Stoneman, a powerful congressman, whose primary caregiver is a biracial woman.

When the Civil War breaks out, at the instigation of northern fanatics, the sons from both families do the right thing and fight for their respective regions. Tragically, the youngest sons from each family die in battle, but, as a hint of what is to come, they die heroically and in each other's arms. Ben Cameron, wounded in battle, is taken to a hospital where his nurse turns out to be none other than Elsie Cameron. For unclear reasons, Ben is sentenced to die, but Elsie and Ben's mother intercede with President Lincoln, who grants a pardon.

Griffith's representation of Lincoln was important and vital to the white supremacist narrative he was trying to convey. Lincoln, of course, was reviled in the South before and during the war. But, after Lincoln's assassination, some southerners came to the conclusion that the fate of the white South would have been much different—and better—if Lincoln had survived. Griffith contributed to this rehabilitation of Lincoln by quoting a declaration that Lincoln had made in Charleston, Illinois, while campaigning for the presidency. For Griffith, these words, the harshest comments Lincoln ever uttered about African Americans, were as good as gold. Following Dixon's lead, Griffith dubbed Lincoln "Great Heart" in the film.

Lincoln's assassination, however, spells doom for the South. Austin Stoneman, modeled so carefully on Thaddeus Stevens that Stoneman, like Stevens, wears a wig and has a biracial housekeeper, grabs power and puts his biracial henchman, Silas Lynch, in charge of Reconstruction. Motivated by lust for power and by lust for Stoneman's daughter, Lynch launches a brutal reign of terror that begins with the enfranchisement of former slaves and the election of illiterate blacks to the legislature, which they control in order to promote legislation legalizing interracial sex. As he worries about the fate of the white South, Ben Cameron takes a walk in the woods and sees a group of white children pull a sheet over their heads to frighten some black youths. Immediately inspired, Ben organizes the Ku Klux Klan.

If any in the audience harbored doubts about the Klan's legitimacy, Griffith took pains to offset them. Ignoring warnings not to leave their house by herself, Ben Cameron's little sister, Flora, heads through the woods to get a bucket of water not realizing that a biracial northern soldier, Gus, has been watching and waiting for her. When Gus declares that he wants Flora to be his wife, she runs for her life with Gus in hot pursuit. She reaches the edge of a cliff and, to save her honor, escapes the would-be rapist by jumping off. When Flora dies in Ben's arms, Ben and the Ku Klux Klan vow revenge. After a short manhunt, the Klan captures Gus and, in a scene not taken from *The Clansman*, but inserted by Griffith, Gus is castrated. His body is then deposited on Silas Lynch's doorstep.

Lynch, with Austin Stoneman's approval, sets out to quash the Klan and calls out the black militia. With a race war under way, Elsie pleads with Lynch to intervene to save the life of Ben Cameron's father, who has been arrested for aiding the Klan. Lynch refuses and tells Elsie that he wants to marry her and make her the queen of a Black Empire that the two of them would rule. When she refuses, Lynch locks her in a room and sets in motion plans for a forced marriage. Meanwhile, with the help of two loyal former slaves,

Dr. Cameron and his wife and daughter, together with Elsie's brother, manage to escape and find refuge in a cabin occupied by white Union war veterans. Led by Ben Cameron, the Klan is mobilized to defeat Lynch and his followers. Amidst this chaos, Austin Stoneman suddenly and unexpectedly appears in Lynch's residence and is informed by Lynch that he is about to marry a white woman. Stoneman congratulates him until, too late, he realizes that this woman is his daughter. Stoneman refuses permission and is taken prisoner along with Elsie. With a forced marriage only moments away, the Klan arrives and rescues Elsie and her father. Then, learning of the black militia's assault on the cabin, the Klan again rides to the rescue and arrives just as black troops are battering down the door and Dr. Cameron has taken out his revolver and put it to his daughter's head to save her from being raped by blacks.

With some audiences standing and applauding the Klan's heroic rescues, *The Birth of a Nation* moved toward conclusion, showing the Camerons and Stonemans at the ocean's edge enjoying a double honeymoon. Love—at least between whites—conquers all. But Griffith does not end his film there. The concluding scenes turn to the Bible for inspiration and, in the grand finale, Jesus, presented as the Prince of Peace, with arms outstretched, makes Griffith's racist renderings of history seem positively divine.[13]

President Woodrow Wilson certainly found something divine about the film. In 1915, as every account of *The Birth of a Nation* notes, Griffith's film became the first feature-length film to be shown in the White House. Wilson was so captivated by the moving picture that he told his old friend Dixon, who had arranged the screening: "It is like writing history with lightning and my only regret is that it is all so terribly true." From the White House, the film traveled the next night to the Supreme Court, where the justices and members of Congress were treated to a special showing. According to Dixon, Chief Justice Edward Douglass White had been reluctant to see the film until Dixon explained its content. Upon hearing that the film extolled the Klan, White exclaimed: "I was a member of the Klan, Sir!" With its manifest lies, historical quarter-truths, and blatant misrepresentations of African Americans (through the use of white actors in blackface), *The Birth of a Nation* rewrote history and trumpeted the rebirth of the Democratic Party as the political party best equipped to ensure the future of racial apartheid in the United States. "Why call it *The Birth of a Nation?*" one reporter asked. "Because it is," Griffith responded. "The Civil War was fought fifty years ago. But the real nation has only existed the last fifteen or twenty years, for there can exist no union without sympathy and oneness of sentiment."[14]

The consequences of the film for African Americans are well known. Police arrested blacks who protested the film. After seeing the film, one white moviegoer reportedly told his female companion: "I should like to kill every nigger I know." African American novelist Ralph Ellison claimed that the film actually promoted the growth of the Klan. Did the film violate, or at least hold the potential to violate, the basic human rights of African Americans? Local and state authorities, along with most African Americans, thought so, and many communities, at the urging of the National Association for the Advancement of Colored People, tried to ban the showing of the film. This led Griffith and his supporters in the press to respond by arguing for the value of artistic freedom. So, was there a cause-and-effect relationship between this film and the hate crimes that followed its showings? Is the evidence as clear as it is in the case of the correlation, say, between cigarette smoking and various forms of cancer? Or is the relationship less one of cause and effect and more one of association? There is no definitive answer. But what is certain is that *The Birth of a Nation* should be considered as a work of ideological innovation that falls in the same tradition as wild west shows and world's fairs. Like these other forms of entertainment, this film provided white audiences with powerful and seemingly authoritative explanations for thinking about American history in ways that lent legitimacy to racist ideology and to the violent acts that flowed from this set of beliefs.[15]

That *The Birth of a Nation*, and film more generally, could be understood in ideological terms was not just a conviction held by African Americans and their few white supporters or by the Dixon-Griffith-Wilson troika that made the film possible. As war expanded in Europe and American involvement grew more likely, government authorities on both sides of the Atlantic began having second thoughts about *The Birth of a Nation*, especially in the wake of the civil unrest generated by the film after its 1915 release in New York City and Boston. By 1916, the U.S. military began worrying about the response of African American troops to the film. In the Panama Canal Zone, where a large number of African American troops were deployed, the government actually prohibited showing the film. But, when it became clear that military authorities had plans to show the film at other military posts, an official with the NAACP expressed his strong opposition to the secretary of war: "If this is true, we want to ask in the name of common social decency for which you have always stood that this be stopped. Colored troops have been giving too good an account of themselves recently to deserve having this vicious attack on their race shown in military posts." Then, after a race riot erupted in Norfolk, Virginia, in 1918, the chief of the military morale section in the U.S. armed forces fired off a letter to his superiors urging that *The Birth of a Nation* not be shown anywhere in the South because it would exacerbate racial hostilities. Indeed, he added, the film should be suppressed "as a military measure." His superiors disagreed, but nonetheless, they were clearly paying attention to the ongoing reactions to the film.[16]

Significantly, these concerns had already been echoed by European allies, especially the French. From the vantage point of the French government, *The Birth of a Nation* was unacceptable, and it was banned from theaters on three counts that proceeded in roughly chronological order. First, when the film was first proposed for release in French theaters in 1915 and 1916, French censors concluded that Griffith's insistence in the final frames of the film that there should be no more wars would undermine public support for the French war effort. Then, as France's situation in the war deteriorated and the military found itself in the position of having to deploy African troops from its West African colonies, censors concluded that the film's depiction of blacks would anger African soldiers and render their loyalty to the war effort highly problematic. Third, once the United States entered the conflict in 1917 and it became clear that African American troops would be deployed along the front lines and be asked to fight in some of the worst battles of the war, French censors, who knew well the protests the film had occasioned in the United States, feared that African American troops would be less than enthusiastic about fighting in a foreign country that allowed them to be demeaned in movie theaters. The French public had to wait until after the war to see Griffith's racist extravaganza. But, in France and throughout most of Europe, with the exception of Germany, where the film "played to huge emotional audiences," the film, perhaps because it was an ongoing source of concern to European imperialists who feared a backlash from their growing populations of colonial subjects, was rarely shown.[17]

No doubt Griffith was not pleased that *The Birth of a Nation* had such a limited showing across most of Europe. But he could take solace from the success he had elsewhere in the world. The film was "thunderously acclaimed" in South Africa; it played to sold-out houses in Australia; and it was a "landslide" success in South America, running for 200 performances at one theater alone in Buenos Aires.[18] The popularity of the film made everyone take notice, including a newly created committee that functioned as the U.S. government's propaganda ministry during the First World War. In its eyes, America's mass cultural products, with *The Birth of a Nation* being the prime case in point, were valuable less for their entertainment value than for their ideological content.

THE CREEL COMMITTEE

As the United States government prepared for war, there was no doubt that American public opinion would require education about America's war aims. Probably at the urging of his friend, journalist Walter Lippmann, President Woodrow Wilson began thinking about creating a propaganda agency that could mobilize American and world public opinion to support America's entry into a "war to end all wars." On April 14, 1917, within hours of asking the U.S. Congress to declare war on Germany, Wilson moved with lightning speed to issue an Executive Order creating the Committee on Public Information (CPI). Headed by George Creel, another long-time friend of Wilson's and a Denver journalist who had been active in a variety of urban reform causes, the CPI set out "to drive home the absolute justice of America's cause, the absolute selflessness of America's aims."[19] Through its massive and efficient mobilization of print, public speaking, exhibition, and motion picture media, the CPI sought to transform already existing modular units of American mass culture into an efficiently running whole that would, in Creel's words, weld the American people into "one white-hot mass."[20] It would be wrong to claim that Creel's Committee gave birth to American mass culture, but there can be no doubt that under its direction American mass culture came of age.

The full scope of the Creel Committee's work is simply staggering to contemplate and impossible to imagine apart from recognizing that it mobilized and coordinated already existing forms of American mass culture into weapons of war and vehicles of U.S. government propaganda. By June 1919, when the CPI was disbanded after the armistice, the organization had grown into, in Creel's words, "a world organization." As Creel put it: "There was no part of the great war machinery that we did not touch, no medium of appeal that we did not employ. The printed word, the spoken word, the motion picture, the poster, the signboard—all these were used in our campaign to make our own people and all other peoples understand the causes that compelled America to take arms in defense of its liberties and free institutions." Through its two major divisions, domestic and foreign, the CPI globalized American culture on an unprecedented scale as part of the "fight for the mind of mankind."[21]

Creel made the scale of the Committee's work clear in his final report to the president as well as the CPI's indebtedness to already existing American mass culture products and practices. Hearkening back to the practices of religious revivalists and the more recent Chautauqua Movement, the Committee deployed 75,000 volunteer speakers who gave 755,190 speeches in 5,200 communities across the United States. All of their activities, Creel noted, were carefully coordinated, as were the 45 conferences on the war that the CPI's division of speakers arranged. The CPI also reached into the history of mass print technologies and marketing, hiring 3,000 writers, including historian Carl Becker, to produce a total of 75 million printed pamphlets designed to promote "America's ideals, purposes, and aims . . ." Another division, one devoted to advertising and drawing on recent developments in this profession, generated millions of dollars of free advertising for the Committee and mobilized artists who produced 1,438 drawings that, through mechanical means, were reproduced as posters and window displays for stores. It was this section that crafted "The Greatest Mother in the World" poster promoting the efforts of the Red Cross. Yet another division drew on the recent history and successes of mass circulation newspapers, creating an official CPI newspaper that went to every U.S. government department. Still another division sought to emulate the success of dime novelists, by persuading novelists and essayists to write feature stories for release in magazines and newspapers around the country. Another division drew on a host of experienced exposition hands to organize exhibits for state fairs and a series of "interallied war expositions" that traveled to dozens of cities across the United States. The CPI also tapped another mass culture resource, cartoons, organizing its own Bureau of Cartoons to help government agencies promote their wartime work. Festivals, pageants, and parades also formed part of the CPI arsenal, especially where the foreign born were concerned. The ultimate event on this front was a Fourth of July celebration organized in 1918 "as a day for the foreign born to demonstrate their loyalty to their adopted country." For this occasion, President Wilson, at the urging of Creel, played host to representatives of 33 ethnic groups who journeyed with Wilson to George Washington's tomb at Mt. Vernon. No less important was the CPI's film section, which bore responsibility for utilizing the film medium for the Committee's "educational" work. This section produced several films, including a seven-reel release entitled *Pershing's Crusaders* that played in more than 3,000 theaters around the nation. CPI officials also contracted with major Hollywood studios to produce shorter films on subjects ranging from the work of engineers to the roles of African Americans and Native Americans in the armed forces. Using already existing film distribution systems, the motion picture section secured showings for its productions in about 80 percent of American theaters.

Creel roundly praised the accomplishments of the CPI's domestic division, but he devoted two-thirds of his final report to the other side of the house, the CPI's foreign division. Its primary functions were divided between its Wireless and Cable Service, its Foreign Press Bureau, and its Motion Picture Service, each of which joined "the fight for world opinion" by disseminating carefully produced information about the United States to a worldwide audience. Since, Creel concluded, most people around the world received information about the United States from foreign newspaper correspondents, who "could not know the nation's heart and soul as a native American could,"[22] the CPI arranged for the direct, daily dissemination of "news"—crafted by CPI experts for foreign consumption—via the wireless and telegraphic cable services of foreign governments. The way this worked was utterly ingenious

Fig. 5-4. Poster generated by the Creel Committee to build support for America's efforts in the First World War. Courtesy of the Library of Congress.

and totally predicated on the preexistence of a mass communication infrastructure already laid by the U.S. Naval Communication Service and foreign governments. As soon as it received CPI materials, the U.S. Naval Communication Service transmitted CPI messages overseas to the French government's wireless station at Lyon, where these messages, in turn, were relayed to London, where CPI agents brought them to the attention of the local media. Through the capacity of U.S. naval wireless systems, the CPI soon had the world at its feet. By 1918, CPI messages were saturating South America and being relayed across the Pacific from San Francisco via Hawaii to the Philippines and then to Guam and from there to Japan, China, and Siberia.

Other sections of the CPI's foreign division mirrored those of the domestic division. In Italy, for instance, CPI special agent and University of Chicago political scientist Charles Merriam organized a "mass education" campaign from his offices in Rome. Each day, wireless dispatches from CPI headquarters in New York City were assembled and provided to Italian newspapers. But their efforts did not stop there. They ordered millions of postcards, thousands of Italian-American friendship buttons, 200,000 American flags, and some 300,000 copies of pamphlets detailing the principles guiding America's war efforts. Speakers, both American and Italian, were mobilized for public lectures. "In some form or other," Creel's *Report* noted, "American educational information was disseminated through 16,000 towns and cities of Italy . . ." Similar successes were reported across Europe, Asia, and Latin America.[23]

Never before had the mass cultural resources of a nation been mobilized on such a scale. The potential for propaganda victories was enormous but also fraught with danger. Precisely because CPI authorities understood that mass cultural products were invested with ideological meanings, they took considerable pains to be sure that both the domestic and foreign divisions censored messages deemed inimical to American and Allied interests. Throughout his life, Creel would claim that CPI activities were "educational and informative only" and that the CPI only "supervised the voluntary censorship" of the press and motion pictures. This was inaccurate. Magazine publishers had to submit copy to CPI censors weeks before publication deadlines; books intended for export had to pass muster before military intelligence officials; and CPI officials collaborated with the U.S. Postal Service to censor mails.[24]

Of particular interest and concern was the relatively new medium of film and the overnight success of American motion pictures overseas. As theater impresario and CPI member P. A. Strachen told President Wilson: "MOTION PICTURES, having become the medium of international expression and speaking a universal language, have in this instance, possibilities for extending the political power and prestige of the UNITED STATES OF AMERICA . . ."[25] Having understood the power of *The Birth of a Nation* to reconstruct a nation along particular ideological lines, Wilson had little difficulty imagining the power of film to reconstruct the world along the lines envisioned by his administration. At the same time, because he was certainly aware of the protests over Griffith's Civil War drama, Wilson could grasp the need to monitor carefully the content of films. The CPI was only too happy to oblige.

In cooperation with U.S. Naval Intelligence (which had experience censoring overseas cables) and the U.S. Customs Service, the CPI set up a Motion Picture Censorship Department with headquarters in New York City. Acting under the authority of the War Trade Board, which had declared celluloid a war materiel subject to export restrictions, the CPI mandated that all films intended for export had to be approved. The guiding principle for approving films was made clear by naval censor G. B. Baker, who noted in one of his reports that "seemingly innocent 'social' messages were capable of carrying concealed information." Motion picture producers, CPI authorities believed, were exporting much more than entertainment; they were exporting images with messages that, however unintentionally, could undermine the Allied cause. As they set about their work, Baker urged his men to follow the "Biblical injunction which enjoins us to be patient with fools."[26]

Fools evidently abounded, and the CPI/naval intelligence team determined to stop them in their tracks. To help with the process, the censorship team established a set of guidelines. Some pertained to depictions of the U.S. military. "In censoring motion pictures for export," they mandated, "expert care should be taken to permit no views of forts, coast defense or other fortifications to leave the country." Furthermore, they insisted, "no pictures which would tend to bring the United States Army into ridicule can be permitted to pass." For instance, films showing "recruits drilling in overalls or civilian garbs must not be permitted." Other guidelines addressed images of American society. Censors were told to be on the lookout for "pictures of breadlines, crowds seeking to purchase coal or other products [that] might be used by the enemy to portray 'Terrible Conditions in the United States.'" Similarly, censors were urged to keep their eyes peeled for images of pacifists and for scenes that would "tend to injure the feelings of neutrals or our allies."[27] "Remember," censors were admonished, "when you classify a picture as educational you signify that it should be counted as one that will aid the cause of the United States and the Allies."[28]

Every morning, around thirty censors, including twenty-three enlisted men, one U.S. naval officer, and representatives from U.S. Customs and the CPI reported to work at an office controlled by the U.S. Customs Service in lower Manhattan. As they reviewed the films assigned to them each day, either alone or in small groups, the men carefully documented their recommendations on index cards that mandated cuts or gave films passing marks. The film "The 13th Labor of Hercules," which showed the demolition of some buildings at the 1915 San Francisco world's fair, caught the attention of one censor who thought the film might be shown abroad "with an ulterior purpose." According to another censor, a Goldwyn production, *The Heart of the Sunset*, contained an objectionable scene of American troops using the "water cure" method of torture against insurgents in the Philippine Insurrection. Goldwyn studios was told to cut the scene before the film would be approved for export. A film produced by Universal Studios, *Ermine of the Yellowstone*, inspired a brief by another censor who raised concerns about "the love affair between a white woman and a half breed Indian and . . . fighting between American soldiers and Indians. The question involved is whether this picture could be used as evidence that the U.S. treated a race inferior in numbers and a prior occupant of American soil in a manner which would stir up antagonistic feeling." Another censor noted: "It could be said that we are preaching liberty to all the world, when we are depriving Indians, an inferior race, not only of liberty, but of their property and exploiting them." "Hence," the censor worried, "Germans could say their doctrine of biology, 'survival of the fittest,' is even true of us." Another film, Paramount's *The Eternal Grind*, with its emphasis on industrial conditions in the United States, attracted the attention of a censor who worried about the film going to Spain, where "at times there have been unsettled labor conditions." A Pathé production, *Little Sister of Everybody*, gained notice because immigrant workers "rise against the owner of the mill where they are employed." A Metro Pictures film, *Her Boy*, was rejected *in toto* because the censor found it "discreditable to American motherhood." A Paralta production ran afoul of a censor because one caption began: "In a nation where success is spelled $ucce$$ . . ." A Triangle film, *The Girl of the Timber Claims*, gained notice because it cast doubts on "the honesty of U.S. government investigations." Another production, about New York politics, was censored because it could "give the impression that the politics of this country are openly corrupt." "Of course," the censor admitted, "they are corrupt, but the less that is known about it abroad, the better off this country will be."[29]

As per their guidelines, censors manifested concern about motion pictures that raised questions about the moral and/or intellectual capacity of the Allies. A Vitagraph production, *A Diplomatic Mission*, might have seemed fairly innocuous. It showed African miners rampaging because they were being mistreated by a German foreman. And, because the village was saved by the arrival of a detachment of American marines, one might suspect that the film would have had little difficulty being passed by censors. But, because the Africans were depicted as being under British control, one censor wondered "why the British are shown as being unable to cope with the situation in their own provinces." Along the same lines and equally troubling was Fox Studios' *The Soul of Buddha*, which showed a scene of the capital of Java with the British flag flying over it. "This," the astute censor observed, "is a glaring error and could be used as anti-British propaganda to show that the British claim to rule everything" when, in fact, Java was under the control of the Dutch.

Of all the American films intended for export during the First World War, perhaps none received greater scrutiny than the films intended for Mexico and Latin America. *Heading South*, for instance, produced by Paramount Studios, was rejected because it was "filled with objectionable Mexican stuff."

Censors rejected another film, *Liberty*, because it was about "Mexican bor-der trouble." Censors cut fifty feet from reel 8 of *Ramona* because it included a scene of a sheriff shooting a Mexican. Why all of this attention to Latin America and especially Mexico? The answer was simple. U.S. authorities feared that German propaganda had already inflamed ordinary Mexicans with memories of the 1846 war with Mexico and, given the recent history of U.S. military excursions in Mexico, the last thing the U.S. wanted to face was a need to redeploy U.S. forces away from the European theater to quell in-surrections along the border with Mexico.

For all of his commanding influence, D. W. Griffith was not immune to the censors' scrutiny. His next major production, *Intolerance*, a multi-reel pro-duction intended to document historical lessons in intolerance—and vindi-cate Griffith in the court of public opinion for the intolerance shown by *The Birth of a Nation*—was also required to meet CPI standards. It did pass, but not without objections that led to cuts before the film could be exported to foreign lands. Censors especially objected to scenes depicting prostitution and terrible housing conditions in the United States, and to scenes depicting the "maltreatment of the workers by State Militia and the killing of many by the entrepreneur's factory guards." Because one of the destinations of the film was Barcelona, Spain, "which," according to CPI censors, "is at present the hotbed of social unrest and anarchism and consequently [Griffith's film] would tend to aggravate the condition there," Griffith was required to excise the offending scenes before the film would be approved for export. Griffith also ran into problems with French censors who insisted that Griffith delete scenes depicting the St. Bartholomew Day massacre. *Intolerance*, one French journalist acidly noted, had become "a victim of intolerance."[30]

It is difficult to learn with any degree of precision the exact amount of cen-sorship imposed on American motion picture exports. We do know that the CPI's Motion Picture Division reviewed about 8,000 films and that most of them did pass the test for patriotism. We also know that many of the films that were censored involved depictions of violence between Mexicans and Anglo-Americans along the U.S./Mexico border. How much film was actu-ally cut? These figures are revealing. In July 1918, 17,779 feet of film was deleted by motion picture producers who had to comply with the recom-mendations of the CPI censorship team or find themselves without access to overseas export markets. But the early summer months were only the be-ginning. In August 1918 alone, some 82,230 feet of film were cut. Clearly, in this war to "make the world safe for democracy," motion pictures required careful intervention by government authorities before publics at home or abroad could be entrusted to come to their own judgments about them.[31]

Anyone who remembered Woodrow Wilson's speech, "The Ideals of America," would not have been surprised.

The First World War ended on November 11, 1918. For the history of American mass culture, it marked a watershed. Under the tutelage of the Creel Committee, American mass culture had come of age as a fully developed, integral component of the American national identity. Moreover, American mass culture had circumnavigated the globe and become a force to be reckoned with in foreign lands. By the end of the war, a chorus of European intellectuals had taken up the challenge of finding meaning in American mass culture, debating its implications for art, and assessing its portent for the practice of democracy in the modern world.

6

DEBATING AMERICAN MASS CULTURE IN
THE UNITED STATES AND EUROPE

By the 1880s, the commercialization of American culture was in full swing, with countless entertainment industries producing products that audiences found both meaningful and pleasurable. This rapid proliferation of industrially produced cultural forms for a mass audience was a source of deep concern in American intellectual circles. E. L. Godkin, for one, editor of *The Nation*, fretted about the "mischievous effects of the pseudo-culture" that had gripped America. As Godkin explained: "A large body of persons has arisen, under the influence of the common-schools, magazines, newspapers, and the rapid acquisition of wealth, who are not only engaged in enjoying themselves after their fashion, but who firmly believe that they have reached, in the matter of social, mental, and moral culture, all that is attainable or desirable by anybody . . . The result is a kind of mental and moral chaos, in which many of the fundamental rules of living, which have been worked out painfully by thousands of years of bitter human experience, seem in imminent risk of disappearing totally." Especially at fault, Godkin insisted, was the "desire to see and own pictures"—photographs and chromolithographs—which could only be pale imitations of authentic culture, which, in his eyes, was "the result of a process of discipline, both mental and moral . . . ; not a thing that can be picked up, or that can be got by doing what one pleases."[1] Godkin was troubled by chromolithographs, but he might just as easily have pointed to developments in theater, literature, or sports to make his argument that mass culture challenged the authority of traditional elites to impose their direction on American culture.

Caught in the throes of the massive economic redirection of the American economy from entrepreneurial to corporate capitalism and the accompanying rise of a consumer-oriented culture, most of America's leading thinkers could not absorb, much less celebrate, the contradictions of American mass culture. An exception was America's self-proclaimed national bard, Walt Whitman.

A product of New York City's antebellum urban artisan culture, Whitman has been aptly described by Miles Orvell as a "cultural sponge," possessing an inexhaustible capacity for absorbing the complexities and contradictions of American society.[2] Like his working-class neighbors, Whitman grew up fascinated by theater and opera. After serving as a book reviewer for the *Brooklyn Eagle*, Whitman determined to write poetry. Proclaiming himself to be "an acme of things accomplish'd" and "an encloser of things to be," he produced *Leaves of Grass*, a veritable lyric opera for the culture that enveloped him. His libretto turned on a simple proposition: *e pluribus unum*, out of many, one.[3]

Twenty years after Alexis de Tocqueville had coined a new word, "individualism," to describe what he believed to be America's distinctive cultural trait, and, in almost the same breath, raised concerns about the despotic potential of the masses in democratic societies, Whitman, in the opening inscription of *Leaves of Grass*, turned Tocqueville on his head. Where Tocqueville had been pessimistic about the future of democracy, dreading democracy's leveling propensities, Whitman delighted in the prospects of individual development within an emerging mass society. "One's-self I sing," Whitman chanted, "a simple separate person, / Yet utter the word Democratic, the word En-Masse." Fully seventy years before the phrase "mass culture" came into general usage in American English, Whitman sensed its presence in American life and embraced it with open arms.[4]

Was there a potential contradiction between democracy and the complex, mechanized urban society that a subsequent generation of sociologists and cultural critics would label with the pejorative term "mass"? Whitman felt those contradictory impulses deeply. "We shall," he wrote in *Democratic Vistas* (1871), "quickly and continually find the origin-idea of the singleness of man, individualism asserting itself, and cropping forth, even from the opposite ideas. But the mass, or lump character, for imperative reasons, is to be ever carefully provided for. Only from it, and from its proper regulation and potency, comes the other, comes the chance of individualism." "The two are contradictory," Whitman conceded, "but our task is to reconcile them." In a footnote, he added: "I have no doubt myself that the two will merge, and will mutually profit and brace each other, and that from them a greater product, a third, will arise. But I feel that at present they and their oppositions form a serious problem and paradox in the United States."[5] His own effort to resolve the challenges that mass culture, democracy, and individualism posed for Americans led Whitman to his distinctive contribution to American culture—a poetic form as fluid as the contours of the culture he traversed through his musings.

As many literary historians have noted, Whitman abandoned classical poetic forms in favor of more open-ended structures that mirrored the energy and seeming formlessness of American culture. "Just as any of you is one of a living crowd," he exulted in "Crossing Brooklyn Ferry," "I was one of a crowd, / Just as you are refresh'd by the gladness of the river and the bright flow, I was refresh'd . . ." To convey his sense of renewal, Whitman pioneered a poetic structure that in its very essence expressed wonder at the inconclusiveness of American culture. As John G. Blair notes, the structure of Whitman's poetry "takes the form of open-ended poetic sequences whose parts are meant to seem implicitly substitutable and latently recombinable." Anticipating the rhetorical structure of mail-order catalogs, Whitman's poetry, in other words, was crafted in forms that perfectly reflected the growing modularity of American culture as a whole, where cultural products like wild west shows or circuses could be assembled, disassembled, and reassembled in seemingly infinite varieties.[6]

In the debate about the meaning of the cultural transformations sweeping America in the late nineteenth century, Whitman lost, at least in the short term. Rendered an invalid by several strokes, he admitted "that I have not gain'd acceptance in my own times." But had Whitman lived one more year, he might have witnessed an event that undermined the categories of "high" and "low" that intellectuals and Americans of genteel persuasion were trying to impose on the American cultural experience. That event, the 1893 Chicago World's Columbian Exposition, the crowning achievement of America's world's fair movement, was, as we have seen, a liminal and leveling moment in the history of American culture.

THE RESPONSE OF AMERICAN INTELLECTUALS

Between 1893 and 1919, with mass culture increasingly becoming synonymous with American culture, American intellectuals, including a new generation of American writers coming of age around the turn of the century, did not exactly emulate Whitman's embrace of America's new cultural forms. Headquartering themselves in Greenwich Village, near the heart of New York's publishing houses, and in the Bohemian district of Chicago, near the 1893 world's fair grounds, this younger generation of cultural rebels thought of themselves as bohemians and called themselves intellectuals, a usage only recently coined by French defenders of Alfred Dreyfus. But as much as they scorned the Victorian cultural productions of their elders as irrelevant to American life, they never abandoned the preceding generation's convictions about the essential rightness of hierarchical cultural categories.[7] As a result, those cultural radicals who called themselves the "Young Americans," including Randolph Bourne, Van Wyck Brooks, Waldo Frank, and Lewis Mumford, continued to harbor deep ambivalence about the impact of mass culture on the future course of American "civilization." In significant ways, their critique of America's "industrial culture" continued the earlier critique of America's "pseudo-culture" developed by E. L. Godkin while anticipating the outpouring of European mass culture criticism that would reach its epitome in the 1920s and 1930s in the chorus of conservative European thinkers led by Max Scheler, José Ortega y Gasset, Oswald Spengler, and Johan Huizinga, as well as the left-leaning contributors to Max Horkheimer's and Theodor Adorno's Frankfurt School. Like these European critics, the Young Americans found fault with much of America's low- and middle-brow culture. But the Young Americans never solely applied a European yardstick of high versus low. On the contrary, they urgently explored the possibility of breaking away *from* European, especially British, culture. They were cultural nationalists in the sense that they cast about for the proper ingredients of a truly American culture, one liberated from British tutelage and the life of cultural derivation. "*New* England," they argued, "was *Old* England transplanted, and weakened in the transplant."[8]

The cultural criticism of the Young Americans emerged in magazines, especially *The New Republic, The New Masses,* and *The Seven Arts.* Despite their avant-garde poetry, reproductions of Ash Can School art, and biting editorials, the Young Americans never took a revolutionary stand against the cultural custodians of Victorian values. Rather, through their instrumentalist view of art, they sought to construct alternative ways of seeing the world and uplifting the masses. For them, the essential problem was not with the Arnoldian category of Culture, but with its misapplication to American circumstances by America's older generation of cultural gatekeepers.

Brooks made the most coherent case for the Young America movement. Raised in an upper-middle-class family that traveled frequently in Europe, Brooks arrived at Harvard predisposed to a way of thinking that equated Europe with Civilization. America, in his eyes, was being pulled in exactly the opposite direction by its "culture of industrialism." In place of a unified national culture, he argued in *America's Coming-of-Age* (1915), American culture had been stretched to the breaking point between two equally shallow extremes: "highbrow" and "lowbrow." By "highbrow," Brooks meant those intellectuals who sought to use America as a proving ground for European ideas. By "lowbrow" he meant American mass cultural forms. The solution, for Brooks, lay somewhere in between the extremes, in a new commitment to cultural pluralism. But as other Young America intellectuals, notably Bourne and Frank, made clear, it did not include mass culture.

For Bourne, the leading voice of the Young America movement until his death in the 1918 influenza epidemic, mass and elite cultures were two halves of the same coin and possessed about as much value as Confederate currency. The movies were a source of deep concern. "I feel even a certain unholy glee at this wholesale rejection of what our fathers reverenced as culture," Bourne confessed in *The New Republic* after seeing a film. "But I don't feel any glee about what is substituted for it. We seem to be witnessing a lowbrow snobbery. In a thousand ways it is as tyrannical and arrogant as the other culture of universities and millionaires and museums." Utterly depressed by the movies, he concluded: "It looks as if we should have to resist the stale culture of the masses as we resist the stale culture of the aristocrat. It is very easy to be lenient and pseudo-human, and call it democracy." Ridiculing "the leering cheapness and falseness of taste and spiritual outlook" of the masses, Bourne wanted something different, namely a distinctive American national culture that would be avowedly exceptional.[9] His quest led him to take up Romain Rolland's urgent plea in the first issue of *The Seven Arts*, sent from war-torn Europe, that it was up to America to form a culture of many cultures, a symphony from all the voices that immigrants brought to its shores. It was also Rolland who, in the same piece, reminded Americans of their cultural high points, as in the work of Walt Whitman, "your Homer," the man who had been among the first to conceive of America's natural cosmopolitanism, it being a nation of nations. And, indeed, in their ruminations on where America might find the source for its cultural reinvigoration, several of these young cultural rebels considered the role the immigrants might play. From European immigration, *The Seven Arts* declared, "has risen some of our most characteristic expression, with the promise of a genuine American art." Therein lay hope for cultural emancipation from England. Out of these immigrant cultures, America might yet realize the promise of transnationalism and produce a unique American culture that would blend cultural nationalism and cosmopolitanism, thus transcending the many nationalisms of Europe, which at the time were at each other's throats, and enable the United States to fulfill its destiny as an exceptional nation among nations.

The major stumbling block in realizing this vision was that the Young Americans could never bring themselves to embrace those very mass cultural forms produced by and for immigrants. Waldo Frank was a case in point. Born into an affluent Jewish family, Frank came of age feeling deeply alienated from his own Jewish cultural traditions and from the "facts of our hideous present." Chief among those facts was the cravenness of American commercial culture, which reduced the masses to a "stupor." In *Our America* (1919), Frank minced few words and anticipated the pessimistic critique of mass culture that was already building on both sides of the Atlantic. "Whitman and his sons cry for their multitudes to be born anew," Frank implored, "and the American powers take every step to preserve them in a state of ignorance, flatulence, and complacency which shall approximate the Herd." Regardless of the medium, film, radio, or jazz, Frank believed America's commercial culture had corroded cultural sensibilities. Like some—but not all—of the later Frankfurt School theorists, he dismissed jazz as a musical score for machine-age values. For Frank, as historian Casey Nelson Blake has explained, "Jazz's popularity was evidence of the totalitarian nature of mass culture, which managed to deflect all protests into harmless channels, drown out all opposing voices, and subdue the agonized conscience with promises of unimagined comfort and illicit pleasures." The only ray of hope he saw was in the ability of film star Charlie Chaplin to blend nostalgia and individualism—virtues, in Frank's opinion, that might serve as antidotes to the machine-induced massification of American society.[10]

Lewis Mumford, who quickly established himself as one of America's leading architectural critics, shared the negative views of Brooks, Bourne, and Frank. In his famous essay "The City," which appeared in Harold E. Stearns's *Civilization in the United States: An Inquiry by Thirty Americans* (1922), Mumford was characteristically direct in his denunciation of the "pseudo-national culture which now mechanically emanates from New York." "The movies, the White Ways, and the Coney Islands," he wrote, "which almost every American city boasts in some form or other, are means of giving jaded and throttled people the sensations of living without the direct experience of life—a sort of spiritual masturbation." What was the result? "So far," he concluded, "we have de-humanized the population."[11]

Between them, the Young America intellectuals determined that mass culture was not authentic Culture and fired a broadside of criticism at urban-centered mass cultural amusements, decrying their lack of authenticity, their debilitating psychological effects, and their propensity to choke out individuality. America's only hope for salvation, they believed, lay with enlightened intellectuals and some immigrant allies, who, in effect, would act as cultural interlocutors, calling attention to the dangers posed by "pseudo" cultural forms and the possibilities of arriving, through artistic creativity, at a spiritually satisfying transnational national culture.

There was, as it turned out, no small measure of irony in the Young American intellectuals' faith in art, for at the very moment Brooks, Bourne, Frank, and Mumford were degrading the worth of mass culture, a growing number of artists were discerning possibilities for cultural creativity and renewal in the beast targeted for extinction by the "smart set" of literary intellectuals. Together with a small number of literary and political radicals, several American artists, especially those associated with the Dadaist movement, ferried Walt Whitman's earlier embrace of urban mass culture across the stormy seas of criticism churned by the Young America crowd and resuscitated the idea that mass culture might harbor democratic possibilities.

Two of the leading advocates of this position were Matthew Josephson and Gilbert Seldes, editors of *Broom* and *Dial*, respectively. Josephson, the future biographer and historian, marched at the forefront of a small, loosely knit group of Dadaists who, rather than shunning mass-produced consumer goods and entertainment, embraced them as solvents that would dissolve outworn formalistic ways of thinking about culture. Inspired by Marcel Duchamp's display of a urinal at an international art exhibition and Joseph Stella's warm embrace of Coney Island in *Battle of Lights, Coney Island* (1913), Dadaist painters like Man Ray began to open the eyes of artists to considering the products of mass culture as worthy of artistic representation.

Seldes, film critic for *The New Republic* and editor of *The Dial*, similarly looked to American mass culture products, especially comic strips and film, to liberate Americans from the debilitating effects of thinking about culture in terms of "high" and "low." These categories, he complained in *The 7 Lively Arts*, reflected the persistence of "a 'genteel tradition' about the arts which has prevented any just appreciation of the popular arts, and . . . these have therefore missed the corrective criticism given to the serious arts, receiving instead only abuse."[12] It was time, Seldes argued, for American intellectuals to celebrate American mass cultural forms as worthy products of a democratic culture and harbingers of the modern age.

For the most part, Seldes's celebratory admonitions fell on deaf ears. Indeed, most American intellectuals rarely moved beyond their disdain for American mass culture and its products. As early as 1899, economist Thorstein Veblen had decried America's "conspicuous consumption" and the "aesthetic nausea" that saturated America's commercial culture. University of Pennsylvania political economist Simon Patten condemned America's popular amusements as "irrational and extravagant, for they sate appetite and deaden acute pain without renewing force or directing vigor toward the day's work." Composer and insurance company executive Charles Ives was no less critical: "But the Camp Meetings aren't the only thing that have gone soft. How about some of the seed of 1776? There are probably several contributing factors. Perhaps the most obvious if not the most harmful element is commercialism, with its influence tending toward mechanization and standardized processes of mind and life (making breakfast and death a little too easy). Emasculating America for money! Is the Anglo-Saxon going 'Pussy'?" The quotation is redolent with a fear of the proud Anglo-Saxon part of the nation becoming effete under the influence of the newly rising culture of consumption and its facile pleasures.[13]

To understand this overwhelming critique of American mass culture by American intellectuals, it is useful to recall that ever since Ralph Waldo Emerson had hitched America's future to a star, many American intellectuals had looked to Europe for models of Civilization and to nature to find the wellsprings for a distinctive American national culture. Precisely because they were, for the most part, both American and urban-based creations, mass cultural forms were hard to swallow. Furthermore, because, as Neal Gabler puts it, entertainment "deposed the rational and enthroned the sensational," American intellectuals perceived mass culture as a direct threat to their cultural authority. "Therein," Gabler writes, "for the intellectuals, lay the utmost danger and deepest despair. They knew that in the end . . . entertainment was less about morality or even aesthetics than about power—the power to replace the old cultural order with a new one, the power to replace the sublime with fun."[14] Not surprisingly, most American intellectuals never really broke from Arnoldian categories of Culture.[15] As much as they may have chafed under the criticisms proffered by Charles Dickens and Matthew Arnold himself, American intellectuals generally accepted the substance of the Europeans' critique, namely, that America lacked real Culture.

EUROPEAN RESPONSES

From the European side, there was a great degree of self-satisfaction in the ongoing critique of the United States as being devoid of real Culture. At the same time, there was growing concern that the American mass cultural camel already had stuck its nose under European canopies of civilization. This was especially clear from reactions of European intellectuals to the world's fairs that swept England and Europe between 1851 and 1900. For instance, writing about the 1855 Paris Universal Exposition, no less a literary figure than Charles Baudelaire asked if the world had become "so americanized . . . as to have lost all notion of the differences that characterize the phenomena of the physical world and the moral, of the natural and the supernatural?" Twelve years later, the Goncourt brothers regarded the world's fair medium itself as the message and termed the 1867 Paris fair "the last blow in what is the americanization of France."[16] By 1901, when W. T. Stead wrote his book, a general concern about "Americanization" had been in the air for at least a generation. Not surprisingly, some of Europe's leading intellectual lights followed the same shipping lanes—and intellectual currents—that Alexis de Tocqueville had traveled earlier in the century and determined to see modern America for themselves.

Among those who traveled to the United States after the Civil War to get a firsthand view of America's multiple challenges to Europe were English literary critic Matthew Arnold, German philosopher Max Weber, and Dutch historian Johan Huizinga. When Arnold visited the United States in the 1880s, he had an established reputation as one of England's leading cultural authorities. When Weber traveled to America to present a paper at the 1904 International Congress on the Arts and Sciences held at the 1904 St. Louis fair, he was just about to publish an essay, "The Protestant Ethic and the

Fig. 6-1. W. T. Stead portrait. Courtesy of the Library of Congress.

Spirit of Capitalism," that would, when expanded into book form, become a mainstay of liberal sociological theory. By the time Huizinga visited the United States in the 1920s, he had already published *The Waning of the Middle Ages* and had taught the first course about American history at Leiden University. Like European intellectuals of all stripes, Arnold, Weber, and Huizinga were preoccupied with understanding how to cope with the forces of political and social revolution in Europe and how modernity, shaped irrevocably by capitalism, would transform European societies. All were preoccupied by questions that concerned what a later generation of social theorists would term "mass society" and its implications for the political and social life of nations. Although they firmly believed that the future would be mapped in London, Paris, and Amsterdam, their deep questions about the meaning of modern life being debated in intellectual circles across Europe inevitably led them to the United States and to the realization that a society without a recognizable Culture might hold some valuable lessons—even if by negative example—for European modernists.

When Tocqueville died in 1856, Matthew Arnold was on the verge of receiving an appointment as professor of poetry at Oxford University. Over the course of the next decade he would publish *Essays in Criticism: First Series* (1865), *Culture and Anarchy* (1869), and several volumes of poetry. By the time of his death in 1888, shortly after returning from his second visit to the United States, Arnold was regarded as one of the leading arbiters of transatlantic Victorian literary taste and cultural values. His judgments mattered—perhaps as much in America as in England, where, try as they might, American intellectuals simply could not overcome feelings of cultural inferiority, especially when measuring the heft of American "civilization" with that of England's.

Arnold's writings about the United States did nothing to allay their feelings. In *Culture and Anarchy*, for instance, Arnold echoed Charles Dickens's earlier scathing denunciations of Americans as being interested in one thing—money. "All their cares, joys, hopes, affections, virtues, and associations," Dickens asserted in *Martin Chuzzlewit*, "seemed to be melted down into dollars." Likewise, Arnold dismissed Americans as "Philistines" with only a limited "spiritual range" and, in an aside about Cornell University, contended that it was founded "on a misconception of what culture truly is" because it was "calculated to produce miners, or engineers, or architects, not sweetness and light." More damning still, Arnold invoked the writings of French critic Ernest Renan, who asserted: "The countries which, like the United States, have created a considerable popular instruction without any serious higher instruction, will long have to expiate this fault by their intellectual mediocrity, their vulgarity of manners, their superficial spirit, their lack of general intelligence." To underscore the point, Arnold insisted: "And when M. Renan says that America, that chosen home of newspapers and politics, is without general intelligence, we think it likely, from the circumstances of the case, that this is so; and that in the things of the mind, and in culture and totality, America, instead of surpassing us all, falls short."[17] In the mounting conflict between unrestrained individualism (anarchy) and Culture ("sweetness and light"), America, Arnold believed, tilted rather precipitously toward the former condition.

Arnold's disdain for the United States did not prevent him from accepting an invitation from steel magnate Andrew Carnegie to lecture there in 1883–84 and again in 1886. In one of these lectures, "Numbers; or, The Majority and the Remnant," subsequently published in his *Discourses in America*, he summed up with his title the growing awareness in Europe that the United States had become a mass society where scale and quantity surpassed quality. To the extent there was hope for "civilization" in the United States, he explained, it rested on the ability of the United States to nurture a "righteous remnant" of cultivated elites who could uplift the masses and on the strength of America's "German stock," the product of "the most moral races of men that the world

Fig. 6-2. Matthew Arnold portrait. Courtesy of the Library of Congress.

has yet seen, with the soundest laws, the least violent passions, the fairest domestic and civic virtues." These were feeble reeds to grasp, especially, as Arnold explained in "Civilisation in the United States," because of the power of the media to influence majority opinion. "I should say," he declared, "that if one were searching for the best means to efface and kill in a whole nation the discipline of respect, the feelings for what is elevated, one could not do better than take the American newspapers." "The masses of Americans," Arnold insisted, suffered a "want of what is elevated and beautiful, of what is interesting." Americans, he contended, lived in a "fool's paradise," believing (thanks to the media and to the gospel of evangelical Protestantism) that they lived in an "elect nation" and were "the chosen people."[18] Although he never used the phrase "mass culture" to describe the United States, Arnold laid out the substance of a racially inflected, media-centered conservative critique of mass culture that would last for more than a century.[19]

Arnold drew on a vast and long-standing reservoir of English and European anti-American sentiment in developing his critical views about American society and culture. He would not have disagreed with the private remarks Austrian psychoanalyst Sigmund Freud made after visiting the United States in 1909 for a series of lectures at Clark University. America, Freud supposedly said, is "a mistake, a gigantic mistake." But, at the turn of the century, there was much more to be said about the United States than this. The point to be made about the United States at the turn of the century, as Heidelberg sociologist Max Weber understood, was not that it had made some wrong turns on the highway to modernity or that it sometimes seemed ridiculous. Rather, one had to open the hood and understand the power of the American socioeconomic engine, because, like it or not, the United States would be the driving force in the new century.

When Harvard philosopher Hugo Munsterberg invited him to present a scholarly paper at the International Congress of Arts and Sciences at the 1904 St. Louis fair, the thirty-nine year-old Weber readily accepted. At the time, while recovering from serious illness and depression, he was finishing an essay that explored the relationship between capitalism and Protestantism. As Wolfgang J. Mommsen points out, Weber's journey to the fair and his tour of the United States proved "pivotally important to the development of his social and political thought."[20]

Like Arnold, Weber drew much of his knowledge about the United States from printed sources. Whether he read Arnold's writings about America is unclear. But, if Weber had been aware of Arnold's views, he would have regarded them as missing the central point about the United States at the end of the nineteenth century—its rapid development into a capitalist global power. When Weber arrived in the United States, he made an extensive tour, visiting major cities along the eastern seaboard as well as New Orleans and Chicago. He met with prominent African Americans, including W. E. B. Du Bois, and visited Indian reservations to better understand the effects of racial segregation. Above all, as Mommsen notes, Weber was interested in the proliferation of religious sects in America and in understanding the relationship between Protestantism and advanced capitalism (like Tocqueville, Weber regarded voluntary associations as one of the keys for unlocking the secrets of the American character and, especially, the emphasis Americans placed on individualism), but his experiences in the United States also sharpened his insights into the rapid development of rational, capitalistic forms of social and economic organization and bureaucracy. In the paper he delivered at the St. Louis Congress, entitled "The Relations of the Rural Community to Other Branches of Social Science," he called attention to the effects of industrial capitalism on rural life and hinted at the broad problems confronting the modern world as the forces of industrialization and democracy collided.

After his stay in St. Louis, a short stay in Oklahoma City confirmed his conviction: "With almost lightning speed everything that stands in the way of capitalistic culture is being crushed."[21]

When Weber returned to Germany, he returned to work on his most important work, *The Protestant Ethic and the Spirit of Capitalism*. When it was published, his excavation of the culture of capitalism—for this is what he sought to understand—bore the unmistakable imprint of his observations about advanced capitalism in the United States. The capitalist social order, he wrote, "is now bound to the technical and economic presuppositions of mechanical, machinelike production, which today determines with irresistible force the lifestyle of all individuals born into this mechanism, *not* only those directly engaged in economic enterprise, and perhaps will determine it until the last ton of fossil coal is burned." Capitalism, Weber argued, had overturned the older, Puritanical "view that the care for external goods should only lie on the shoulders of the saint like 'a light cloak, which can be thrown aside at any moment.'" In modern times, he insisted, "fate decreed that the cloak should become an iron cage."[22] For Weber, one of the fundamental conditions of modern life was entrapment, if not entombment, in an "iron cage" of standardized cultural productions that left modern human beings in desperate circumstances searching for meaning. He wondered aloud if life in the future would be one of "mechanized petrification, embellished with a sort of convulsive self-importance."[23]

Weber was critical of the United States (a twenty-story hotel in New York City made Weber wonder if he and his wife were "not cut off from the good earth as though they were in the tower of a prison? Undoubtedly one could take ill and die without anyone caring!"). At the same time, he had no doubt about America's potential to dominate the world. On the eve of America's entry into the First World War, he declared: "The rise of the United States to world dominance was as unavoidable as that of ancient Rome after the Punic Wars."[24] For Weber, the Americanization of the world was already an accomplished fact.

More critical than Weber was his Russian contemporary, the writer Maxim Gorky. In 1906, Gorky visited the United States and became so depressed by what he saw that his friends took him to Coney Island to cheer him up. Their intentions backfired. "Boredom," as he put it in the title of the piece he wrote for an American magazine, was Coney Island's chief effect. "The visitor is stunned," he wrote, "his consciousness is withered by the intense gleam; his thoughts are routed from his mind; he becomes a particle in the crowd. People wander about in the flashing, blinding fire intoxicated and devoid of will. A dull-white mist penetrates their brains, greedy expectation envelopes their souls. Dazed by the brilliancy the throngs wind about like dark bands in the surging sea of light, pressed upon all sides by the black bournes of night . . . The people screw up their eyes, and smiling disconcertedly crawl along the ground like the heavy line of a tangled chain." The upshot? Visitors "drink in the vile poison with silent rapture. The poison contaminates their souls. Boredom whirls about in an idle dance, expiring in the agony of its inanition."[25] If this was the future, the Americanization of the world would result in only one outcome: degradation.

Like Gorky, Weber, and Arnold, Dutch historian Johan Huizinga found little solace in America's modernizing project and in its rapid ascent to power. During the First World War, Huizinga took the bold step of offering a course on American history at Leiden University—one of the first such courses taught anywhere in Europe. His readings on American history led to the writing of *Man and the Masses in America*, which appeared in 1918, just as he was in the process of completing his classic book *The Waning of the Middle Ages*. Then, following a trip to the United States in 1926, he published a sequel, *Life and Thought in America*. Together, they deepened the well of European pessimism about American life and its basis in mass culture.

The title of his first book on the United States accurately summed up his central argument and feelings about the United States and encapsulated the more general attitude being expressed by other European intellectuals like Ortega y Gasset in Spain, Oswald Spengler in Germany, and Georges Duhamel in France. Refining the arguments by German sociologists about the triumph of *Gesellschaft* over *Gemeinschaft* societies, Huizinga declared that in the United States the machine trumped humanity and had created a society where "matter rules and the spirit is doomed to superficiality." True enough, he argued, American techniques of mass production had reached a stage unequaled elsewhere in the world, but "mass production and machine industry mean cultural impoverishment." Department stores and installment buying, he insisted, had ushered in an era of "modern feudalism" where consumer goods substituted for human relationships. Newspapers, advertising, and cinema—all of these mass cultural products had the effect of debasing the intellect because "intellectual content has ceased to have any commercial value." As disturbing as he found newspapers and advertising, he unleashed his harshest criticism against cinema. Film, he conceded, might have some merit as an art form, but its effects were overwhelmingly negative:

> The film provides the people with a standard of beauty in the romantic forms they covet. It creates a necessarily limited and crude code of expression and imagination, and it does so in accordance with a purely commercial attitude. It develops from already existing low taste a catchy, crudely romantic, sensation, gruesome, and low-comedy taste, and then mechanically delivers

Fig. 6-3 and Fig. 6-4. During Johann Huizinga's incumbency as president of Leiden University, every year, on the occasion of the university's *dies natalis,* a drawing was made presenting Huizinga in the role of historical persons that figured in his work. Here we see him in Dutch academic regalia and as Uncle Sam. Courtesy of the Leiden University Library.

> such an excess of satisfactions in this taste that it raises it to a cultural norm
> of the very greatest weight . . . When we accept the art of the cinema as the
> daily spiritual bread of our time, we acknowledge the enslavement by the
> machine into which we have fallen.

Everywhere he looked, even in libraries, Huizinga found intellectual degradation. Conceding that the Dewey decimal system of book classification might make it easier to find books, Huizinga cautioned that "the perils of intellectual mechanization are hidden in every overly ingenious and technically perfect system of classification." Reflecting on America in the second decade of the twentieth century, Huizinga pronounced that the triumph of "the Masses" over "Man" was an accomplished fact, a sad reality, and a cause for deep pessimism.[26]

His visit to the United States six years later did nothing to change his mind. The "mechanization of culture" had so eroded powers of concentration and eliminated time for reflection that Americans had been reduced to communicating in slogans. More menacing was the growing emphasis on "standardization" which, in the United States, was "not just an industrial necessity," but "an ideal of civilization."[27] Everything was now standardized in American culture, so much so, in fact, that:

Among us Europeans who were traveling together in America, in a striking solidarity of Latins, Teutons, and Slavs, there rose up repeatedly this pharisaical feeling: We all have something that you lack; we admire your strength but do not envy you. Your instrument of civilization and progress, your big cities and your perfect organization, only make us nostalgic for what is old and quiet, and sometimes your life seems hardly to be worth living, not to speak of your future.

Huizinga, like his fellow European antimodernists, was a cultural pessimist who was convinced, as one historian has explained, that "never did American culture challenge the individual to pause and reflect, to find coherence and meaning, to consummate rather than merely to consume." Mass culture, Huizinga concluded, only worsened America's already existing propensities toward cultural depravity and made it essential for Europeans to keep U.S. cultural influences at arm's length.[28]

As influential as it was, Huizinga's argument—and the arguments of other cultural conservatives—did not entirely persuade a younger generation of European intellectuals. The Italian Communist Antonio Gramsci, for instance, had little sympathy for European intellectuals and their glib criticism of American culture. Responding to a review of Sinclair Lewis's *Babbitt*, Gramsci took the offensive: "[European intellectuals] laugh at Babbitt and are amused at his mediocrity, his naive stupidity, his automatic way of thinking and his standardized mentality. They do not even ask the question: are there Babbitts in Europe?" Indeed, Gramsci declared, Babbitts abounded in Europe: "They belong to a historical gradation inferior to that of the American Babbitt: they are a national weakness, whereas the American one is a national strength."[29] Or, on another occasion, Gramsci took issue with a contemporary critic who, in 1929, had asserted: "Americanism is swamping us. I think that a new beacon of civilization has been lit over there." For Gramsci, such criticism missed the point. "The problem," he wrote, "is rather this; whether America, through the implacable weight of its economic production (and therefore indirectly), will compel or is already compelling Europe to overturn its excessively antiquated economic and social basis." Bourgeois critics of Americanization missed its revolutionary dimensions, and their criticism merely represented "an unconscious attempt at reaction on the part of those who are impotent to rebuild and who are emphasizing the negative aspects of the revolution." American culture, Gramsci argued, was not "a new type of civilisation," but "an organic extension and an intensification of European civilisation, which has simply acquired a new coating in the American climate." Salvation for the masses of Europeans, he believed, would not come from "Americanism" or from its bourgeois critics. Rather, it is the oppressed "who 'must' find for themselves an 'original,' and not Americanised, system of living, to turn into 'freedom' what today is necessity." What Gramsci admired about American society was its industrial efficiency and modernity, both of which, he believed, "will compel or [are] already compelling Europe to overturn its excessively antiquated economic and social basis."[30]

Huizinga's arguments also provoked disagreement closer to home. In the Netherlands, a group of young cultural critics, because of their admiration for film as a potentially new art form, sought to separate the conservative critique of mass culture, with which they disagreed, from the critique of the United States, which they found more persuasive. For these younger intellectuals, especially those with interests in film, Huizinga's arguments about the cinema could not have been more wrong-headed. Younger intellectuals tended to hail the advent of new art forms, like film and photography, that harnessed techniques of mechanical reproduction for purposes of reaching a mass audience. Where Huizinga had perceived, in the mechanization of culture, a tension between the promise of a democratic art and its fake realization as mass culture, the younger generation's advocacy of film centered precisely on the technical conditions of film production. If film to them held a promise, it was one of a restored union between the worlds of technical invention and artistic creation, between culture and the machine, which had been so long disconnected. During the First World War, the machine had visited its destructive potential upon the world of European culture. But at the same time, in the huge collective endeavor of the belligerents, a new appreciation of the machine had arisen as the harbinger of a new technical civilization. No longer could intellectuals, in their role as cultural critics and guardians, afford to ignore the novel sense of exhilaration, of nervous speed and energy, which technology had spawned. And film to them was the perfect new medium to convey this novel existential awareness. Rather than rejecting film as a mere technical contraption, unable ever to provide more than shallow entertainment to the masses, or continuing the spurious division between a highbrow sphere of cultured life and the lowbrow realm of the engineer, the younger intellectual generation made film the object of critical reflection. They were aware that film had not yet realized its full artistic potential. Their responsibility, as they saw it, was to nurture this fledgling art form, to create a new critical language, develop a new aesthetics, and educate the larger public.

Theirs was always a struggle on more than one front. There was the aspect of a generational struggle, of a younger generation defiantly challenging the dominant forms of discourse in the marketplace of ideas. Where Huizinga, and people of his generation and cast of mind, still tended to cling to a dichotomous, if not Manichaean, view of the life of the mind in a mechanized world, many of the younger generation had radically adopted the machine as a powerful ingredient of contemporary culture. The latter position was generational rather than ideological. Across the political spectrum, younger writers defended film against its many detractors.

Thus, in *Communisme*, the theoretical journal of the Dutch Communist Party, G. de Waal argued a position which was no doubt ideologically correct, but which at the same time reads like a highly original defense of industrial film production. Against all those who held that film as an art was doomed given the industrialization and standardization of its production, he argued in favor of large-scale, industrial production as the only mode compatible with prevailing forces of production. Against the elitists who favored films made for a happy few in small artisan shops and ateliers, he used essentially the same argument, pointing out that their views represented an outdated stage of development. What was wrong, according to him, was not the mode of production, but its capitalist auspices. The profit motive as the main force behind film production prevented film from realizing its full potential.

Others, not as far to the left, were equally sanguine in their views of film as a mechanical art. Thus, L. J. Jordaan, a socialist and one of the early film scholars in the Netherlands, saw technology as the most crucial characteristic of his time. It had deeply affected the conditions of everyday life yet had been ignored as an object for cultural reflection. Film incorporated precisely the spirit of the age of technology and, like technology, would be there to stay. In a piece full of martial metaphors—and tellingly entitled "The Struggle for the Silver Screen"—he called upon intellectuals to take film seriously and to provide critical guidance to the general public through the press. The forum that Jordaan had chosen for this plea was the short-lived cultural journal *NU* (*NOW*), which, not unlike *The Seven Arts* ten years earlier in the United States, was meant as a call for the revitalization and rejuvenation of cultural life. As one of its two editors, the socialist A. M. de Jong, put it in the introduction to the first issue, art could no longer be the private act of single individuals: "The watchword of the new age: 'Brotherhood!' echoes around the world. It is the call of a young, passionate breed, ready for every sacrifice, not for their own greatness, but on behalf of the common weal . . ."[31]

Thus Jordaan, in the piece cited above, pointed out that the struggle for the silver screen ("one of the most urgent problems of our time—of NOW!") not only meant a struggle with outside opponents but should imply an inner purge as well: "It means, amongst many other things, a struggle against 'Americanism'—against the senseless and mindless transplant of the insipid, childish mentality and the overflowing energy of a young, and newly-marketed culture onto our old, experienced and weary state of mind." In a later issue of *NU* Jordaan takes up the theme once again and makes it his central argument. The piece is entitled "Americanism and the Film." "We, children of the old Europe, do not like the Americans . . . We do not like them, because the best in us rebels against this: our culture and our tradition." "To us this white brother 'over there' remains a boisterous, narrow, conceited, arrogant and very vulgar upstart. Altogether a relative whom we wish well, as long as he does not force himself upon us. Precisely this, we are sorry to say, has been happening in recent years, in most emphatic ways, through film." At the very moment when film, "in its nobler forms"—needless to say, Jordaan was think-ing of German, French, and Russian films—was beginning to gain accept-ance among the more educated classes and when it was becoming a cultural force in its own right, the American film industry had gained hegemonic control of world film production. Through this, a mentality is exported world-wide, "made in America." "Now this is fatal, absurd, intolerable!" If Europe is a house, "old, decrepit perhaps, but venerable," illuminated by the luster of Rembrandt, Bach, Beethoven, Dante, and Shakespeare, it is invaded by a stranger "who, shamelessly, pins 'pictures' of soapbox beauties on the walls, and fills the rooms with the blare of the Charleston and the Dirty-Dig." Not only were the masses held in thrall, a case of "chronic mass poisoning," intel-lectuals with an interest in film had to endure this deluge as well.[32]

Jordaan's was one of the more unsubtle blasts in the chorus of anti-Americanism in the 1920s. In early 1925 the literary and cultural monthly journal *De Stem* conducted a survey of the views which Dutch intellectuals held about film. The editors set the tone by calling film a wicked witch, "swollen by all the evil juices of our civilization." The negative replies, not surprisingly, were many, stressing film's mechanical, naturalistic, and stan-dardizing elements. American films were the main culprits. The young poet Slauerhoff was willing to give film a chance on condition that in the next twenty-five years the importation of films from the United States would be stopped. In the same year, 1925, at a conference on "the movie theater prob-lem," organized by the VCSJ, a Christian youth organization, H. C. Verkruy-sen, the director of an art school in Haarlem, denied the possibility of film ever developing into an art form. Again, his arguments were mainly aimed at American films. As the 1927 manifesto of the Amsterdam Film League, drawn up by one of its founding members, J. Scholte, put it: "Once every hundred times we see: film. For the rest we see: movies. The herd, the commercial regime, America, kitsch."[33] Another co-founder, Menno ter Braak, also had his less subtle moments. In a piece which he wrote as editor of an irreverent Amsterdam student weekly, *Propria Cures*, his rallying cry was: "Europe for the Europeans." With true crusading zeal he called for the culture of old Eu-rope to be defended to the last breath. "Mind bestows life, Americanism kills." "Americanism makes man into a senseless machine, . . . a coin gone smooth.

Fig. 6-5. Menno ter Braak portrait. Courtesy of Gemeentearchief Amsterdam.

It penetrates everything, erodes everything, depraves everything to the core."
In 1930, as film critic of one of the leading Dutch quality papers, he wrote a
piece entitled "'Americanism' in the Film World." His tone is more Olympian,
his judgment equally harsh. It was the lasting achievement of American
films, naively unaware of rival art forms, simply produced for the entertainment of the masses, to have stumbled upon the basic rules of cinematic movement, "when Europeans were still clumsily training their lenses on the
Comédie Française, or were pinning their hopes to eerily expressive décors."
Without the naiveté of Americans (ter Braak presents them here almost as
noble savages), without their lack of inner conflict, film-as-art, "which is so
dear to the more complicated Europeans, would have foundered on the rocks
of other art forms." Yet for the further development of a serious film culture,
America had become an encumbrance. Or, more precisely, not America, but
Americanism. Americanism, as a mental habitus, had far extended beyond

the geographic confines of a particular country. In the far-flung standardization of film production in America, "it may have reached its most threatening heights, yet as a mentality it can be found elsewhere." It is the mentality "of the commonplace, of the cliché."[34]

What is rather remarkable in all this fevered elevation of American culture as the central threat to everything that these authors held dear is not the cultural survival reflex itself. It is rather the language in which they cast the main contours of the conflict. It is not Dutch culture which is threatened by Americanism. It is European culture, Euro-pe-an-ism. There is much irony in this. If one of the most potent effects of the rising challenge of American culture was the reactivation of a variety of national discourses in Europe, using Europe rather than their varied national contexts as their frame of reference, European critics of America have much to thank America for. Yet this point is usually overlooked.

It is not just the smaller national cultures in Europe which tended to cast their critique of America in European terms, although it may have been more frequent there. Among the leading critics of Americanism in Germany and France as well, the main contrast as they construed it was between "America" and "Europe." Yet—and this is not without irony either—the Europe that we see invoked in French writings (for instance by Duhamel or André Siegfried) or in German writings (by, e.g., Spengler, Adolf Halfeld, or Hermann Keyserling) is always cast in either a characteristic French or German light. French authors tended to project typically French views of a creative individualism onto the larger European screen in order to highlight the contrast to the American standardization of production, which aimed at the average tastes of the masses. German authors rather tended to argue in terms of the collective "Soul" of the "Kulturvolk" as the central defining element of the civilization of the "Abendland"—the West. That, in their view, constituted the central European antithesis to Americanism.

As it unfolded in Europe, especially among a younger generation of intellectuals, the debate about American mass culture had rather less to do with mass culture *per se* than with its American-ness. By the 1930s, as Victoria de Grazia has argued, European governments were becoming more assertive about taking specific measures to protect and nurture their own nationally based film production companies.[35] But, ironically, Hollywood productions never lost their allure among Europeans, who showed their cinematic preferences by plunking down their national currencies for Hollywood productions.

While ordinary Europeans may have been drawn to American films, it is clear that in the first third of the twentieth century European intellectuals found little positive to say about American mass culture. Indeed, it is worth noting, by way of conclusion, that the group of German scholars who combined in 1923 to form the Institute for Social Research in Frankfurt, better known as the Frankfurt School, effectively ignored American mass culture in their early writings despite their avowed interest in studying the development of mass society. For sociologist Max Horkheimer, philosopher Theodor Adorno, psychologist Erich Fromm, and philosopher Herbert Marcuse, and—at a distance—literary critic Walter Benjamin, American mass culture was almost distasteful beyond words. As one recent scholar has explained: "Their traditional cultural arrogance led the Germans to interpret American society as 'the cultural grade of zero' of a mechanized civilization 'devoid of any spiritual qualities.'"[36] Ironically, this same mechanized civilization would provide a home for Frankfurt School intellectuals when the Nazis forced them into exile in the 1930s.

By the First World War, as far as intellectuals on both sides of the Atlantic were concerned, American mass culture was akin to the proverbial 900-lb. gorilla at the dinner table. It would just not go away no matter how hard one might wish. Its presence was unmistakable and unavoidable and a source of much concern and condemnation. Not until the United States and Europe cycled through a Depression, a Second World War, and a Cold War, would a later generation of intellectuals determine to renew an affair with mass culture that Walt Whitman had started almost a full century earlier. As Rob Kroes has recently put it: "If mass culture has provided people with the rituals and ceremonies for the celebration of their collective identities, its time has now come to be celebrated in its own right."[37] Not everyone would agree, but it is clear that, in the present, discussions of mass culture, especially about the contradictory implications of ideologically laden forms of mass culture for the future of democratic practices, have intensified, making it all the more important to understand the history of American mass culture in all of its complexities, beginning with the realization that its presence was fully felt and already under critical scrutiny a full generation before the American cultural onslaught occasioned by the Marshall Plan.

AMERICANIZATION: BALANCING OUR VIEWS, STEADYING OUR GAZE

When, in the fall of 1918, the young Russian composer Igor Stravinsky put the finishing touches to a piece of music in his Paris studio, there was a pounding noise in his ears. Briefly, he feared he had been afflicted with the same disease as his illustrious predecessors, Beethoven and Schumann. As it turned out, what he heard was the distant roar of guns blazing away to announce the end of World War I on the western front. American troops had critically weighed in to break the stalemate of trench warfare. In their wake would follow the sights and sounds of a faraway American culture. In the following years, they would take the culture of cosmopolitan centers like Paris and Berlin by storm. Ironically, the piece that Stravinsky had just completed was written in the quiet before the storm, yet it drew on an American musical form, ragtime. It was his second attempt. The year before, in his *Soldier's Tale* (*L'histoire du soldat*), he had already used the ragtime idiom, but this time his aim was more ambitious. He wanted to render a portrait of the ragtime, the way that before him Chopin had written portraits of waltzes, not as music to be danced to, as real waltzes, but portraits catching the essence of a dance form. Amazingly, Stravinsky had never heard ragtime played. All he had were notes taken by his friend, the young Swiss conductor Ernest Ansermet, who on a visit to New York had listened to the music and taken notes on paper, trying to catch its syncopated rhythms and typical melodic lines. Stravinsky's rendition produced a strangely stilted music, typical more of the composer's idiom than of the original. Yet something about ragtime, distant, indirect, and mediated as his knowledge of the music was, must have struck the composer as worthy of integration into his continuing quest for innovation of the European musical idiom.

What are we to make of this? Clearly we have a case here of European music appropriating a musical form originating in America and one that was highly popular there. Yet there was not even direct exposure to it in Stravinsky's case. What he may have heard internally was a musical invention—so to speak—an imagined music. Yet, distant and distorted as the echo of the American original must have been, still some of its vitality and pulse must have been preserved and must have appealed to Stravinsky. With the more direct exposure to forms of American popular music in the years immediately following World War I, the pattern of reception did not basically change. A European avant-garde in musical composition, although more knowledgeable about the sound of the American original, preserved their essentially eclectic attitude to it, sampling what they liked, using it as they saw fit, twisting and bending its meaning. French composers like Debussy, Ravel, and Milhaud, a German composer like Kurt Weil, or Russian composers like Shostakovich or Prokofiev were influenced by American jazz and dance music. If there was an acknowledged Americanness in what they appreciated, it was the sound of American modernity, of the pulse of its big cities, freewheeling and demotic, a new urban musical vernacular. In the artistic ferment in Europe's avant-garde centers in the 1920s, the sounds (and sights, as in Fritz Lang's *Metropolis*, conjuring up a metropolitan cityscape based on an inner imaginary New York, as imaginary as Stravinsky's ragtime) from America were only one source of inspiration among many others, to be sampled and bent at will. When Darius Milhaud wrote his music for the ballet *The Creation of the World*, he produced moments when the sonority of his music is reminiscent of his American contemporary Gershwin. Yet what Milhaud may have recognized in American jazz was a mediated Africa, more than the authentic self-expression of America. To Milhaud it may have had the same dark appeal that African folk art had to modern painters like Picasso. There are many ironies here. Gershwin, yearning to write music that could vie with its European high-art models while it was at the same time authentically American, drew on American jazz precisely because it was American, not African.

The sounds and sights of American modernity blended in well with a European avant-garde that explored the aesthetics of its contemporary machine culture. Americans working in Paris fully partook of this feverish activity. American composer George Antheil wrote the music for French director René Clair's films, and for the *Ballet Mécanique* (1927), resounding with the pounding rhythms of industrial machinery.[38] Others, not artists but members of a political and anticapitalist intelligentsia, were equally captivated by America's mastery of machines and the breakthrough in productive capacity it had brought. Socialists like Gramsci or the Belgian Herman de Man, instigator of the idea of democratic planning in European socialism, or German labor leaders, all appreciated American capitalism's promise of ushering in the era of affluence for the mass of consumers, which according to Marx could only follow the ultimate revolution of Communism. If Marx, in his journalistic writings from America for the German press in the early 1880s, had already acknowledged America as the leading capitalist power, he saw in the labor unrest of the time the harbinger of the Communist revolution. Now, in the 1920s, Socialists felt they saw the world moving from an age of scarcity into Marx's promised era of abundance under capitalist auspices. If they looked at America, they also felt they were beholding the future. As so often before, America appeared as a culture venturing out like a latter-day Prometheus into terrain where Europeans feared to tread. If America held the promise of political democracy in the eyes of many Europeans, with equal rights for all, it also, particularly in the 1920s, appeared to lead the way toward a "democracy of goods," producing a plethora of goods for consumption by the many. The central narrative ploy in much American advertising of the period helped to create this cherished self-image among Americans, while projecting a tempting model for emulation across the Atlantic. If America at the time and in later years emphasized freedom of choice, it was always in the dual sense of the political choice of individual citizens and of the economic choice of individual consumers. In that sense the 1920s foreshadowed America's later more concentrated effort through the Marshall Plan to educate Europeans economically and to help them concentrate their minds on economic growth and mass consumption. Cultural conservatives, such as Huizinga, André Siegfried, or Von Halfeld, may have bemoaned the negative impact of the ongoing mechanization of Western civilization, by which workers were turned into machines. Others—many of them on the Left—had taken their first positive cues from industrial America in the immediate post–World War I years.

The Americanness and modernity—and they are truly two sides of the same coin—of the Machine Age fascinated and inspired many Europeans. Its beat was picked up by artists as expressive of the spirit of the time; its organizational techniques were studied, adapted, and adopted by European entrepreneurs and labor leaders. Are these various forms of creative reception all equally indicative of a process of Americanization? They are not, is the short answer. But let us sit back and consider the possible range of meanings of the word Americanization.

Clearly, in the case of Stravinsky and other modernist composers, the very eclecticism in their use of American material almost logically precludes labeling it a case of Americanization. What they did is instead a case of cultural reception, and a very interesting one to boot. In their sampling approach to bits and pieces of American culture, what happened was that they picked up fragments from popular culture and made them work in a self-consciously high-brow context, radically changing their meaning. If anything, they Europeanized what they borrowed. And this a continuing story. When jazz was produced as mere entertainment in the United States, going in one ear and out the other, European aficionados in France, Germany, and other countries developed a critical language and a canon. This allowed them to make critical distinctions, between genres and styles, between levels of achievement, and to trace lines of influence and innovation. Rather than merely consuming what they liked, they brought the music to cultural consummation. In other words they wove the music into typically European patterns of analytical and critical appreciation.[39]

In the case of European capitalists taking over American ways of production, distribution, marketing, and advertising, things are different. There indeed we might see the outcome as a case of the Americanization of the European industrial process. The word then appears in the particular sense that Stead gave it, when he spoke of the "Americanization of the World." His focus was specifically on the American business acumen that disseminated American commodities across the world. Perhaps we should broaden his focus and conceive of American business practices as a game that others can learn to play. When they do, they play according to American rules, while at the same time competing with their American fellow industrialists.

Yet, as we have seen, the word Americanization is used by many others, with a different analytical thrust. It was a French coinage initially, cultural critics like Baudelaire and the Goncourt brothers wielding the term in response to their exposure to forms of American material culture displayed at various world's fairs in Paris. As they used the term, it was in defense of cultural values which they saw threatened, if not already eroded, by the materialism of American civilization. The word Americanization in cases like these is a shorthand diagnostic term for changes occurring in countries other than the United States. Whether or not the diagnosis is correct, whether or not the dismal changes might have occurred autonomously, without any American agency, America serves as the rhetorical tool to visualize and situate the origin of what would otherwise be the outcome of anonymous forces, beyond human control and comprehension. America in that connection is like the devil in Christian demonology; had it not already existed, it would have to be invented.

What the many European uses of the word Americanization as a term of critical rejection should teach us is that there is hardly ever a one-to-one relation between the ideological program of American culture as Americans willfully project it abroad, and the ideological reading given to it at the receiving end. One ideology that we have repeatedly uncovered in the American attempts at projecting a hegemonic reading of what American society is all about is that of a white, male republic, based on current ideas of racial hierarchy and racial purity. As the example of Buffalo Bill's Wild West made clear, European publics were quick to pick up the resonance with European ideas of empire and white supremacy. But most European constructions of what made American civilization tick ignored this point and, fearing its expansionism and appeal to the European masses, focused on other aspects, such as its materialism and cultural erosiveness.

Much as the word Americanization may be of non-American vintage, we should never forget that its first and obvious thrust is toward America and American culture. Americanizing America was the most urgent and obvious task for the new nation in its new Republic. No single definition was ever uncontested. Throughout American history there has been a continuing tug of war about inclusiveness versus exclusiveness, in terms of gender, class, and race, or about the universalism of its founding ideals versus the particularism of entrenched group interests vying for cultural hegemony. In that sense, President Woodrow Wilson was a two-faced Janus, standing at America's door. One face, looking inward, and whose features we explored in this book, was of the supporter of the white man's republic; the other face, looking outward, was of the messianic American seeing an Americanization of the world along the lines of a universalist American creed of democracy and the self-determination of nations. This second face is the face that the outside world responded to, in skepticism or enthusiasm.

We should also emphasize that the ideology of the white man's republic, informing much of America's mass cultural pageants, was not the only message carried by early American mass culture. Much of it arose as an entrepreneurial response to a mass demand for leisure-time pursuits, for good clean fun, and entertainment. Again, the terrain was always contested, but the general storyline is one of smaller communal groups, like working-class neighborhoods, or ethnic groups, seeking control of their own collective entertainment, in early film, in early radio, but in the end slowly but surely being incorporated into larger mass publics. But even so, the messages these mass publics were exposed to always to a large extent aimed at what the masses wanted to see and enjoy. Part of the reason why so much of American mass culture traveled so well to other national publics was precisely the expertise that the American culture industry had developed in appealing to a mass audience across class, regional, and ethnic lines within the American nation.

INTERNATIONAL SPECTATOR SPORTS: AN EXCEPTION TO OUR STORY?

The story we have told in this book explores the early rise of forms of American mass culture and their dissemination across the globe to Europe. One form of mass entertainment seems to resist being incorporated into the story, though: international spectator sports. Undeniably, they are a form of mass culture. People in the hundreds of thousands each weekend flock to playing fields across the globe to cheer on their teams, and millions more watch them perform on their television screens. Yet the games played across the globe are only to a limited extent of American origin. Few Europeans understand American football or are able to get excited about it: vice versa, Americans can hardly suppress a yawn when invited to watch European soccer. How to account for this peculiar geographic containment of enthusiasms and excitement?

Admittedly, from a larger perspective both Americans and non-Americans fully partake of a form of mass entertainment, spectator sports. The distinction is not to be found at this general level. We would have to go back in history in order to account for the global dissemination of specific forms of spectator sports. In an astute study, Dutch sociologist Maarten van Bottenburg suggests this explanation. Most spectator sports as we now know them were codified and standardized in the late nineteenth century, at a time when the British Empire was at its height. They were all initially forms of upper- or middle-class leisure exercise. This alone must have added a certain snob appeal to middle-class people on the European continent or in Latin America who more generally oriented their tastes toward British models. Within the Empire, the ruling colonial elites played these games, but they were instrumental in whetting appetites among their colonial subjects for adopting these games for their own enjoyment. Many were the unintended outcomes.[40] In a recent book on cricket in India and Pakistan, Ramachandra Guha explores the leveling effect cricket had on established caste lines on the Indian subcontinent.[41] It was not America but class-conscious Britain that had a democratizing effect on its colonial subjects. More generally, though, the story, as Bottenburg tells it, is of the rapid adoption of these essentially British sports among social elites first, followed by lower classes later on. American sports like football or baseball show a similar story from their early codification to their later mass dissemination. Yet parallel as their histories are, they remained contained within the spheres of cultural radiance of their mother countries. Bottenburg's explanation for this lack of cross-radiance is in terms of preemption. The established appreciation of specific sports preempted the adoption of rival ones. Rules of the game had grown too far apart to make for appreciation across cultural lines dividing America and Britain. Sports in both cultural empires henceforth developed in relative isolation, separating publics on either side of the divide. Never mind that America uses terms like World Series to trumpet its sports contests, it cannot hide the stark fact that, in Europe, American sports have not gone global.

There may yet be a different explanation for the divide in public appreciation of sports between America and elsewhere around the globe. It is perhaps to be found in typically American characteristics of sports like football and baseball that may jar with cultural habits elsewhere. As John Blair has convincingly argued, both sports have a typical modular form, consisting of individual plays, that reflects a more general modular approach to cultural forms in the United States. This family likeness was only reinforced when television began to broadcast games. Like so many other forms of American culture, television itself uses a modular approach to its broadcasting time, cutting it up for a jumble of different messages, commercials crucially among them. American sports and American television thus make for an ideal fit. In Europe, on the other hand, cultural appreciation is for a game continually unfolding, for narrative flow rather than dramatic spasms. Baseball has made inroads in countries like Italy and the Netherlands. American football, however, is struggling to gain a foothold, much the way that European soccer is in America, yet in terms of successfully established mass spectator sports the overall picture is still one of a cultural divide between the United States and Europe.

CONCLUSION

The proper conclusion to this book would be another book—one that carries the story of American mass culture across the divide of the Second World War and into the present. That is far beyond the scope of what we set out to do, and there are several excellent studies that have at once deepened and broadened our knowledge of American mass culture as it took root in various hybrid forms around the globe after the First World War. Yet it would be unfair not to share our thoughts about what we think the implications of our study are for understanding American mass culture as it continued to evolve past the Second World War and into the present.

To understand the presence, power, contradictions, and imaginative possibilities of American mass culture—and mass culture more generally—it is worth recalling the experiences of a young Jewish girl, Anne Frank, who found refuge from the horrors of the Nazi occupation of the Netherlands in a "secret annex" built into a house on the Prinsengracht in Amsterdam's city center. As she recorded in her *Diary*, and as her family and friends recalled after her tragic death in a Nazi concentration camp, Anne loved movies. Just before she moved with her family to the Prinsengracht residence, Anne's father found a way around a Nazi-issued law that prohibited Jews from attending movie theaters. For Anne's thirteenth birthday party, her father acquired a motion picture projector, brought it home, and showed an American film featuring the heroic antics of the dog Rin-tin-tin. The next day, Anne recorded in her diary: "This morning I lay in the bath thinking how wonderful it would be if I had a dog like Rin-tin-tin. I'd call him Rin-tin-tin too, and I'd take him to school with me, where he could stay in the caretaker's room or by the bicycle racks when the weather was good." Less than a month later, when Anne entered her bedroom in the annex, she noted: "Thanks to father—who brought my entire postcard and film-star collection here be-

Fig. conc.-1. Anne Frank's wall with a portion of her "star collection." Courtesy of the Anne Frank Institute.

forehand—and to a brush and pot of glue, I was able to plaster the walls with pictures. It looks much more cheerful."

Anne's "star collection" included some European film celebrities like Lily Bouwmeester and Heinz Ruhmann, but her wall also featured a number of notable American actors, including Robert Stack, Rudy Vallee, Norma Shearer, and Sally Eilers. For two years, friends kept her supplied with film magazines, talked with her about the films they saw, and gave her friend Peter van Pels, whose family shared the secret annex with the Franks, a picture of Greta Garbo. So taken was Anne with movies during the dark days of the war, one friend of the family recalled, that she "spread out her collection of movie pictures and looked at the beautiful faces. She discussed with every listener she could find about movies and movie stars." Then, shortly before her family's hiding place was betrayed and Anne was deported to the Bergen-Belsen concentration camp, she penned a short story in which she flew from the Netherlands to Hollywood, met famous actors, and ultimately became a model for a tennis equipment firm. At the end of the story and in her diary,

Anne noted that her Hollywood-centered dreams were passing fancies and that she "was cured once and for all of my delusions of fame."[1]

There are several points to be made about Anne Frank's embrace of the film medium and of Hollywood in particular. First, her diary makes clear that Europeans were well-acquainted with American mass culture before the liberation of Europe by American and Allied forces. Like countless numbers of her peers, Anne Frank came of age in an atmosphere swirling with American cultural products. Indeed, as we have shown in this book, the presence of American mass culture in Europe dates back to the late nineteenth century and stirred debate among European intellectuals well before the Frankfurt School was organized in 1923. What follows from this conclusion is that the European encounter with American mass culture after the Second World War needs to be understood as part of a cumulative and complex history of American cultural transmissions and European cultural receptions that occurred as part of the ongoing nation-building processes that gave form to the modern world in the nineteenth and early twentieth centuries.

In so concluding, we do not mean to minimize the significance of the Marshall Plan for transmitting American mass culture to Europe. Through exhibitions of American consumer products (most famously at American trade shows that featured American consumer products), American movies (by 1951, well over half the movies playing in Europe were produced by Hollywood), and American music (notably through Willis Conover's radio program *Music U.S.A.*, with tens of millions of listeners), all sponsored by the U.S. government, postwar planners sought to win the hearts and minds of Europeans and to create a bulwark against Soviet Communism.[2] But it is important to understand that mass culture served as an instrument for promoting American values well before the *First* World War. That those who planned the reconstruction of Europe after the *Second* World War looked to American mass cultural forms to further their cause should not be surprising. Since the Civil War, mass culture had been vital to efforts to rebuild the American nation and to "Americanize" millions of immigrants. During the First World War, the U.S. government's Creel Committee made American mass culture the centerpiece of its efforts to construct a world that would be safe for democracy and American exports. Little wonder, given the devastation of Europe during the Second World War and given their knowledge of the capacity of American mass cultural forms to influence public opinion, that planners seeking to reconstruct postwar Europe would give their work a cultural turn and regard American mass culture as vital to their efforts.

Another point to be made about Anne Frank's enthusiasm for Hollywood celebrities turns on this question: Was her fondness for her "star collection" escapist? The answer is yes, but in a particular sense. Confronted with the absolute terror of mounting totalitarianism, her flights of fantasy were just that—flights into dream worlds of alternative futures.[3] But labeling mass culture as simply "escapist" begs too many questions about points of departure, final destinations, and ports of call along the way to be a terribly useful analytical category.

A related issue is that it is insufficient to focus on Anne Frank's collection of celebrities as evidence only of the impact of American mass culture on Europe. As important as categories of cultural transmission and impacts may be, we have also argued that it is a mistake to neglect cultural receptions, or how cultural meanings are constructed by individuals and groups to advance their own interests. Let us take the long view.

Over the course of the "American Century," as the twentieth century is sometimes called, it is undeniable that the United States assumed a centrality in world affairs that can rightly be called imperial. Like Rome in the days of the Roman empire, the United States has become the center of webs of control and communication that span the world. Its cultural products reach the far corners of the world, communicating American ways and views to people elsewhere, while America itself remains relatively unaware of cultural products originating outside its national borders. If for such reasons we might call the United States imperial, it is so in a number of ways. It is imperial in the economic sphere, in the political sphere, and in the cultural sphere. Indeed, these forms of imperialism overlap to a considerable extent. For instance, America, in its role as the new political hegemon after the Second World War, could restructure markets and patterns of trade through the Marshall Plan, which guaranteed American firms access to European markets. Political imperialism, in short, could promote economic imperialism. At the same time, opening European markets for American commerce also meant preserving access for American cultural exports, such as Hollywood movies. Conversely, as carriers of an American version of the "good life," American cultural products, from cars to movies, from clothing styles to kitchen appliances, all actively doubled as agents of American cultural diplomacy. Trade, in short, translated back into political imperialism. And so on, in endless feedback loops.

It would be easy to end our discussion here. American mass culture = American imperialism. So is it proven. But imperial ambitions do not always result in imperial successes. As they have tried to accommodate themselves to their diminished role and place in the world, European countries have at times opted to resist particular forms of America's imperial presence. In recent years, France is the most telling case. It chose to resist political imperialism by ordering NATO out of the country; it warned against America's economic imperialism through Jean Jacques Servan-Schreiber's *Le défi américain*

(The American Challenge); and it briefly tried to prevent *Jurassic Park* from being released. Some French critics tried to prevent EuroDisney from opening
on the outskirts of Paris, seeing both *Jurassic Park* and EuroDisney as cases of
American cultural imperialism that threatened French cultural identity. More
recently, in the context of the war in Iraq, acts of violence have been directed
against emblems of American mass culture like McDonald's restaurants.

Resistance, however, is only one strategy for responding to American mass
culture. Selective appropriation is another. There is no doubt that from the
high rhetoric of its political ideals to the golden glow of McDonald's arches,
from Bruce Springsteen to the Marlboro Man, American culture washes
across the globe. But it does so in mostly disentangled bits and pieces, for
others to recognize and pick up, and to re-arrange into a setting expressive
of their own individual identities, or identities they share with peer groups.
Thus, while teenagers have adorned their own bedrooms with the iconic faces
of Hollywood or rock music stars in order to provide themselves with a most
private place for reverie and games of identification, they have also been engaged in a construction of private worlds that they share with countless others. In the process they have re-contextualized and re-semanticized American
culture to make it function within expressive settings of their own making.[4]

While there is no doubt that by the close of the First World War American
mass cultural forms were sweeping Europe and parts of Asia, their power did
not automatically command allegiance to "the American way." At the point of
reception, whether among American audiences or other people around the
globe, there is much creativity and inventiveness when it comes to mass culture. Audiences do not passively imbibe the messages of mass cultural media.[5]
Yet making audience creativity and inventiveness the whole story would be
as fallacious as a focus centered solely on the schemes and designs of the creators and transmitters of mass culture products.[6] In *Buffalo Bill in Bologna*,
we have aimed for balance on two counts: first, we have tried to restore some
balance to the historical record by showing that American mass culture was
running at full throttle before the First World War; second, we have tried to
balance our account of the capacity of American mass culture to overwhelm
other cultural systems with a perspective that stresses the capacity of individuals to make meaning out of their own lives. We have tried, in short, to
recognize both the power of American mass culture and its limits.

BIBLIOGRAPHICAL ESSAY

To understand why the subject of mass culture has been a source of so much controversy, the best place to begin is with the extensive literature on the "mass culture debate." There are two excellent introductions to this debate about how best to think about mass culture. Patrick Brantlinger's *Bread and Circuses: Theories of Mass Culture as Social Decay* (1983) examines the historical roots of the idea that mass culture fundamentally erodes and debases culture, while Salvador Giner's *Mass Society* (1976) surveys the sociological literature that underpins the mass society debate.

Older, but still insightful, are the writings of the intellectuals who, in the early 1920s, formed what came to be known as the "Frankfurt School" of cultural criticism. By calling attention to the power of the "culture industry" as an instrument of political domination, Max Horkheimer, Theodor Adorno, and Herbert Marcuse, among others, saw the rise of mass culture as the handmaiden of totalitarianism. The best synopsis of their views is found in Horkheimer and Adorno's *Dialectic of Enlightenment* (1944), trans. John Cumming (1972). The Frankfurt School should not be viewed monolithically. Walter Benjamin, for one, emphasized how mechanically reproduced cultural forms carried the potential of social transformation. See his "The Work of Art in the Age of Mechanical Reproduction," in *Illuminations*, trans. Harry Zohn, ed. Hannah Arendt (1969). The best overview of the Frankfurt School is Martin Jay's *The Dialectical Imagination: A History of the Frankfurt School and the Institute of Social Research, 1923–1950* (1973).

Equally important are the perspectives offered in the 1950s by Dwight MacDonald, Clement Greenberg, Irving Howe, and Mary McCarthy, captured by Bernard Rosenberg and David Manning White's *Mass Culture: The Popular Arts in America* (1957). The views of this later generation of New York Intellectuals echoed many of the presuppositions of the Van Wyck Brooks crowd but tended to be far more pessimistic if only because they took mass culture more seriously. Equally worth reading in this light are Daniel J. Boorstin's *The Image; or, What Happened to the American Dream* (1962) and Herbert Gans's *Popular Culture and High Culture: An Analysis and Evaluation of Taste* (1974). For a good review of this literature, see Eugene Lunn, "Beyond 'Mass Culture': *The Lonely Crowd*, the Uses of Literacy, and the Postwar Era," *Theory and Society* 19 (1990): 63–86. Also useful is T. J. Jackson Lears, "Mass Culture and Its Critics," in Mary Kupiec Cayton et al., eds., *Encyclopedia of American Social History*, vol. 3 (1993), pp. 1591–1609.

More recently, the theoretical literature about mass culture has also been enriched by two convergent streams of cultural theory: Antonio Gramsci's theory of cultural hegemony and the cultural studies movement that came to life in the United Kingdom in 1960s and 1970s and spread to the United States in the 1970s and 1980s. Gramsci's theory of cultural hegemony has been the subject of intense discussion. In addition to Gramsci's own *Prison Notebooks* (1971), trans. Joseph A. Buttigieg and Antonio Callari (1992), useful introductions include Geoff Eley's "Reading Gramsci in English," *European History Quarterly* 14 (1984): 441–478; Robert Bocock's *Hegemony* (1986); T. J. Jackson Lears's "The Concept of Hegemony," *American Historical Review* 90 (1985): 567–593; and James C. Scott, *Weapons of the Weak: Everyday Forms of Peasant Resistance* (1985); special issue on Stuart Hall, *Journal of Communication Inquiry* 10 (Summer 1986): 3–129; and Richard Butsch, "Introduction: Leisure and Hegemony in America," in Butsch, ed., *For Fun and Profit: The Transformation of Leisure into Consumption* (1990), pp. 3–27. As an analytical concept, "hegemony" may be most helpful for understanding what Dick Hebdige, in *Subculture: The Meaning of Style* (1979), has called the "moving equilibrium" between those with relatively more and those with relatively less access to political and economic power and for understanding the role of ideology in shaping cultural values.

Gramsci's theories were central to—but not the sole influence on—the British cultural studies movement that coalesced around the Birmingham Centre for Contemporary Cultural Studies under the direction of Stuart Hall. In addition to Gramsci, British cultural studies drew on a number of continental thinkers, especially French structuralists. For introductions to British cultural studies, consult Stuart Hall, "Cultural Studies: Two Paradigms," in *Culture, Ideology, and Social Process*, ed. Tony Bennett et al. (1981), pp. 567–593; Richard Johnson, "What Is Cultural Studies Anyway?" *Social Text* 16 (1986/1987): 38–80; Stuart Hall, "The Emergence of Cultural Studies and the Crisis of the Humanities," *October* 53 (1990): 11–23; Graeme Turner, *British Cultural Studies: An Introduction* (1990). One should also become familiar with the *Working Papers in Cultural Studies* published by the Centre for Contemporary Cultural Studies.

The reception by American scholars of Gramscian ideas about culture and ideology as well as those developed by the British cultural studies movement and French structuralists and deconstructionists will one day become the subject of a fascinating dissertation that asks why American intellectuals, liv- . ing in the nation that served as the fount of mass culture, became so dependent upon European theoretical constructs for understanding their own culture. When that study is written, it will surely take note of Eugene Genovese's *In Red and Black: Marxian Explorations in Southern and Afro-American History* (1971), one of the first American publications to make use of Gramscian ideas. Cultural studies, which seems, of late, to have stolen some of the thunder from the American Studies movement, first found a home in departments of communications and mass media in American universities. For valuable introductions to the American corollary to the British cultural studies movement, one should consult James W. Carey, *Communication as Culture: Essays on Media and Society* (1988); Chandra Mukerji and Michael Schudson, *Rethinking Popular Culture: Contemporary Perspectives in Cultural Studies* (1991); and Lawrence Grossberg, Cary Nelson, and Paula Treichler's weighty *Cultural Studies* (1992).

Gramscian studies and cultural studies are not the only theoretical underpinnings for contemporary academic discussions about mass culture. There is a wealth of literature to be found in anthropology and literary criticism as well. Starting points include, in anthropology: Clifford Geertz, *The Interpretation of Cultures* (1973), and James Clifford, *The Predicament of Culture: Twentieth-Century Ethnography, Literature, and Art* (1988); in literary criticism: Frederic Jameson, *The Political Unconscious: Narrative as a Socially Symbolic Act* (1981), and Terry Eagleton, *Criticism and Ideology: A Study in Marxist Literary Theory* (1975).

Many of these studies point to the importance of reconsidering the positions staked out by many American intellectuals during the Cold War who either proclaimed or anticipated, to borrow from the title of Daniel Bell's book, *The End of Ideology* (subtitled *On the Exhaustion of Political Ideas in the Fifties* and published in 1960). As a growing number of studies are showing, ideology, far from being diluted by the rise of mass culture, has been integral to its success. On the importance of ideology, see, in particular, John B. Thompson's *Ideology and Modern Culture: Critical Social Theory in the Era of Mass Communication* (1990); Alexander Saxton's *The Rise and Fall of the White Republic: Class Politics and Mass Culture in Nineteenth-Century America* (1990); and Terry Eagleton's *Ideology: An Introduction* (1991). On the subject of cultural and ideological representation, see Hanna Fenichel Pitkin, *The Concept of Representation* (1967), and W. J. T. Mitchell, "Representation," in *Critical Terms for Literary Study* (1990): 11–22.

Many issues central to the debate about mass culture are also featured in scholarly journals, including *American Quarterly, Critical Inquiry, Critical Theory, Cultural Studies, Journal of Communication, Journal of Communication Inquiry, Journal of Popular Culture, Representations,* and *Telos.*

The mass culture debate also intersects with questions about the nature and function of popular culture. Some scholars, notably John Fiske in *Understanding Popular Culture* (1989), entirely reject the concept of mass culture, arguing that meanings are primarily made by the consumers rather than the producers of cultural products. Scholars like Janice Radway in *Reading the Romance: Women, Patriarchy, and Popular Literature* (1984) and Ien Ang in *Watching Dallas: Soap Opera and the Melodramatic Imagination* (1982), trans. Della Couling (1985), have emphasized the liberatory potential of literary and televised soap operas. These "cultural populists," as John Clarke terms them in "Pessimism versus Populism: The Problematic Politics of Popular Culture," in Butsch, *For Fun and Profit,* pp. 28–44, offer a much needed corrective to the line of argumentation offered by Horkheimer and Adorno. But those drawn to the "populist" perspective should read two important skeptics. Donald Lazere, who edited *American Media and Mass Culture: Left Perspectives* (1987), wrote a short comment, "Mass Culture and Its Audience," *Journal of Communication* 39 (1989): 131–133, in which he notes that however valuable audience-centered studies have become, "they fail to indicate any substantial shift in control of media—or politics or wealth—away from the male corporate elite" (132). Steven Watts, in "The Idiocy of American Studies: Poststructuralism, Language, and Politics in the Age of Self-Fulfillment," *American Quarterly* 43 (1991): 625–660, is more blunt, asking "does the *content* of a commercialized American popular culture—MTV and romance novels, video games and McDonalds, Disneyland and *Reader's Digest*—truly nurture the seeds of revolution?" "Sensible people," Watts remarks, "might be suspicious" (pp. 650–651).

The major difficulty confronting historians, of course, is that interrogating the past is not the same as conducting an ethnographical survey in the present. Interviews with follow-up questions for the person being interviewed are generally impossible. Historical research, moreover, is complicated by the unavailability of sources—many of which were deemed by libraries to lack sufficient "cultural" importance to merit preservation. To recite just one horror story, about forty years ago, a major research library on the West Coast threw away many of its records for the midway entertainments at the 1915 San Francisco fair because they were too bulky to move to new storage facilities and because they had received too little attention from scholars. Today, these papers would be regarded as a gold mine for information about the organization of entertainment in the early years of the twentieth century, but, at the time they were tossed, the study of popular culture had not attained the same degree of legitimacy as it has today.

Among the works that ushered in a new appreciation for the importance of cultural history are Richard Hoggart, *The Uses of Literacy: Aspects of Working-Class Life with Special Reference to Publications and Entertainments* (1957); Robert Mandrou, *De la culture populaire aux XVIIe et XVIIIe siècles: La bibliothèque bleue de Troyes* (1964); E. P. Thompson, "Patrician Society, Plebeian Culture," *Journal of Social History* 7 (1974): 382–405; Natalie Zemon Davis, *Society and Culture in Early Modern France: Eight Essays* (1975), and her *The Return of Martin Guerre* (1983); Robert Jacques Beauroy et al., eds., *The Wolf and the Lamb: Popular Culture in France: From the Old Regime to the Twentieth Century* (1977); Richard D. Altick, *The Shows of London* (1978); Emmanuel Le Roy Ladurie's *Carnival in Romans*, trans. Mary Feeney (1979); and Robert Darnton *The Great Cat Massacre and Other Episodes in French Cultural History* (1984). These helped pave the way for the proliferation of studies under the banner of "new cultural history." See Lynn Hunt, "Introduction: History, Culture, and Text," in *The New Cultural History*, ed. Lynn Hunt (1989), pp. 1–22.

The development of popular culture studies in the United States took form in an atmosphere of contention, described by Ray B. Browne's *Against Academia: The History of the Popular Culture Association/American Culture Association and the Popular Culture Movement, 1967–1988* (1989). Browne, along with Russel Nye, Carl Bode, and Philip Durham, played a pivotal role in organizing the Popular Culture Association in 1971 and in arranging for the publication of the *Journal of Popular Culture*, which has become one of the major outlets for scholarship in the field. Since its inception, the Popular Culture Association has expanded to include the American Culture Association and the *Journal of American Culture*.

At the same time the Popular Culture Association was taking form, Russel B. Nye published *The Unembarrassed Muse: The Popular Arts in America* (1970), the first comprehensive history of "the arts of commercial entertainment" (preface) in the United States. With its detailed surveys of a vast range of cultural media from the colonial period through the Cold War, Nye's book remains a standard work in the field. Its bibliography, while dated, is still superb.

Another scholarly outlet that, over the years, has made room for work about popular culture, especially American literature, is *The American Quarterly*. True to its origins in American literary studies, the route carved out by American Studies practitioners initially followed the inspiration of Henry Nash Smith's *Virgin Land: The American West as Symbol and Myth* (1950). Smith's classic study, perhaps more than any other, lent legitimacy to the study of popular literature and, in so doing, to the study of popular culture more generally. One might usefully compare and contrast Smith's seminal

BIBLIOGRAPHICAL ESSAY | 180

work with a more recent slant on mass culture, John G. Blair's *Modular America: Cross-Cultural Perspectives on the Emergence of an American Way* (1988).

The upsurge of scholarship in mass and popular culture began to be reflected in professional historical journals as well, especially in the context of the historiographical revolution associated with the "new social history" generated in the 1960s and 1970s. Students of American history would be especially well advised to work through the indices at the back of each issue of the *Journal of American History* for recent articles and doctoral dissertations produced in areas related to cultural history.

There are several reference publications that also provide useful overviews of secondary literature: Don B. Wilmeth, *American and English Popular Entertainment: A Guide to Information Sources* (1980), as well as his *Variety Entertainment and Outdoor Amusements: A Reference Guide* (1982); Larry N. Landrum, *American Popular Culture: A Guide to Information Sources* (1982); Katherine Fishburn, *Women in Popular Culture: A Reference Guide* (1982); Arthur Frank Wertheim, ed., *American Popular Culture: A Historical Bibliography* (1984); M. Thomas Inge, *Concise Histories of American Popular Culture* (1982), as well as his *Handbook of American Popular Literature* (1988) and *Handbook of American Popular Culture*, 2nd ed. (1989); and Christopher Geist, *Directory of Popular Culture Collections* (1989).

Concerning the origins of American mass culture, Alexis de Tocqueville's *Democracy in America* (1835, 1840), trans. Henry Reeve, should be read in conjunction with Abraham S. Eisenstadt, ed., *Reconsidering Tocqueville's Democracy in America* (1988). Tocqueville never used the term "mass culture," but his description of America's political culture in the 1830s points to the economic, political, and religious conditions that facilitated the rise of mass culture in the United States.

There is, of course, an enormous body of literature on each of these aspects of American life. The most informative for purposes of this study have been George Rogers Taylor, *The Transportation Revolution: 1815–1860* (1951); Paul Johnson, *A Shopkeeper's Millennium: Society and Revivals in Rochester, New York, 1815–1837* (1978); Donald G. Matthews, "The Second Great Awakening Considered as an Organizing Process," *American Quarterly* 21 (1969): 24–43; Richard Hofstadter, *The Idea of a Party System: The Rise of Legitimate Opposition in the United States, 1780–1840* (1969); Richard P. McCormick, *The Second American Party System: Party Formation in the Jacksonian Era* (1966); Sean Wilentz, *Chants Democratic: New York City and the Rise of the American Working Class, 1788–1850* (1984); Carl Bode, *The Anatomy of American Popular Culture, 1840–1861* (1960); and Russel Blaine Nye, *The Cultural Life of the New Nation, 1776–1830* (1960).

The idea of considering the set of developments associated with the transportation revolution as a revolution in communication comes from Carey's *Communication as Culture* and Daniel J. Czitrom's *Media and the American Mind: From Morse to McLuhan* (1982).

Far and away the best effort to synthesize these developments in antebellum America and explicitly link them with the rise of American mass culture is Saxton's *The Rise and Fall of the White Republic*. This work, with its powerful thesis that ideological formulations about race were central to the development of mass culture, is essential reading. Saxton's analyses of the popular press, blackface minstrelsy, and Jacksonian theater have integrated the study of politics and culture in ways that few others have attempted.

Another key work is Lawrence W. Levine's *Highbrow/Lowbrow: The Emergence of Cultural Hierarchy in America* (1988). With its richly textured histories of American theater—including a brilliant chapter on William Shakespeare in America—opera, and museums, Levine explores the shifting and contested terrain of American cultural development over the course of the nineteenth century. Equally far-reaching is Michael Kammen's *American Culture, American Tastes: Social Change and the 20th Century* (1999).

There are other notable histories of American theater in its many manifestations, especially Albert F. McLean, Jr., *American Vaudeville as Ritual* (1965); David Grimsted, *Melodrama Unveiled: American Theater and Culture, 1800–1850* (1968); Frederick F. Snyder, "American Vaudeville—Theatre in a Package: The Origins of Mass Entertainment" (Ph.D. diss., 1970); Robert Toll, *Blacking Up: The Minstrel Show in Nineteenth-Century America* (1974); Gunther Barth, *City People: The Rise of Modern City Culture in Nineteenth-Century America* (1980); Peter G. Buckley, "To the Opera House: Culture and Society in New York City, 1820–1860" (Ph.D. diss., 1984); Robert William Snyder, "The Voice of the City: Vaudeville and the Formation of Mass Culture in New York Neighborhoods, 1880–1930" (Ph.D. diss., 1986); and Robert C. Allen, *Horrible Prettiness: Burlesque and American Culture* (1991). On the physical organization of the theater, see Claudia D. Johnson, "That Guilty Third Tier: Prostitution in Nineteenth-Century American Theaters," in *Victorian America*, ed. Geoffrey Blodgett and Daniel Walker Howe (1976). On efforts to control theater audiences, see Bruce A. McConachie, "Pacifying American Theatrical Audiences, 1820–1900," in Butsch, *For Fun and Profit*, pp. 47–50.

P. T. Barnum was virtually synonymous with the world of nineteenth-century popular amusements. Two excellent studies are Neil Harris, *Humbug: The Art of P. T. Barnum* (1973; reprint, 1989), and A. H. Saxon, *P. T. Barnum: The Legend and the Man* (1989). In addition, Barnum authored several versions of his *Autobiography*, thus, as Harris points out, presenting consumers with a choice about which of his life stories to follow. American dime museums are still awaiting comprehensive historical treatment. For a model study of urban amusements in the eighteenth and nineteenth centuries, consult Altick's *Shows of London*, cited earlier. Other insightful studies include Paul Bouissac, *Circus and Culture: A Semiotic Approach* (1976); Rosemarie Garland Thomson, ed., *Freakery: Cultural Spectacles of the Extraordinary Body* (1996); Bluford Adams, *E Pluribus Barnum: The Great Showman and the Making of U.S. Popular Culture* (1997); Robert Bogdan, *Freak Show: Presenting Human Oddities for Amusement and Profit* (1988); James W. Cook, *The Arts of Deception: Playing with Fraud in the Age of Barnum* (2001); and Benjamin Reiss, *The Showman and the Slave: Race, Death, and Memory in Barnum's America* (2001).

The history of American photography is drawing increased scholarly attention. The best study is Alan Trachtenberg's *Reading American Photographs: Images as History, Mathew Brady to Walker Evans* (1989). Insightful analysis is also provided by Miles Orvell's *The Real Thing: Imitation and Authenticity in American Culture, 1880–1940* (1989) and the essays in David E. Nye and Mick Gidley's *American Photographs in Europe* (1994).

Like photography, film was a newly invented medium of visual mass communication. As technical media they were the first typical carriers of a culture increasingly geared toward what Walter Benjamin called "mechanical reproduction." A new field of academic exploration—New Media—looks at photography, film, and later radio, television, and the Internet, from the perspective of their early years. It explores the rival uses and experimental approaches to these new media, in terms of their production, distribution, and consumption. William Uricchio published an exemplary study with Roberta E. Pearson, *Reframing Culture: The Case of the Vitagraph Quality Films* (1993). Nanna Verhoeff, one of his students, is the author of "After the Beginning: Westerns Before 1915" (Ph.D. diss., 2002).

On the development of America mass culture in the late nineteenth and early twentieth centuries, several works stand out: Henry Nash Smith, ed., *Popular Culture and Industrialism, 1865–1890* (1967); Neil Harris, ed., *The Land of Contrasts: 1880–1901* (1970), and his *Cultural Excursions: Marketing Appetites and Cultural Tastes in Modern America* (1990); Robert C. Toll, *The Entertainment Machine: Show Business in Twentieth-Century America* (1982); Alan Trachtenberg, *The Incorporation of America: Culture and Society in the Gilded Age* (1982); Donna R. Braden, *Leisure and Entertainment in America* (1988); Mick Gidley, ed., *Modern American Culture: An Introduction* (1993); and David Nasaw, *Going Out: The Rise and Fall of Public Amusements* (1993).

The significance of world's fairs has been recounted by a growing number of scholars. Good introductions are to be found in Burton Benedict et al., *The Anthropology of World's Fairs: San Francisco's Panama-Pacific International Exposition of 1915* (1983); Robert W. Rydell, *All the World's a Fair: Visions of Empire at American International Expositions, 1876–1916* (1984), and his introductory essay to *The Books of the Fairs* (1992); John E. Findling and Kimberly D. Pelle, eds., *Historical Dictionary of World's Fairs and Expositions, 1851–1988* (1990); and Robert W. Rydell and Nancy E. Gwinn, eds., *Fair Representations: World's Fairs and the Modern World* (1994). There is a growing scholarly literature on world's fairs. The best starting point is the online bibliography compiled by Alexander Geppert, "International Exhibitions, Expositions Universelles, and World's Fairs, 1851–1951: A Bibliography," http://www.lib.csufresno.edu/subjectresources/specialcollections/worldfairs/secondarybiblio.pdf.

On the Chicago World's Columbian Exposition, students should contrast the interpretation provided by Rydell, in *All the World's a Fair*, with that offered by James B. Gilbert in *Perfect Cities: Chicago's Utopias of 1893* (1991). Additional insights are afforded by Carolyn Kinder Carr and George Gurney, eds., *Revisiting the White City: American Art at the 1893 World's Fair* (1993), and Neil Harris et al., *Grand Illusions: Chicago's World's Fair of 1893* (1993). An especially insightful treatment of world's fairs is Warren Susman's "Ritual Fairs," *Chicago History* 12 (Fall 1983): 4–9.

Wild West shows have been the subject of several recent studies: Sarah J. Blackstone, *Buckskins, Bullets, and Business: A History of Buffalo Bill's Wild West* (1986); Joseph G. Rosa and Robin May, *Buffalo Bill and His Wild West: A Pictorial Biography* (1989); Paul Reddin, *Wild West Shows* (1999); and Joy Kasson, *Buffalo Bill's Wild West: Celebrity, Memory, and Popular History* (2000). Kasson's cultural biography is an important supplement to Don Russell's *The Lives and Legends of Buffalo Bill* (1960). For an insightful examination of the broader influence of Cody and the Wild West on European attitudes toward race, see Louis S. Warren, "Buffalo Bill Meets Dracula: William F. Cody, Bram Stoker, and the Frontiers of Racial Decay," *American Historical Review* 107 (2002): 1124–57. Information about women who performed in wild west shows can be found in Sarah Wood-Clark's *Beautiful Daring Western Girls: Women of the Wild West Shows* (1991). The manuscript and photographic archives of the Buffalo Bill Historical Center in Cody, Wyoming, have much to offer investigators interested in pursuing this subject.

John Kasson's pathbreaking *Amusing the Million: Coney Island at the Turn of the Century* (1978) has laid the basis for scholarly investigations of the rise of amusement parks at the turn of the century. In addition to Kasson's study, readers should consult the special section of the *Journal of Popular Culture* 15 (1981): 56–179; Robert E. Snow and Dave E. Wright, "Coney Island: A Case Study of Popular Culture and Technical Change," *Journal of Popular Culture* 9 (1976): 960–975; Raymond M. Weinstein, "Disneyland and Coney Island: Reflections on the Evolution of the Modern Amusement Park," *Journal of Popular Culture* 26 (1992): 131–164; Judith A. Adams, *The American Amusement*

Park Industry: A History of Technology and Thrills (1991); and Woody Register, *The Kid of Coney Island: Fred Thompson and the Rise of American Amusements* (2001). Useful bibliographies have also been compiled in the Architecture Series Bibliography produced by Vance Bibliographies in Monticello, Illinois (see esp. nos. A1318 and A1052). Those interested in popular amusements at the turn of the century can ill afford to miss Edwin E. Slosson, "The Amusement Business," *Independent* 57 (21 July 1904): 134–139; and Frederic Thompson, "Amusing the Million," *Everybody's Magazine* 19 (September 1908): 378. Those interested in forward linkages into the world of Disney theme parks should consult Michael J. Smith's "Back to the Future: EPCOT, Camelot, and the History of Technology," in *New Perspectives on Technology and American Culture*, ed. Bruce Sinclair (1986), pp. 69–79; and Mike Wallace's "Mickey Mouse History: Portraying the Past at Disney World," *Radical History Review* 32 (1985): 33–57; and Steven Watts, *The Magic Kingdom: Walt Disney and the American Way of Life* (1997).

Circuses are finally beginning to receive their due from cultural historians. Especially important is Janet Davis, *The Circus Age: Culture and Society under the Big Top* (2002). One should also consult the books by Fred Dahlinger, Jr., especially his *Trains of the Circus, 1872–1956* (2000).

There is a substantial body of literature on the history of the film industry. Useful starting points include Robert Sklar, *Movie-made America: A Cultural History of American Movies* (1976); Tina Balio, ed., *The American Film Industry* (1976); Lary May, *Screening Out the Past: The Birth of Mass Culture and the Motion Picture Industry* (1980); Charles Musser, *The Emergence of Cinema: The American Screen to 1907* (1990); Eileen Bowser, *The Transformation of Cinema, 1907–1915* (1990); and Steven J. Ross, *Working-Class Hollywood: Silent Film and the Shaping of Class in America* (1998). An excellent analysis of D. W. Griffith's *The Birth of a Nation* is provided by Michael P. Rogin, *Ronald Reagan, the Movie, and Other Episodes in Political Demonology* (1987). One should also consult Robert Lang, ed., *The Birth of a Nation: D. W. Griffith, Director* (1994), and Jane M. Gaines, *Fire and Desire: Mixed-Race Movies in the Silent Era* (2001).

With respect to the early years of radio, three studies are indispensable: Susan J. Douglas, *Inventing American Broadcasting, 1899–1922* (1987); Lizabeth Cohen, *Making a New Deal: Industrial Workers in Chicago, 1919–1939* (1990); and Mary Murphy, *Mining Cultures: Men, Women, and Leisure in Butte, 1914–1941* (1997).

One of the most controversial subjects in cultural history and cultural studies turns on the question of how meaning is constructed. Studies of cultural institutions, like fairs and wild west shows, have often assumed a one-to-one correspondence between intentions of media creators and audience responses, in rather the same way college professors often assume that what they have said in a lecture has been understood by students in the way the instructors intended. That grounds exist for questioning such assumptions is patently clear—both in the classroom and in the historical record. Under the threefold influences of the new social history of the 1960s and 1970s, which endeavored to give voice to people—especially the poor, women, and people of color—who had hitherto been voiceless in historiography, the British cultural studies movement, and the deconstructionist school of literary criticism, some historians became increasingly skeptical of top-down models of cultural history. See John Clarke's essay and the volume by Lawrence Grossberg cited above as well as Tania Modleski's introduction to her *Studies in Entertainment: Critical Approaches to Mass Culture* (1986) for recent concerns about the directions cultural meanings flow. For seminal works in the new social history, see E. P. Thompson, "Patrician Society, Plebeian Culture" (cited above), and his monumental *The Making of the English Working Class* (rev. ed., 1977), as well as Herbert G. Gutman's essays gathered in *Work, Culture, and Society in Industrializing America: Essays in American Working-Class and Social History* (1976).

Several historians have emphasized the contested terrain of American society and the struggles by different groups to resist impositions of meaning from above. Roy Rosenzweig's *Eight Hours for What We Will: Workers and Leisure in an Industrial City, 1870–1920* (1983) is one model study of working-class engagement with the rise of mass culture which should be read in conjunction with David Glassberg's *American Historical Pageantry: The Uses of Tradition in the Early Twentieth Century* (1990). Others include Michael Denning's *Mechanic Accents: Dime Novels and Working-Class Culture in America* (1987) and Susan B. Davis's *Parades and Power: Street Theatre in Nineteenth-Century Philadelphia* (1986). Along with Steven J. Ross, "Struggles for the Screen: Workers, Radicals, and the Political Uses of Silent Film," *American Historical Review* 96 (1991): 333–367, and Francis Couvares, *The Remaking of Pittsburgh: Class and Culture in an Industrializing City, 1877–1919* (1984), these works make clear that the rise of mass culture was anything but an automatic process and that resistance was often rooted in ethnic and working-class traditions.

As a growing number of scholars have pointed out, mass culture was engendered both by producers and consumers. Pivotal works on this subject include Karen Halttunen, *Confidence Men and Painted Women: A Study of Middle-Class Culture in America, 1830–1870* (1982); Elizabeth Ewen, *Immigrant Women in the Land of Dollars: Life and Culture on the Lower East Side, 1890–1925* (1985); Gail Bederman, *Manliness and Civilization: Cultural History of Gender and Race in the U.S.* (1995); Kathy Peiss, *Cheap Amusements: Working Women and Leisure in Turn-of-the-Century America* (1986), and her essay "Commercial Leisure and the 'Woman Question,'" in Butsch, *For Fun and Profit*, pp. 105–117.

Many of these studies are part of a broader discussion about the rise of consumerism in the late nineteenth and early twentieth centuries. In addition to Lizabeth Cohen's *Making a New Deal*, mentioned above, see especially Stuart Ewen and Elizabeth Ewen, *Channels of Desire: Mass Images and the Shaping of American Consciousness* (1982); Richard Wightman Fox and T. J. Jackson Lears, eds., *The Culture of Consumption: Critical Essays in American History, 1880–1980* (1983); William Leach, "Transformations in a Culture of Consumption: Women and Department Stores," *Journal of American History* 71 (1984): 319–342, and his *Land of Desire: Merchants, Power, and the Rise of a New American Culture* (1993); Susan Porter Benson, *Counter Cultures: Saleswomen, Managers, and Customers in American Department Stores, 1890–1940* (1986); Thomas J. Schlereth, *Cultural History and Material Culture: Everyday Life, Landscapes, Museums* (1990); and, David E. Nye and Carl Pedersen, eds., *Consumption and American Culture* (1991).

There are many studies of American intellectuals between 1865 and 1920, but few historians have probed the relationship between American intellectuals and the rise of mass culture. As interest in the subject grows, historians may discover that among intellectuals, scientists were much quicker than literary intellectuals to hop aboard the mass culture bandwagon. One might reflect specifically on the large role of scientists, especially anthropologists, in organizing midway-type ethnological shows at world's fairs. See, for example, Curtis Hinsley, "The World as Marketplace: Commodification of the Exotic at the World's Columbian Exposition, Chicago, 1893," in *Exhibiting Cultures: The Poetics and Politics of Museum Display*, ed. Ivan Karp and Steven D. Lavine (1991), pp. 344–365; and Robert W. Rydell, "The Open (Laboratory) Door: Scientists and Mass Culture," in *High Brow Meets Low Brow: American Culture as an Intellectual Concern*, ed. Rob Kroes (1988), pp. 61–84.

For background on American intellectuals during this period, readers should consult Henry Steele Commager, *The American Mind: An Interpretation of American Thought and Character Since the 1880s* (1950); Perry Miller, ed., *American Thought: Civil War to World War I* (1954); Stow Persons, *American Minds: A History of Ideas* (1958), Henry F. May, *The End of American Innocence: A Study of the First Years of Our Own Time, 1912–1917* (1959); George M. Fredrickson, *The Inner Civil War: Northern Intellectuals and the Crisis of the Union* (1965); George W. Stocking, Jr., *Race, Culture, and Evolution: Essays in the History of Anthropology* (1968); James B. Gilbert, *Work without Salvation: America's Intellectuals and Industrial Alienation, 1880–1910* (1977); T. J. Jackson Lears, *No Place of Grace: Antimodernism and the Transformation of American Culture, 1880–1920* (1981); Jean-Christophe Agnew, "The Consuming Vision of Henry James," in Fox and Lears, *The Culture of Consumption*, pp. 65–100; James T. Kloppenberg, *Uncertain Victory: Social Democracy and Progressivism in European and American Thought, 1870–1920* (1986); and George Cotkin, *Reluctant Modernism: American Thought and Culture, 1880–1900* (1992).

Works that focus more specifically on the reaction of American intellectuals to mass culture include James Hoopes, "The Culture of Progressivism: Croly, Lippmann, Brooks, Bourne, and the Idea of American Artistic Decadence," *Clio* 7 (1977): 91–111; Leslie Fishbein, *Rebels in Bohemia: The Radicals of the Masses, 1911–1917* (1982); Miles Orvell, *The Real Thing: Imitation and Authenticity in American Culture, 1880–1940* (1989), which contains an excellent overview of Walt Whitman's stance toward mass culture; Kroes, *High Brow Meets Low Brow,* cited earlier; Casey Nelson Blake, *Beloved Community: The Cultural Criticism of Randolph Bourne, Van Wyck Brooks, Waldo Frank, and Lewis Mumford* (1990); James B. Gilbert, "Mass Culture and the Romance of American Pluralism," and Brett Gary, "Modernity's Challenge to Democracy: The Lippmann-Dewey Debate," both in *Cultural Transmissions and Receptions: American Mass Culture in Europe,* ed. Rob Kroes et al. (1993), pp. 24–34, 35–36. Two additional works offer important assessments of American intellectuals' responses to mass culture and have been valuable for our own thinking about the subject: Andrew Ross, *No Respect: Intellectuals and Popular Culture* (1989); and Paul R. Gorman, "The Development of an American Mass Culture Critique, 1910–1960" (Ph.D. diss., 1990).

Not to be missed, of course, are the writings of the intellectuals themselves. Walt Whitman was virtually alone in expressing enthusiasm for American mass culture. His attitudes unfold in *Leaves of Grass* (1855) and *Democratic Vistas* (1871). For a contrary perspective, see E. L. Godkin, "Chromo-civilization," *The Nation* (17 and 24 September 1874), and William Dean Howells, *Criticism and Fiction* (1891).

Challenging the authority of Victorian standard-bearers were the Young America crowd, who published much of their criticism in such magazines as *The Masses, The New Republic,* and *The Seven Arts.* In his famous *America's Coming-of-Age* (1915), Van Wyck Brooks drew his line in the sand between "highbrow" and "lowbrow" expressions of culture. Randolph Bourne's criticism has been compiled in Carl Resek, ed., *War and the Intellectuals: Collected Essays, 1915–1919* (1964). Waldo Frank's *Our America* (1919) contains some of his most pointed criticisms of American mass culture. Lewis Mumford's own voluminous writings constitute a bibliographic task in themselves. His outlook is neatly encapsulated in "The City," in Harold E. Stearns, ed., *Civilization in the United States: An Inquiry by Thirty Americans* (New York, 1922). Gilbert Seldes, *The 7 Lively Arts* (1924; rev. 1957), tried to defend mass entertainments, but his efforts were undercut by his racism. The writings of Simon Patten and Thorstein Veblen should also be consulted. Patten, in *The New Basis of Civilization* (1907), suggested that amusements could form the basis of a new civilization in American, while Veblen, in *The Theory of the Leisure Class* (1899), scorned America's turn toward conspicuous consumption.

The cultural criticism of European intellectuals with specific reference to mass culture is being revisited by scholars on both sides of the Atlantic. See, for instance, Kroes, *Cultural Transmissions and Receptions*, and Brantlinger, *Bread and Circuses*, both cited earlier. Also see Rob Kroes, *If You've Seen One, You've Seen the Mall: Europeans and American Mass Culture* (1996). Seminal works in this area also include Roger Rollin, ed., *The Americanization of the Global Village: Essays in Comparative Popular Culture* (1989); Emily S. Rosenberg, *Spreading the American Dream: American Economic and Cultural Expansion, 1890–1945* (1982); Vanessa R. Schwartz, *Spectacular Realities: Early Mass Culture in Fin-de-siècle Paris* (1999); Reinhold Wagnleitner and Elaine Tyler May, eds., *"Here, There and Everywhere": The Foreign Politics of American Popular Culture* (2000); and multiple works by Victoria de Grazia, including *The Culture of Consent: Mass Organization of Leisure in Fascist Italy* (2002).

The work of European specialists in American Studies is invaluable for providing a transatlantic perspective on American mass culture. Richard Pells has provided a useful introduction in *Not Like Us: How Europeans Have Loved, Hated, and Transformed American Culture Since World War II* (1997), especially chapter 4 and the bibliography. The scholarship produced by European and British American Studies Associations is invaluable. The papers from the European Association for American Studies conferences under the general editorship of Rob Kroes and published by the VU University Press in Amsterdam deserve the notice of every serious student interested in putting American culture in a transatlantic context. Rob Kroes and Robert Rydell co-directed an international research undertaking at the Netherlands Institute for Advanced Studies in the Humanities and Social Sciences that produced several collections of essays: Rob Kroes, Robert W. Rydell, and Doeko F. J. Bosscher, eds., *Cultural Transmissions and Receptions: American Mass Culture in Europe* (1993); Rydell and Gwinn, *Fair Representations*, and Nye and Gidley, *American Photographs in Europe*, both cited above; and David W. Ellwood and Rob Kroes, eds., *Hollywood in Europe: Experiences of a Cultural Hegemony* (1994).

To sum up, there is an impressive body of scholarship about mass culture generally and excellent historical studies of particular aspects of American mass culture. But, at the beginning of the twenty-first century, there is much left to learn about the origins and universalizing propensities of American mass culture and its implications for democratic practices around the globe.

NOTES

INTRODUCTION

1. Gertrude Stein, *Everybody's Autobiography* (New York: Random House, 1937), p. 289.

2. "Oxford Union to Hear Noted Environmentalist," *International Herald Tribune*, 6 November 1994, p. 20.

3. Mark Isaak, "Curiosities of Biological Nomenclature: Etymologies," http://home .earthlink.net/~misaak/taxonomy/taxEtym.html.

4. Information about Aziz is from *All Things Considered*, National Public Radio, 24 April 2003. On Junichiro Koizumi and Lionel Jospin, see *Entertainment and Media*, "Japanese Pm Sings Elvis with Cruise," *Guardian Newspapers*, 28 August 2003, http:// www.buzzle.com/editorials/8-28-2003-44774.asp.

5. With respect to Stalin, one might also recall the Soviet leader's support for showing the 1940 film *The Grapes of Wrath* across the Soviet Union because he thought it would hammer home the message of human destitution under capitalism. Soviet audiences may have taken note of this message, but they were also impressed that, in America, the peasants had automobiles. Historian Kenneth Jackson shared this anecdote at the 2003 Organization of American Historians Annual Meeting. For revealing insights into the subversive potential of American mass culture icons, see the art exhibition "Forbidden Art: The Postwar Russian Avant-Garde."

6. "America's cultural domination has intensified even as its power in other domains has waned," writes David Rieff in "Global Culture: The Paradox of U.S. Dominance," *International Herald Tribune*, 5 January 1994.

7. For an insightful discussion of the reasons for using the term "mass culture" to describe American culture in the late nineteenth century, see especially Richard Ohmann, *Selling Culture: Magazines, Markets, and Class at the Turn of the Century* (New York: Verso, 1996), pp. 11–19. Jill Forbes also asks an interesting question in the title of her essay "Popular Culture and Mass Culture—A War of Position?" in *Australian Journal of French Studies* 35 (January–April 1998): http://elecpress.monash.edu/french/1998_1/forbes.html.

8. Patrick Brantlinger, *Bread and Circuses* (Ithaca: Cornell University Press, 1983); Max Horkheimer and Theodor W. Adorno, *Dialectic of Enlightenment* (1944), trans. John Cumming (New York: Continuum, 1987); Stephen Heath and Gillian Skirrow, "An Interview with Raymond Williams," in *Studies in Entertainment: Critical Approaches to Mass Culture*, ed. Tania Modleski (Bloomington: Indiana University Press, 1986), pp. 3–17;

John Fiske, *Understanding Popular Culture* (Boston: Unwin Hyman, 1989); Michael Denning, "The End of Mass Culture," *International Labor and Working-Class History* 37 (1990): 4–18; and "The Ends of Ending Mass Culture," in ibid., pp. 63–67.

9. On the etymology of "mass culture" see Paul R. Gorman, *Left Intellectuals and Popular Culture in Twentieth-Century America* (Chapel Hill: University of North Carolina Press, 1996), p. 193, n. 4.

10. Susan G. Davis, *Parades and Power: Street Theatre in Nineteenth-Century Philadelphia* (Berkeley: University of California Press, 1986), p. 181, n. 37; Dick Hebdige, *Subculture: The Meaning of Style* (London: Methuen, 1979), p. 15.

11. T. J. Jackson Lears, "The Concept of Cultural Hegemony," *American Historical Review* 90 (1985): 567–93. The work of Stuart Hall and Frederic Jameson is also important here. See Frederic Jameson, "Reification and Utopia in Mass Culture," *Social Text* 1 (1979): 130–48; Stuart Hall, "Notes on Deconstructing 'the Popular,'" in *People's History and Socialist Theory*, ed. Raphael Samuel (London: Routledge & Kegan Paul, 1981), pp. 227–40. See also *Stuart Hall: Critical Dialogues in Cultural Studies*, ed. David Morley and Kuan-Hsing Chen (New York: Routledge, 1996), and Todd Gitlin, "Television's Screens: Hegemony in Transition," in *American Media and Mass Culture: Left Perspectives*, ed. Donald Lazere (Berkeley: University of California Press, 1987), pp. 240–265.

12. Contrast, for instance, the perspectives of Neil Postman, *Amusing Ourselves to Death* (London: Methuen, 1985), with James C. Scott, *Weapons of the Weak: Everyday Forms of Peasant Resistance* (New Haven: Yale University Press, 1985); George Lipsitz, *Rainbow at Midnight: Labor and Culture in the 1940s* (Urbana: University of Illinois Press, 1994); and Andrew Ross, *No Respect: Intellectuals and Popular Culture* (New York: Routledge, 1989).

13. Stuart Ewen, *Captains of Consciousness: Advertising and the Social Roots of the Consumer Culture* (New York: McGraw-Hill, 1976); Stuart Ewen, *All Consuming Images: The Politics of Style in Contemporary Culture* (New York: Basic Books, 1988). See also Lawrence M. Friedman, *The Horizontal Society* (New Haven: Yale University Press, 1999), p. 240; and Susan Strasser, *Satisfaction Guaranteed: The Making of the American Mass Market* (Washington, D.C.: Smithsonian Institution Press, 1989), pp. 286–291. One might also consult David D. Kirkpatrick, "Big Retailers Shaping Cultural Tastes," *International Herald Tribune*, 19 May 2003.

14. Robert Darnton, "Five Theses on Cultural Transmission," *Intellectual History Newsletter* 11 (June 1989): 3–4. See also the excellent discussion of "mass culture" and "popular culture" by T. J. Jackson Lears and Peter G. Buckley in *The Encyclopedia of American Social History*, ed. Mary Kupiec Cayton et al., vol. 3 (New York: Charles Scribner's Sons, 1993), pp. 1591–1625.

15. This point is made in "Questions of Cultural Exchange: The NIAS Statement on the European Reception of American Mass Culture," in *Cultural Transmissions and Receptions: American Mass Culture in Europe*, ed. Rob Kroes, Robert W. Rydell, and Doeko F. J. Bosscher (Amsterdam: VU University Press, 1993), pp. 324–325. The "NIAS Statement" was co-authored by David Ellwood, Mel van Elteren, Mick Gidley, Rob Kroes, David E. Nye, and Robert W. Rydell.

16. Michael Kammen, *American Culture, American Tastes: Social Change and the Twentieth Century* (New York: Alfred A. Knopf, 1999), p. 267, n. 34. He also argues that mass culture is not the right category for thinking about late nineteenth-century America "because major differences of class and race remained so powerful (and combustible) throughout the century. Many factors were required to make mass culture genuinely

'mass,' and one of them was a waning and resultant diminution of class consciousness, class distinctions, and class-related tastes" (p. 63). See also pp. 166–168.

17. Reyner Banham, "The Wilderness Years of Frank Lloyd Wright," in Mary Banham et al., *A Critic Writes: Essays by Reyner Banham* (Berkeley: University of California Press, 1996), p. 138.

18. David Haward Bain, *Empire Express: Building the First Transcontinental Railroad* (New York: Viking, 1999), p. 664.

19. We are not the first to suggest that institutions of American mass culture were firmly in place in the late nineteenth century. See, for instance, Ohmann, *Selling Culture*, ch. 2, and Neal Gabler, *Life the Movie: How Entertainment Conquered Reality* (New York: Alfred A. Knopf, 1998).

20. David Kunzle, *The History of the Comic Strip: The Nineteenth Century* (Berkeley: University of California Press, 1990), p. 378.

21. On the transatlantic telegraph cable, see John Steele Gordon, *A Thread Across the Ocean: The Heroic Story of the Transatlantic Cable* (New York: Walker & Co., 2002).

22. For a brief introduction to Muzak, see Hiromi Hosoya and Markus Schaefer, "Brand Zone," in *Harvard Design School Guide to Shopping*, ed. Chuihua Judy Chung et al. (Köln: Taschen, 2001), p. 170.

23. The phrase "massification of leisure" is from Bill Brown, *The Material Unconscious: American Amusement, Stephen Crane, and the Economies of Play* (Cambridge: Harvard University Press, 1996), p. 7.

CHAPTER ONE

1. See, for example, Lawrence W. Levine, *Highbrow/Lowbrow: The Emergence of Cultural Hierarchy in America* (Cambridge: Harvard University Press, 1988), p. 33.

2. Walt Whitman, "Passage to India," in *Leaves of Grass, and Selected Prose*, ed. Sculley Bradley (San Francisco: Rinehart, 1949), p. 341. Whitman originally wrote the poem in 1868 and revised it in 1871.

3. Alan Trachtenberg, *The Incorporation of America: Culture and Society in the Gilded Age* (New York: Hill & Wang, 1982).

4. Emily Rosenberg, *Spreading the American Dream: American Economic and Cultural Expansion, 1890–1945* (New York: Hill & Wang, 1982), pp. 25–26. McKenzie quoted in ibid., p. 21. See also Mira Wilkins, *The Emergence of Multinational Enterprise: American Business Abroad from the Colonial Era to 1914* (Cambridge: Harvard University Press, 1970), and her *The Maturing of Multinational Enterprise: American Business Abroad from 1914 to 1970* (Cambridge: Harvard University Press, 1974).

5. Trachtenberg, *The Incorporation of America*, passim.

6. Seymour Martin Lipset, *The First New Nation: The United States in Historical and Comparative Perspective* (New York: Basic Books, 1963).

7. Alexander Saxton, *The Rise and Fall of the White Republic: Class Politics and Mass Culture in Nineteenth-Century America* (New York: Verso, 1997).

8. Ibid.

9. In addition to Saxton's account of blackface minstrelsy in ibid., see Robert C. Toll, *Blacking Up: The Minstrel Show in Nineteenth-Century America* (New York: Oxford University Press, 1974); and Eric Lott, *Love and Theft: Blackface Minstrelsy and the American Working Class* (New York: Oxford University Press, 1993).

10. Levine, *Highbrow/Lowbrow*, p. 40.

11. Ibid., pp. 64–66; see also Peter G. Buckley, "To the Opera House: Culture and

Society in New York City, 1820–1860," (Ph.D. diss., State University of New York at Stony Brook, 1984).

12. This account of P. T. Barnum draws on Neil Harris, *Humbug: The Art of P. T. Barnum* (Chicago: University of Chicago Press, 1973). For more recent accounts of P. T. Barnum, see especially A. H. Saxon, *P. T. Barnum: The Legend and the Man* (New York: Columbia University Press, 1989); Bluford Adams, *E Pluribus Barnum: The Great Showman and U.S. Popular Culture* (Minneapolis: University of Minnesota Press, 1997); Benjamin Reiss, *The Showman and the Slave: Race, Death, and Memory in Barnum's America* (Cambridge: Harvard University Press, 2001); and James W. Cook, *The Arts of Deception: Playing with Fraud in the Age of Barnum* (Cambridge: Harvard University Press, 2001).

13. Daniel J. Boorstin, *The Image; or, What Happened to the American Dream* (Harmondsworth, UK: Penguin Books, 1961), p. 213.

14. Harris, *Humbug*, p. 12.

15. Robert Toll, *On with the Show: The First Century of Show Business in America* (New York: Oxford University Press, 1976), pp. 265–293. We are indebted to this account for much of what follows about the vaudeville industry.

16. Russel Nye, *The Unembarrassed Muse: The Popular Arts in America* (New York: Dial Press, 1970), p. 170.

17. Toll, *On with the Show*, pp. 272–273.

18. Eric Hobsbawm and Terence Ranger, eds., *The Invention of Tradition* (Cambridge: Cambridge University Press, 1983).

19. Joseph R. Conlin, *The Morrow Book of Quotations in American History* (New York: William Morrow, 1984), p. 32.

20. See especially Janet M. Davis, *The Circus Age: Culture and Society under the American Big Top* (Chapel Hill: University of North Carolina Press, 2002).

21. *The Plantation Darkey at the Circus*, Ringling Brothers Circus Route Book, 1895–96 (no imprint), Circus World Museum Library, Baraboo, Wisconsin.

22. *Official Programme of Ringling Bros.' World's Greatest Shows. Season of 1893* (no imprint), p. 31, from Circus World Museum Library.

23. The standard biography of William Cody is Don Russell, *The Lives and Legends of Buffalo Bill* (Norman: University of Oklahoma Press, 1960).

24. David E. James, "Rock and Roll in Representations of the Invasion of Vietnam," *Representations*, no. 29 (Winter 1990), pp. 78–79, quoted in *Modernity and Mass Culture*, ed. James Naremore and Patrick Brantlinger (Bloomington: Indiana University Press, 1991), p. 19.

25. Sarah J. Blackstone, *Buckskins, Bullets, and Business: A History of Buffalo Bill's Wild West* (New York: Greenwood Press, 1986), p. 47. See also, Roger A. Hall, *Performing the American Frontier, 1870–1906* (Cambridge: Cambridge University Press, 2001).

26. Ibid., pp. 18–21.

27. Jonathan Martin, "'The Grandest and Most Cosmopolitan Object Teacher': Buffalo Bill's Wild West and the Politics of American Identity, 1883–1899," *Radical History Review* 66 (1966): 92–134. Paul Reddin, *Wild West Shows* (Urbana: University of Illinois Press, 1999); Joy Kasson, *Buffalo Bill's Wild West: Celebrity, Memory, and Popular History* (New York: Hill & Wang, 2000). The phrase "people of plenty" is from David M. Potter, *People of Plenty: Economic Abundance and the American Character* (Chicago: University of Chicago Press, 1954). The phrase "empire as a way of life" is from William A. Williams, *Empire as a Way of Life* (New York: Oxford University Press, 1980).

28. Sarah Wood Clark, *Beautiful Daring Western Girls: Women of the Wild West Shows* (Cody, WY: Buffalo Bill Historical Center, 1985).

29. Ibid., p. 8.

30. L. G. Moses, *Wild West Shows and the Images of American Indians, 1883–1933* (Albuquerque: University of New Mexico Press, 1996).

31. Henry Nash Smith, *Virgin Land: The American West as Symbol and Myth* (Cambridge: Harvard University Press, 1950).

32. Saxton, *Rise and Fall of the White Republic*, pp. 322–332; Michael Denning, *Mechanic Accents: Dime Novels and Working-Class Culture in America* (New York: Verso, 1987), p. 17.

33. Saxton, *Rise and Fall of the White Republic*, pp. 322–332.

34. Denning, *Mechanic Accents*, pp. 50–52.

35. John G. Cawelti, *Apostles of the Self-Made Man* (Chicago: University of Chicago Press, 1965), pp. 101–123.

36. Saxton, *Rise and Fall of the White Republic*, pp. 343–344.

37. Jane P. Tomkins, *West of Everything: The Inner Life of Westerns* (New York: Oxford University Press, 1992).

38. Denning, *Mechanic Accents*, pp. 201–213.

39. Mick Gidley and David E. Nye, "American Photographs in Europe," in *American Photographs in Europe*, ed. David E. Nye and Mick Gidley (Amsterdam: VU University Press, 1994), p. 3.

40. Brown, *The Material Unconscious*, p. 144.

41. "Photographic Phases," *New York Times*, 21 July 1862, p. 5.

42. Ibid.

43. Trachtenberg, *The Incorporation of America*, passim.

44. John C. Ropes, "The War as We See It Now," *Scribner's Magazine* 9 (June 1891): 778, 785.

45. Brown, *The Material Unconscious*, p. 148.

46. Judith Babbitts, "Made in America: A Stereoscopic View of the United States," in Nye and Gidley, pp. 42–43.

47. Rob Kroes, *Them and Us: Questions of Citizenship in a Globalizing World* (Urbana: University of Illinois Press, 2000), ch. 4.

48. Peter C. Marzio, *The Democratic Art: Pictures for a 19th-Century America* (Boston: David R. Godine, 1979), p. xi; Thomas J. Schlereth, "Country Stores, County Fairs, and Mail-Order Catalogues: Consumption in Rural America," in *Consuming Visions: Accumulation and Display of Goods in America, 1880–1920*, ed. Simon J. Bronner (New York: W. W. Norton, 1989), pp. 339–375.

49. On the rise of department stores, see William Leach, *Land of Desire: Merchants, Power, and the Rise of a New American Culture* (New York: Pantheon, 1993); Rosalind H. Williams, *Dream Worlds: Mass Consumption in Late Nineteenth-Century France* (Berkeley: University of California Press, 1982); and Gunthar Barth, *City People: The Rise of Modern City Culture in Nineteenth-Century America* (New York: Oxford University Press, 1980), ch. 4; Leach, pp. 22–26.

50. Stuart Ewen and Elizabeth Ewen, *Channels of Desire: Mass Images and the Shaping of American Consciousness* (New York: McGraw-Hill, 1982), p. 69.

51. Leach, *Land of Desire*, p. 23.

52. Ibid., p. 11.

53. Kathy Peiss, *Cheap Amusements: Working Women and Leisure in Turn-of-the-Century New York* (Philadelphia: Temple University Press, 1986).

54. The classic statement of this position is found in Richard Wightman Fox and T. J. Jackson Lears, eds., *The Culture of Consumption: Critical Essays in American History, 1880–1980* (New York: Pantheon, 1983).

55. Edward Bellamy, *Looking Backward* (1888; reprint, New York: New American Library, 1960), p. 80.

CHAPTER TWO

1. A good starting point for understanding these issues is Eric Foner, *Reconstruction: America's Unfinished Revolution, 1863–1877* (New York: Harper & Row, 1988).

2. Aram A. Yengoyan, "Culture, Ideology, and World's Fairs: Colonizer and Colonized in Comparative Perspective," in *Fair Representations: World's Fairs and the Modern World*, ed. Robert W. Rydell and Nancy E. Gwinn (Amsterdam: VU University Press, 1994), pp. 62–83; Penelope Harvey, *Hybrids of Modernity: Anthropology, the Nation State, and the Universal Exhibition* (New York: Routledge, 1996).

3. On American world's fairs in the Victorian period, see Robert W. Rydell, *All the World's a Fair: Visions of Empire at American International Expositions, 1876–1916* (Chicago: University of Chicago Press, 1984), and Robert W. Rydell, John E. Findling, and Kimberly D. Pelle, *Fair America: World's Fairs in the United States* (Washington, D.C.: Smithsonian Institution Press, 2000), ch. 1.

4. James Gilbert, *Perfect Cities: Chicago's Utopias of 1893* (Chicago: University of Chicago Press, 1991), ch. 4.

5. Rydell, *All the World's a Fair*, ch. 1.

6. Levine, *Highbrow/Lowbrow*, p. 132.

7. Roy Rosenzweig, *Eight Hours for What We Will: Workers and Leisure in an Industrial City, 1870–1920* (Cambridge: Cambridge University Press, 1983), p. 27.

8. Ibid., p. 58.

9. Mary Murphy, *Mining Cultures: Men, Women, and Leisure in Butte, 1914–41* (Urbana: University of Illinois Press, 1997); and Lizabeth Cohen, *Making a New Deal: Industrial Workers in Chicago, 1919–1939* (Cambridge: Cambridge University Press, 1990).

10. John W. Baer, *The Pledge of Allegiance: A Centennial History, 1892–1992* (Annapolis, MD: J. W. Baer, 1992), pp. 28–46. Margaret Miller, *I Pledge Allegiance* (Boston: Christopher Publishing House, 1946), passim.

11. Ibid., 19–21.

12. The so-called "Balch salute" could also be recited: "We give our Heads! and our Hearts! to our Country! One Language! One Flag!" See John T. Rodgers, "Authorship of the Pledge of Allegiance to the Flag: A Report," Library of Congress, July 18, 1957.

13. Baer, *Pledge of Allegiance*, pp. 20–21.

14. Rodgers, "Authorship of the Pledge," p. 6.

15. Robert Rydell, "The Pledge of Allegiance," *Rendezvous* 30 (1996), pp. 13–26.

16. Ibid., 10, 15.

17. Ibid., 16.

18. Ibid., 16–17.

19. Ibid., 17.

20. One of the sidelights in the history of the Pledge is the debate over its authorship. Both Miller and Baer provide details. Rogers authoritatively argues that the au-

thor was Bellamy, not Upham. It seems clear that both men contributed to the Pledge; Bellamy probably wrote the words; Upham probably scripted the gesture.

21. "The Official Programme for the National School Celebration of Columbus Day," *The Youth's Companion* 65 (8 September 1892): 446–447.

22. "The Celebration Begun," *New York Times*, 20 October 1892: 1–2.

23. There is no small amount of controversy about the Midway. See Rydell, *All the World's a Fair*, ch. 2, and Gilbert's counterargument in *Perfect Cities*, pp. 82–130. See also Meg Armstrong, "'A Jumble of Foreignness': The Sublime Musayums of the Nineteenth-Century Fairs and Expositions," *Cultural Critique* (Winter 1992–93): 199–250.

24. "Through the Looking Glass," *Chicago Tribune*, 1 November 1893, p. 9.

25. On African Americans and the fair, see Robert W. Rydell, "Introduction," in Ida B. Wells et al., *The Reason Why the Colored American Is Not in the Columbian Exposition*, ed. Robert W. Rydell (Champaign and Urbana: University of Illinois Press, 2000); and Christopher Robert Reed, *"All the World Is Here!": The Black Presence at White City* (Bloomington: Indiana University Press, 2000).

26. Quotes are from Wells, *The Reason Why*, pp. 8–9, 79–80.

27. Robert W. Rydell, "'Darkest Africa': African Shows at America's World's Fairs, 1893–1940," in *Africans on Stage*, ed. Bernth Lindfors (Bloomington: Indiana University Press, 1999), pp. 135–155.

28. Gilbert, *Perfect Cities*, pp. 82–130.

29. James Carey, *Communication as Culture: Essays on Media and Society* (Boston: Unwin Hyman, 1988), pp. 227–228. Information on the Sunday closing issue is from Robert W. Rydell, "Rediscovering the 1893 Chicago World's Columbian Exposition," in *Revisiting the White City: American Art at the 1893 World's Fair*, ed. Carolyn K. Carr et al. (Washington, D.C.: National Museum of American Art, 1993), pp. 44, 48.

30. Andrew Carnegie, "Value of the World's Fair to the American People," *The Engineering Magazine* 6, no. 4 (January 1894): 421–422.

31. Tony Bennett, *The Birth of the Museum* (New York: Routledge, 1995), p. 62.

32. Carnegie, "Value of the World's Fair," p. 422.

33. John G. Blair, *Modular America: Cross-Cultural Perspectives on the Emergence of an American Way* (New York: Greenwood Press, 1988), p. 3.

CHAPTER THREE

1. John Kasson, *Amusing the Million: Coney Island at the Turn of the Century* (New York: Hill & Wang, 1978), p. 58 and passim.

2. Woody Register, *The Kid of Coney Island: Fred Thompson and the Rise of American Amusements* (New York: Oxford University Press, 2001).

3. Judith A. Adams, *The American Amusement Park Industry: A History of Technology and Thrills* (Boston: Twayne Publishers, 1991), esp. ch. 3.

4. Dave Walter, "Beautiful Columbia Gardens," *Montana: The Magazine of Western History* 73, no. 5 (October 1985): 22–27; see also Robert W. Rydell, "The Culture of Imperial Abundance: World's Fairs in the Making of American Culture," in Bronner, *Consuming Visions*, pp. 191–216.

5. Adams, *The American Amusement Park Industry*, p. 47; Peiss, *Cheap Amusements*, p. 137; Kasson, *Amusing the Million*, pp. 105–108; and Register, *The Kid of Coney Island*, pp. 16, 21; Stephen Drucker, "Las Vegas, Theme City," *New York Times*, 13 February 1994.

6. Lary May, *Screening Out the Past: The Birth of Mass Culture and the Motion Picture*

Industry (New York: Oxford University Press, 1980), chs. 2–3; Daniel Czitrom, *Media and the American Mind: From Morse to McLuhan* (Chapel Hill: University of North Carolina Press, 1982). Good introductions to the early years of American cinema include Robert Sklar, *Movie-Made America: A Cultural History of American Movies* (New York: Vintage Books, 1976); Garth Jowett, *Film, the Democratic Art: A Social History of American Film* (Boston: Little, Brown, 1976) ; and Charles Musser, *The Emergence of Cinema: The American Screen to 1907* (New York: Scribner, 1990).

7. May, *Screening Out the Past*, p. 37.

8. Steven J. Ross, *Working-Class Hollywood: Silent Film and the Shaping of Class in America* (Princeton: Princeton University Press, 1998), p. 102.

9. Ibid., ch. 1.

10. Nye, *The Unembarrassed Muse*, p. 173. See also Toll, *On with the Show*, chs. 7–10; and Robert C. Allen, *Horrible Prettiness: Burlesque and American Culture* (Chapel Hill: University of North Carolina Press, 1991).

11. Toll, *On with the Show*, p. 317.

12. William Lawrence Slout, "The Repertoire Tent Show from Its Beginning to 1920" (Ph.D. diss., UCLA, 1970).

13. G. Brown Goode, "The Museums of the Future," *Annual Report of the U.S. National Museum* (Washington, D.C.: U.S. Government Printing Office, 1898), pp. 243–262.

14. Schlereth, "Country Stores," pp. 367–368.

15. Good introductions to the history and cultural function of advertising in America are Roland Marchand, *Advertising the American Dream: Making Way for Modernity, 1920–1940* (Berkeley: University of California Press, 1985), and Jackson Lears, *Fables of Abundance: A Cultural History of Advertising in America* (New York: Basic Books, 1994).

16. Kunzle, *The History of the Comic Strip*, p. 377. See especially M. Thomas Inge, *Comics as Culture* (Jackson: University Press of Mississippi, 1990), passim. Much of what follows is derived from Inge's work.

17. Nye, *The Unembarrassed Muse*, pp. 216–220; M. Thomas Inge, ed., *Concise Histories of American Popular Culture* (Westport, CT: Greenwood Press, 1982), pp. 73–77; and Inge's "Comic Art," in *Handbook of American Popular Culture*, vol. 1., ed. M. Thomas Inge (Westport, CT: Greenwood Press, 1978), pp. 77–102 .

18. Kammen, *American Culture, American Tastes*, pp. 168–170.

19. For a good overview of the American comic strip, see Bill Blackbeard, *The Smithsonian Collection of Newspaper Comics* (Washington, D.C.: Smithsonian Institution Press, 1977). On "Krazy Kat," see Franklin Rosemont, "Surrealism in the Comics I: Krazy Kat (George Herriman)," in *Popular Culture in America*, ed. Paul Buhle (Minneapolis: University of Minnesota Press, 1987), pp. 119–127. On the influence of the comics on American English, see Inge, *Comics as Culture*, pp. 17–27; and Bill Bryson, *Made in America: An Informal History of the English Language in the United States* (New York: Perennial, 2001), pp. 198–199, and "It All Started with a Kid," *International Herald Tribune*, 10 April 1995.

20. Bradford W. Wright, *Comic Book Nation: The Transformation of Youth Culture in America* (Baltimore: Johns Hopkins University Press, 2001).

21. Bloom sadly destroyed many of his papers. The best account of his life remains his autobiography: *The Autobiography of Sol Bloom* (New York: G. P. Putnam, 1948).

22. David Ewen, *The Life and Death of Tin Pan Alley* (New York: Funk and Wagnalls, 1964), pp. 17–18. See also Richard Crawford, *A History of America's Musical Life* (New York: W. W. Norton, 2001), ch. 24.

23. Charles K. Harris, *After the Ball: Forty Years of Melody* (New York: Frank-

Maurice, 1926), pp. 20–21; Gilbert Tompkins, "The Making of a Popular Song," *Munsey's Magazine*, August 1902, pp. 745–748; Ewen, *The Life and Death of Tin Pan Alley*, p. 124; Isaac Goldberg, *Tin Pan Alley: A Chronicle of the American Popular Music Racket* (New York: John Day Co., 1930), ch. 8.

24. Ewen, *The Life and Death of Tin Pan Alley*, pp. 123–124.

25. Crawford, *A History of America's Musical Life*, ch. 27; Porter Emerson Brown, "Tin Pan Alley," *Hampton's Broadway Magazine* 21 (October 1908), p. 456.

26. Lewis A. Erenberg, *Steppin' Out: New York Nightlife and the Transformation of American Culture, 1890–1930* (Chicago: University of Chicago Press, 1981), p. 258.

27. Susan J. Douglas, *Inventing American Broadcasting, 1899–1922* (Baltimore: Johns Hopkins University Press, 1987). Although they concentrate on a later period, two excellent works on early radio are the aforementioned Murphy, *Mining Cultures*, ch. 6, and Cohen, *Making a New Deal*, esp. pp. 142–143.

28. Douglas, *Inventing American Broadcasting*, passim.

29. Paul Wilson Clark, "Major General George Owen Squier: Military Scientist" (Ph.D. diss., Case Western University, 1974); and the Web site for Muzak, http://www.muzak.com/. See also Jerri Ann Husch, "Music of the Workplace: A Study of Muzak Culture" (Ph.D. diss., University of Massachusetts, 1984); and Joseph Lanza, *Elevator Music* (New York: Picador, 1994).

CHAPTER FOUR

1. W. T. Stead, *The Americanization of the World; or, The Trend of the Twentieth Century* (New York and London: Horace Markley, 1901), pp. 1, 354–356, 396.

2. See, for instance, the notices and reviews of the book that Stead provided in his magazine, *The [London] Review of Reviews*, throughout 1902.

3. Quotation attributed to Clemenceau in *Saturday Review of Literature* (1 December 1945), as noted in *Columbia World of Quotations* (New York: Columbia University Press, 1996), entry 12632.

4. Henry Adams, *The Education of Henry Adams* (Boston: Houghton Mifflin, 1918; reprint, 1973), pp. 381–382, 388.

5. The best short introduction to the Paris fair of 1900 is Robert W. Brown, "Paris 1900," in *Historical Dictionary of World's Fairs and Expositions, 1851–1988*, ed. John E. Findling and Kimberly D. Pelle (New York: Greenwood Press, 1990), pp. 155–164. Lengthier treatments include Richard D. Mandell, *Paris 1900: The Great World's Fair* (Toronto: University of Toronto Press, 1967); Debora L. Silverman, *Art Nouveau in Fin-de-siècle France: Politics, Psychology, and Style* (Berkeley: University of California Press, 1989); and Diane P. Fischer, "The 'American School' in Paris: The Repatriation of American Art at the Universal Exposition of 1900" (Ph.D. diss., City University of New York, 1993).

6. Adams, *The Education of Henry Adams*, p. 380.

7. Frederick Jackson Turner, *The Significance of the Frontier in American Life*, ed. Harold P. Simonson (1893; New York: Frederick Ungar, 1966), p. 57.

8. B. D. Woodward, "The Exposition of 1900," *North American Review* 170 (April 1900): 473.

9. "Reply of Mr. A. Picard to Commissioner-General Ferdinand W. Peck . . . October 15, 1898," National Archives, Record Group 43, Box 1, entry 1279, f. affairs.

10. "The United States at the Fair," *New York Times*, 17 June 1900, p. 19; Woodward, "The Exposition of 1900," p. 476.

11. "Cuban Exhibit in Paris," *New York Times*, 16 March 1900, p. 7. See also *Exposi-*

tion Universelle Internationale de 1900 à Paris. Catalogue spécial officiel de Cuba (Paris: Prieur et Dubois, 1900).

12. Ferdinand Peck to John Hay, 7 July 1899, U.S. National Archives, Records of the Bureau of Insular Affairs, Record Group 350, Entry 5, f. 906-1 and 906-2. These issues cropped up again at the 1901 Buffalo fair. See "Flag for Cuban Exhibits," *Buffalo Enquirer*, 28 June 1900, clipping, Buffalo and Erie County Historical Society, Pan-American Scrapbooks.

13. Richard Nelson Current and Marcia Ewing Current, *Loie Fuller: Goddess of Light* (Boston: Northeastern University Press, 1997).

14. Woodward, "The Exposition of 1900," p. 475.

15. "Correspondent Challenged," *New York Times*, 9 June 1900, p. 6; "Nationality in Art," *New York Times*, 17 June 1900, p. 20.

16. Fischer, "The 'American School' in Paris," p. 177.

17. Walter Benjamin, "The Work of Art in the Age of Mechanical Reproduction," in *Illuminations*, trans. Harry Zohn, ed. Hannah Arendt (New York: Schocken Books, 1969).

18. "Three Annexes of the United States," *The Nineteen Hundred* 10, no. 6 (June 1900): 17–18; Eugène-Melchior de Vogüé, "The Exposition of 1900," *The Living Age* 10 (26 January 1901): 208.

19. "Three Annexes," pp. 17–18; *Report of the Commissioner-General for the United States to the International Universal Exposition, Paris, 1900* (Washington: Government Printing Office, 1901), vol. 1., 69.

20. Burton Benedict, "The American Exhibition of 1887: How Buffalo Bill Captured London," *World's Fair* 5 (Spring 1985): 1–4.

21. Ibid., p. 3.

22. There are many accounts of these incidents. See, for instance, Joseph G. Rosa and Robin May, *Buffalo Bill and His Wild West: A Pictorial Biography* (Lawrence: University of Kansas Press, 1989), pp. 102–137; and Don Russell, *The Lives and Legends of Buffalo Bill* (Norman: University of Oklahoma Press, 1960), ch. 23.

23. William F. Cody, *Story of the Wild West and Camp-Fire Chats* (Philadelphia: Historical Publishing Co., 1888), p. 737.

24. Quoted in Rosa and May, *Buffalo Bill*, p. 125.

25. Paul Reddin, *Wild West Shows* (Urbana: University of Illinois Press, 1999), pp. 94–95.

26. Ibid., pp. 101–102. See also, Louis S. Warren, "Buffalo Bill Meets Dracula: William F. Cody, Bram Stoker, and the Frontiers of Racial Decay," *American Historical Review* 107 (2002): 1124–1157.

27. Reddin, p. 102; Rosa and May, *Buffalo Bill*, pp. 143–144; Kasson, *Buffalo Bill's Wild West*, pp. 85–88.

28. Kasson, *Buffalo Bill's Wild West*, pp. 88–91; Reddin, *Wild West Shows*, pp. 104–110.

29. Christian F. Feest, ed., *Indians and Europe: An Interdisciplinary Collection of Essays* (Lincoln: University of Nebraska Press, 1999).

30. Heribert Frhr. Von Feilitzsch, "Karl May: The 'Wild West' as Seen in Germany," *Journal of Popular Culture* 27 (1993): 183. Rudolf Conrad, "Mutual Fascination: Indians in Dresden and Leipzig," in Feest, *Indians and Europe.*

31. Daniele Fiorentino, "'Those Red-Brick Faces'—European Press Reactions to the Indians of Buffalo Bill's Wild West Show," in Feest, *Indians and Europe*, p. 410.

32. John Sears, "Bierstadt, Buffalo Bill, and the Wild West in Europe," in Kroes, Rydell, and Bosscher, *Cultural Transmissions and Receptions*, pp. 3–15.

33. Quoted in Naila Clerici, "Native Americans in Columbus's Home Land: A Show within the Show," in Feest, *Indians and Europe*, p. 415.

34. José Martí, *Martí on the U.S.A.*, ed. Luis A. Baralt (Carbondale: Southern Illinois University Press, 1966), p. 143.

35. Quoted in Russell, *The Lives and Legends of Buffalo Bill*, pp. 371–372.

36. Gisela Maler-Sieber, *Völkerkunde, die uns angeht* (Gütersloh: Bertelsmann, 1978), pp. 22–24.

37. Quoted in Conrad, "Mutual Fascination," p. 463.

38. Quoted in Peter Bolz, "Life among the 'Hunkpapas': A Case Study in German Indian Lore," in Feest, *Indians and Europe*, p. 481.

39. "Deep in the Heart of Bavaria," *International Herald Tribune*, 16 April 2004, p. 8.

40. Babbitts, "Made in America," p. 54.

41. Quoted by David E. Haberstich, "American Photographs in Europe and Illusions of Travel," in Nye and Gidley, *American Photographs in Europe*, p. 59.

42. Quoted by Maren Kröger, "From Sublime Vision to 'The Thing in Itself': American Art Photography at German Exhibitions, 1893–1929," in Nye and Gidley, *American Photographs in Europe*, p. 96.

CHAPTER FIVE

1. Kristin Thompson, *Exporting Entertainment: America in the World Film Market, 1907–34* (London: British Film Institute, 1985), chs. 2–3.

2. May, *Screening Out the Past*, pp. 55–58; Eileen Bowser, *The Transformation of Cinema, 1907–1915* (New York: Charles Scribner's Sons, 1990), pp. 48–52.

3. Ronald T. Takaki, *Iron Cages: Race and Culture in 19th-Century America* (New York: Alfred A. Knopf, 1979).

4. Raymond Allen Cook, *Fire from the Flint: The Amazing Careers of Thomas Dixon* (Winston-Salem, NC: John F. Blair, 1968), passim.

5. F. Garvin Davenport, Jr., "Thomas Dixon's Mythology of Southern History," *Journal of Southern History* 36 (1970): 350–367; Cook, *Fire from the Flint*, p. 105.

6. Thomas Dixon, *The Leopard's Spots: A Romance of the White Man's Burden—1865–1900* (New York: Doubleday, Page & Co., 1903), quoted in Davenport, "Thomas Dixon's Mythology," pp. 355–358.

7. Thomas Dixon, *The Clansman: An Historical Romance of the Ku Klux Klan* (New York: A. Wessels, 1907), pp. 81, 371, 374.

8. Woodrow Wilson, *A History of the American People* (New York: Harper & Brothers, 1902), pp. 49, 50, 64.

9. Ibid., pp. 212–213.

10. Woodrow Wilson, "The Ideals of America," *Atlantic Monthly* 90 (1902), pp. 726, 730–732.

11. Ibid., pp. 731, 734.

12. Fred Silva, ed., *Focus on "The Birth of a Nation"* (Englewood Cliffs, NJ: Prentice Hall, 1971), pp. 3, 46, 42; Michael Rogin, *Ronald Reagan, the Movie and Other Episodes in Political Demonology* (Berkeley: University of California Press, 1987), p. 201.

13. For brief plot and content synopses, see Silva, *Focus on "The Birth of a Nation,"* pp. 169–173.

14. Wilson, quoted in Rogin, *Ronald Reagan*, p. 192; ibid., pp. 161–183; Cook, *Fire from the Flint*, p. 172; "D. W. Griffith, Producer of the World's Biggest Picture," in *Focus on D. W. Griffith*, ed. Harry M. Geduld (Englewood Cliffs, NJ: Prentice Hall, 1971), pp. 27–28. Our thanks to Prof. Dan Flory for the last reference.

15. Assistant Secretary to Mr. W. W. Wright, 28 May 1918, Library of Congress, Manuscripts Division, NAACP Papers, Box C, f. 311; Ralph W. Ellison, *Shadow and Act* (New York: Random House, 1953), p. 275, quoted in Nickieann Fleener-Marzec, "D.W. Griffith's *The Birth of a Nation:* Controversy, Suppression, and the First Amendment as It Applies to Filmic Expression, 1915–1973" (Ph.D. diss., University of Wisconsin, 1977), p. 10. For Griffith's and Dixon's reactions to efforts to ban the film, see Silva, *Focus on "The Birth of a Nation,"* pp. 90–98.

16. Roy Nash to Secretary of War, 31 August 1916, National Archives, Record Group 94, Adjutant General's Office, Document File 2455681, filed with 2019608, in Richard Wood and David Culbert, eds., *Film and Propaganda in America*, vol. 1, *World War I* (New York: Greenwood Press, 1990), p. 65.

17. Seymour Stern, *The Birth of a Nation*, special supplement, *Sight and Sound* (July 1945), Museum of Modern Art, vertical files, f. "Birth of a Nation." See also Jean de Baroncelli, "Naissance d'une nation," *Le Monde*, 14 December 1970, Paris, Centre National de la Cinématographie, clipping, vertical files.

18. Seymour Stern, *Cinemages*, special issue no. 1 (1955), D. W. Griffith Papers, Museum of Modern Art, microfilm, reel 36; Thompson, *Exporting Entertainment*, pp. 78–79.

19. [George Creel], *Complete Report of the Chairman of the Committee on Public Information* (Washington, D.C.: Government Printing Office, 1920), p. 1.

20. Creel quoted in Stephen Vaughn, *Holding Fast the Inner Lines: Democracy, Nationalism, and the Committee on Public Information* (Chapel Hill: University of North Carolina Press, 1980), p. 21. See also George Creel, *How We Advertised America: The First Telling of the Amazing Story of the Committee on Public Information That Carried the Gospel of Americanism to Every Corner of the Globe* (New York: Harper & Brothers, 1920).

21. *Complete Report of the Chairman*, p. 2; *How We Advertised America*, p. 99.

22. *How We Advertised America*, p. 109.

23. *Complete Report of the Chairman*, passim.

24. Vaughn, *Holding Fast the Inner Lines*, pp. 212–232.

25. P. A. Strachen quoted in James D. Startt, "American Film Propaganda in Revolutionary Russia," *Prologue* 30 (Fall 1998): 168.

26. G. B. Baker, [report], n.d., National Archives, Record Group 45, Naval Records Collection, DC-Censorship, Box 110, f. George Burr Baker's Personal Letters, f. 3.

27. [Memo: Motion Picture Censorship], n.d., National Archives, Record Group 45, Subject File 1911–1927, Box 111, f. DC Correspondence.

28. [Film Censorship Bureau, General Bulletin No. 7], 12 September 1918, National Archives, Record Group 38, entry 212.

29. Information about the censorship of particular films is taken from index cards found in National Archives, Record Group 63, CPI, Division of Foreign Picture Service, Box 1, E-246; and from "Reports of Films Censored," found in National Archives, Record Group 38, entry 212.

30. *Le Temps*, clipping [ca. 1916–1920s], Paris, Centre National de la Cinématographie, clipping, vertical files.

31. "Report of Films Censored," [5 August 1918], National Archives, Record Group 38, entry 212.

CHAPTER SIX

1. E. L. Godkin, "Chromo-civilization," *The Nation*, 17 September 1874 and 24 September 1874.

2. Miles Orvell, *The Real Thing: Imitation and Authenticity in American Culture, 1880–1940* (Chapel Hill: University of North Carolina Press, 1989), p. 4.

3. Walt Whitman, "Song of Myself," in *Leaves of Grass and Selected Prose*, p. 69.

4. Ibid., "Inscriptions," p. 1. Alexis de Tocqueville, *Democracy in America* (1835; New York: Doubleday, 1969).

5. Whitman, *Leaves of Grass and Selected Prose*, p. 498.

6. Blair, *Modular America*, pp. 51–66.

7. Gorman, *Left Intellectuals*, pp. 53–54. See also his dissertation, "The Development of an American Mass Culture Critique, 1910–1960" (Ph.D. diss., University of California, 1990). We are indebted to both of these insightful works. Also valuable is T. J. Jackson Lears, "Mass Culture and Its Critics," in Cayton, *Encyclopedia of American Social History*, vol. 3, pp. 1591–1609.

8. "American Independence and War," *The Seven Arts*, supplement to the April issue (May 16, 1917), quoted in Rob Kroes, *If You've Seen One, You've Seen the Mall: Europeans and American Mass Culture* (Champaign: University of Illinois Press, 1996), p. 55.

9. Randolph Bourne, "Trans-National America," *Atlantic Monthly* 118 (July 1916), reprinted in Bourne, *War and the Intellectuals: Collected Essays, 1915–1919*, ed. Carl Resek (New York: Harper Torchbooks, 1964), p. 114; "The Heart of the People," *New Republic* 3 (3 July 1915): 233, reprinted in Bourne, *War and the Intellectuals*, pp. 171–174; Bourne, "American Independence and War," *The Seven Arts* 2 (August 1917): 524. The last piece, editorial in form, presents arguments commonly used in Randolph Bourne's contributions.

10. Casey Nelson Blake, *Beloved Community: The Cultural Criticism of Randolph Bourne, Van Wyck Brooks, Waldo Frank, and Lewis Mumford* (Chapel Hill: University of North Carolina Press, 1990), p. 272.

11. Lewis Mumford, "The City," in *Civilization in the United States: An Inquiry by Thirty Americans*, ed. Harold E. Stearns (New York: Harcourt, Brace and Co., 1922), p. 13.

12. Gilbert Seldes, *The 7 Lively Arts* (1924; New York: Sagamore Press, 1957), p. 295.

13. Thorstein Veblen, *The Theory of the Leisure Class* (1899), reprinted in *The Portable Veblen*, ed. Max Lerner (New York: Viking Press, 1948), p. 206. Ives quoted in J. Kirkpatrick, ed., *Charles Ives: Memos* (New York: Norton, 1972), p. 161; Simon Patten, *The New Basis of Civilization* (New York: Macmillan, 1913), p. 123.

14. Gabler, *Life the Movie*, p. 21.

15. James Hoopes, "The Culture of Progressivism: Croly, Lippman, Brooks, Bourne, and the Idea of American Artistic Decadence," *Clio* 7 (1977): 91–111.

16. Quoted in D. Lacorne et al., eds., *L'Amérique dans les têtes* (Paris: Hachette, 1986), p. 61.

17. Matthew Arnold, *Culture and Anarchy*, reprinted in *The Complete Prose Works of Matthew Arnold*, vol. 5., ed. R. H. Super (Ann Arbor: University of Michigan Press, 1965), pp. 241–245.

18. Matthew Arnold, *Discourses in America* (New York: Macmillan, 1906), pp. 25, 69–70. Arnold "Civilisation in the United States," in Super, *The Complete Prose Works*, pp. 366–367.

19. See, for instance, Samuel Lipman's "Why Should We Read *Culture and Anarchy*?" in Matthew Arnold, *Culture and Anarchy*, ed. Samuel Lipman (New Haven: Yale Univer-

sity Press, 1994), p. 220. Reflecting on late twentieth-century American culture, Lipman observes: "Harrowingly, what links all these anarchies—rich and poor, white and black, young and old—is a triumphant popular culture that glorifies, and profits from, the depiction of bestial acts. The children of the affluent are provided by their parents with all the paraphernalia that brutal and sadistic entertainment can devise; the children of the poor—*vide* the propaganda for rap culture—are told that the representation of lust and murder is 'their' culture, one that they should take pride in as it is made available, at colossal profits, for everyone of whatever economic and social condition."

20. Wolfgang J. Mommsen, "Max Weber in America," *American Scholar* 69, no. 3 (Summer 2000): 103.

21. Quoted in Marianne Weber, *Max Weber: A Biography*, trans. and ed. Harry Zohn (New York: John Wiley & Sons, 1975 [original German ed., 1926]), p. 293.

22. Max Weber, quoted in Lawrence A. Scaff, *Fleeing the Iron Cage: Culture, Politics, and Modernity in the Thought of Max Weber* (Berkeley: University of California Press, 1989), p. 88.

23. Max Weber, *The Protestant Ethic and the Spirit of Capitalism* (London: G. Allen & Unwin, 1930).

24. Weber, *Max Weber*, p. 281; Weber, quoted in Mommsen, "Max Weber in America," p. 110.

25. Maxim Gorky, "Boredom," *Independent* 43 (8 August 1907): 309–317.

26. Johan Huizinga, *America: A Dutch Historian's Vision from Afar and Near*, trans. and ed. Herbert H. Rowan (New York: Harper and Row, 1972), pp. 89–118. This is the only English translation of Huizinga's two books on the United States.

27. Ibid., pp. 233–337.

28. Ibid., p. 312.

29. Antonio Gramsci, *Selections from Cultural Writings*, ed. David Forgacs and Geoffrey Nowell-Smith, trans. William Boelhower (Cambridge: Harvard University Press, 1985), pp. 278–280.

30. Antonio Gramsci, *Selections from the Prison Notebooks*, ed. and trans. Quintin Hoare and Geoffrey Nowell Smith (New York: International Publishers, 1971), p. 317.

31. A. M. de Jong, "Ter Inleiding [Introduction]," *NU* 1 (October 1927), p. 8.

32. L. J. Jordaan, "De strijd om het witte doek [The Struggle for the Silver Screen]," ibid., pp. 71–75.

33. *Manifest Film Liga Amsterdam* (Amsterdam: Film Liga, 1927).

34. M. ter Braak, *De Propria Curesartikelen, 1923–1925*, ed. Carel Peters (The Hague: Bzztôh, 1978), pp. 216–217; "'Amerikanisme' in de filmwereld," *Nieuwe Rotterdamsche Courant*, Feb. 15, 1930.

35. Victoria de Grazia, "Mass Culture and Sovereignty: The American Challenge to European Cinemas," *Journal of Modern History* 61 (March 1989), pp. 53–87.

36. Ulrich Ott, *Amerika ist Anders* (1991), quoted in Philipp Gassert, "Between Political Reconnaissance Work and Democratizing Science: American Studies in Germany, 1917–1953," *Bulletin of the German Historical Institute* 32 (Spring 2003): 38.

37. Rob Kroes, "Americanization and Cultural Imperialism: American Mass Culture and the European Sense of History," in *Ceremonies and Spectacles: Performing American Culture*, ed. Teresa Alves, Teresa Cid, Heinz Ickstadt (Amsterdam: VU University Press, 2000), p. 110.

38. The full French title of the ballet is telling: *Ballet pour instruments mécaniques et*

percussion (1924), and so are its instruments: 3 xylophones, 4 bass drums, tam-tam, 2 pianos, sirens, 7 bells, 3 airplane propellers, and 16 player pianos.

39. Frenchman Charles Delaunay, brother of the modernist painter Robert, was among the first to treat jazz as a serious art form. The jazz avant-garde pianist Thelonious Monk would later dedicate a piece to him, ironically entitled "Delaunay's Dilemma."

40. M. van Bottenburg, *Global Games*, trans. Beverley Jackson (Urbana: University of Illinois Press, 2001), p. 184. See also Blair, *Modular America*, pp. 81–94.

41. Ramachandra Guha, *A Corner of a Foreign Field: The Indian History of a British Sport* (London: Picador, 2003). See also C. L. R. James, *Beyond a Boundary* (London: Hutchinson, 1963), and the discussion by Mark Naison, "Sports and the American Empire," in Lazere, *American Media and Mass Culture*, pp. 499–515.

CONCLUSION

1. *The Diary of Anne Frank: The Revised Critical Edition*, ed. David Barnouw and Gerrold Van Der Stroom, trans. Arnold J. Pomerans, B. M. Mooyaart-Doubleday, and Susan Massotty (New York: Doubleday, 1986), pp. 776–779. "Nicole Caspari's Anne Frank Website," http://www.nicole-caspari.de/annefrank/e_film01.html.

2. Richard Pells, *Not Like Us: How Europeans Have Loved, Hated, and Transformed American Culture Since World War II* (New York: Basic Books, 1997); D. W. Ellwood, "The Impact of the Marshall Plan on Italy; The Impact of Italy on the Marshall Plan," in Kroes, Rydell, and Bosscher, *Cultural Transmissions and Receptions*, pp. 100–124.

3. For elaboration on this matter, see Raymond Williams, *Problems in Materialism and Culture* (London: Verso, 1980), pp. 38–40.

4. Reinhold Wagnleitner and Elaine Tyler May, eds., *"Here, There and Everywhere": The Foreign Politics of American Popular Culture* (Hanover: University Press of New England, 2000).

5. For a recent argument to this effect, see Philippe Legrain, "Cultural Globalization Is Not Americanization," *Chronicle of Higher Education* (9 May 2003): B7–B10. There is also a growing body of very interesting scholarship on the reception of American mass culture in Japan. See, for instance, Miriam Silverberg, "Constructing the Japanese Ethnography of Modernity," *Journal of Asian Studies* 51 (1992): 30–54; Barbara Hamill Sato, "The *Moga* Sensation: Perceptions of the *Modan Garu* in Japanese Intellectual Circles during the 1920s," *Gender and History* 5 (1993): 363–381; Miriam Silverberg, "Constructing a New Cultural History of Prewar Japan," and H. D. Harootunian, "America's Japan/Japan's Japan," in *Japan in the World*, ed. Masao Miyoshi and H.D. Harootunian (Durham, N.C.: Duke University Press, 1993), pp. 115–143 and 196–221; and Jeffrey E. Haines, "Media Culture in Taisho Osaka," in *Japan's Competing Modernities: Issues in Culture and Democracy, 1900–1930*, ed. Sharon A. Minichiello (Honolulu: University of Hawaii Press, 1998), pp. 267–287. We are grateful to Professor Brett Walker for these references.

6. For recent articulations of the argument that mass culture restricts rather than expands freedom, see Carl Hiaasen, *Team Rodent: How Disney Devours the World* (New York: Ballantine, 1998); and David D. Kirkpatrick, "Big Retailers Shaping Cultural Tastes," *International Herald Tribune*, 19 May 2003, p. 6.

INDEX

Page numbers in boldface type refer to illustrations.